Using R for Data Analysis in Social Sciences

Using R for Data Analysis in Social Sciences

A Research Project-Oriented Approach

QUAN LI

OXFORD
UNIVERSITY PRESS

OXFORD
UNIVERSITY PRESS

Oxford University Press is a department of the University of Oxford. It furthers
the University's objective of excellence in research, scholarship, and education
by publishing worldwide. Oxford is a registered trade mark of Oxford University
Press in the UK and in certain other countries.

Published in the United States of America by Oxford University Press
198 Madison Avenue, New York, NY 10016, United States of America.

Library of Congress Cataloging-in-Publication Data
Names: Li, Quan, 1966– author.
Title: Using R for data analysis in social sciences : a research
project-oriented approach / Quan Li.
Description: New York, NY : Oxford University Press, [2018]
Identifiers: LCCN 2017010031| ISBN 9780190656225 (pbk.) |
ISBN 9780190656218 (hardcover) | ISBN 9780190656232 (updf) |
ISBN 9780190656249 (epub) Subjects: LCSH: Social sciences–Research–Data
processing. | Social sciences–Statistical methods. | R (Computer program language)
Classification: LCC H61.3 .L52 2018 | DDC 330.285/5133–dc23
LC record available at https://lccn.loc.gov/2017010031

3 5 7 9 8 6 4 2

Paperback printed by Marquis, Canada
Hardback printed by Bridgeport National Bindery, Inc., United States of America

CONTENTS

6. Regression Diagnostics and Sensitivity Analysis   206

7. Replication of Findings in Published Analyses   263

8. Appendix: A Brief Introduction to Analyzing Categorical Data and Finding More Data   302

LIST OF FIGURES

LIST OF TABLES

ACKNOWLEDGMENTS

Five original tables from four different journal articles are reprinted in the book for replication exercises. The articles include (1) Iversen, Torben, and David Soskice, 2006, "Electoral Institutions and the Politics of Coalitions: Why Some Democracies Redistribute More Than Others," American Political Science Review 100(2): 165–81, Table A1. Copyright: Cambridge University Press. (2) Frankel, Jeffrey A., and David Romer, 1999. "Does Trade Cause Growth?" American Economic Review 89(3): 379–99, Table 3. Copyright: American Economic Association. (3) Braithwaite, Alex. 2006. "The Geographic Spread of Militarized Disputes," Journal of Peace Research 43(5): 507–22, Table I and Table II. Copyright: SAGE Publications. (4) Bénabou, Roland, Davide Ticchi, and Andrea Vindigni, 2015, "Religion and 'Innovation'" American Economic Review 105(5): 346–51, Table 2. Copyright: American Economic Association. Permissions to reprint the relevant tables in Iversen and Soskice (2006) and Braithwaite (2006) have been acquired and licensed from Cambridge University Press and SAGE Publications. Jeffrey Frankel, Roland Bénabou, and American Economic Association deserve special thanks for graciously granting me permission to reprint the relevant tables in their articles for free.

Figures 1 through 4 in F. J. Anscombe's "Graphs in Statistical Analysis," published in 1973 in The American Statistician 27(1): 17–21, have been adapted and used with permission of the publisher, Taylor & Francis Ltd http://www.tandfonline.com.

This book would not have been possible without the encouragement, help, and support of many students, colleagues, and friends. My undergraduate students in Polimetrics and Senior Research Seminar at Texas A&M University gave me the first impetus to write this book. Many students taking those two courses, especially Jacob King and Alex Goodman, caught typos and mistakes in earlier drafts. During the summer of 2016, Scarlet Amo, Corbin Cali, Chandler Dawson, and Elizabeth Gohmert experimented with using an earlier version of the manuscript to self-study R for data analysis. They provided detailed reports on each chapter and completed independent application papers. Their input has dramatically changed and improved how various materials in the book are now presented and structured. I thank them for their extraordinary work and effort. My graduate assistants, Molly Berkemeier, Kelly McCaskey, and Austin Johnson, provided excellent editorial assistance. My colleagues and friends, Tiyi Feng, Ren Mu, Erica Owen, and Carlisle Rainey, read parts of an earlier draft and provided valuable feedback and suggestions.

Many people at Oxford University Press have helped to make this manuscript possible and better. Scott Parris, who was the editor for my first book by Cambridge University Press, had been patiently encouraging and prodding me to finish this book until his retirement from Oxford. Happy retirement, Scott! Before retiring from Oxford, Scott handed my case to Anne Dellinger. Anne's enthusiasm and encouragement were the main reason that I decided to stay with Oxford. After Anne departed from Oxford, David Pervin became my editor and offered sound advice. Scott's assistant Cathryn Vaulman and David's assistants Emily Mackenzie and Hayley Singer took care of many of the logistic issues in the process. Debbie Ruel corrected many errors and did a great job during copy editing, and Lincy Priya patiently dealt with my requests and smoothly handled the production of my book. Xun Pang and Jude Hays provided valuable comments and suggestions that helped to make the book enormously better.

Finally, my greatest debt of gratitude is owed to my wife, Liu, and my two children, Ellen and Andrew. Without their unyielding support, constant inquiry, and even reading parts of the book and checking my R code, I would not have finished the project. This book is dedicated to them!

INTRODUCTION

This book seeks to teach senior undergraduate and beginning graduate students in social sciences how to use R to manage, visualize, and analyze data in order to answer substantive research questions and reproduce the statistical analysis in published journal articles. Over the past several decades, statistical analysis training has become increasingly important for undergraduate and graduate students in many disciplines within social and behavioral sciences, such as economics, political science, public administration, business, public health, anthropology, psychology, sociology, education, and communication. With rapid progress in statistical computing, proficiency in using statistical software has become almost a universal requirement, albeit to varying degrees, in statistical methods courses. Popular software choices include: SAS, SPSS, Stata, and R. While SAS, SPSS, and Stata all have accessible introductory textbooks targeting students in social sciences, such textbooks on R are rare.

Compared with commercial packages like SAS, SPSS, and Stata, R has at least three strengths. It is a well-thought-out, coherent system that comes with a suite of software facilities for data management, visualization, and analysis. In addition, to meet emerging needs, a large community of R users constantly develops new open source add-on packages, already reaching over 10,000. Finally, perhaps the greatest perk of the software is that it is free. This financial benefit cannot be over-emphasized. Cash-strapped college students often find themselves relying on lab computers for access to SAS, SPSS, and Stata, or constrained by the limitations of the student versions of those commercial packages. Even postgraduation, many find it difficult to convince their employers to purchase a particular commercial package they know for their everyday use.

There are many reasons why R is preferred to other statistical software packages in higher education. But R's greatest handicap to its widespread use in the social sciences is its steep learning curve. While the market has produced numerous books on R at various levels, introductory textbooks that focus on the needs of students in the social sciences are not easy to find. This book seeks to fill this void.

This book distinguishes itself from other introductory R or statistics books in three important ways. First, it intends to serve as an introductory text on using R for data analysis projects, targeting an audience rarely exposed to statistical programming. The rationale for emphasizing the introductory nature of this book is simple; it is driven by the needs and heterogeneity of the student body we often come across in classroom teaching in social science departments. Unlike students in math and statistics, many student users of R in social sciences have no experience in any computing language or programming software, and many will never achieve a higher level of programming beyond what is necessary for their everyday use in R. However, students in social sciences will find that the opportunity to use R for data manipulation, visualization, and analysis frequently presents itself in various courses and future careers. Hence, they need to become proficient at accomplishing common tasks in data manipulation, visualization, and analysis using R, without getting overly technical. In this respect, existing introductory texts on R programming that do not involve statistics tend to be overly comprehensive in coverage and are often geared toward students in math, statistics, sciences, and engineering, thus intimidating most social science students. Alain Zuur, Elena Ieno, and Erik Meesters' *A Beginner's Guide to R* and Philip Spector's *Data Manipulation with R* are good examples. Their target audiences often are students in math, statistics, sciences, and engineering majors who have more experiences in programming than fellow classmates in social sciences.

This book, in contrast, adopts a minimalist approach in teaching R. It covers only the most important features and functions in R that one will need for conducting reproducible research projects, with other materials moved to chapter appendices or removed from consideration completely. R is extremely flexible, almost always allowing multiple solutions to one programming task. While this is a strength, it does challenge beginning R users rarely exposed to computer programming. The minimalist approach adopted here will present typically one way to deal with a task in the main part of a chapter, leaving other stuff to a section called "Miscellaneous Questions for Ambitious Readers." As a result, the minimalist approach should flatten the steep learning curve—a commonly noted disadvantage of R—thereby improving the software's accessibility to undergraduates and similar audiences. Organizationally, this book breaks down chapters into small sections that mimic lab sessions for students. Each chapter focuses on only the essential R functions one needs to know in order to manipulate, visualize, and analyze data to accomplish some primary statistical analysis tasks. In the end, through this minimalist approach, the reader will accumulate enough R knowledge and skills to complete a course research project and to self-study more advanced R materials if necessary.

A second unique feature of this book is its emphasis on meeting the practical needs of students using R to conduct statistical analysis for research projects driven by substantive questions in social sciences. In addition to homework assignments and problem sets, statistical methods courses in social sciences often require the completion of a full-blown, substantively motivated research project. Such training is critical if statistical knowledge is to prove to be of any value and relevance to substantive courses and students' future careers. Ideally, students can utilize completed statistical analysis papers as writing samples to showcase their quantitative skills in their graduate school or job applications.

In practice, to accomplish such a project on a substantive question, a student has to collect, clean, and manipulate data, visualize and analyze data systematically to address the question asked, and report findings in an organized manner. Many R books for introductory statistics tend to emphasize the R codes for statistical techniques, giving insufficient attention to the pre-analysis needs of users as well as the process of completing a research project. For example, John Verzani's *Using R for Introductory Statistics* and Michael Crawley's *Introductory Statistics Using R* are two popular texts in this category. Data preparation is not linked to particular research projects that address substantive questions.

In contrast, this book is written under the premise that the reader uses R primarily to address some substantive question of interest. This leads to several notable differences from other introductory statistics books using R. This book begins with the use of R to get an original raw dataset into a condition appropriate for statistical analysis, thus emphasizing how to deal with various issues that arise in such a process. Next, instead of starting with the interactive use of R, which is typical in other textbooks, this book gives exclusive attention to writing and executing R programs. This approach allows easy verification, recollection, and replication of analysis, and it is almost always how things are done in actual reproducible research. Students following this approach will write many well-documented R codes that address a variety of practical issues such that they can save those programs for future reference. Last but not least, the use of R in this book is closely integrated into a prototypical process that consists of a sequence of elements: a substantive question to be answered, a hypothesis that answers the question, the logic of statistical inference behind the empirical test of the hypothesis, the test statistic for statistical inference represented in mathematical notation and implemented computationally in R, and the presentation of findings in an organized manner. The emphasis is on an in-depth understanding of why we do statistical analysis and how R fits into actual empirical research. Hence, this research process- or project-oriented approach ought to significantly increase the likelihood that students will actually use R to solve problems in their future courses and careers.

A third unique feature of this book is its emphasis on teaching students how to replicate statistical analyses in published journal articles. Scientific progress requires previous findings be replicable and replicated; scientific education, like in physics and chemistry, always includes lab exercises that replicate previous experiments. As social scientific knowledge becomes increasingly evidence-based and relies on extensive data analysis, learning to replicate published results is a necessary step for undergraduates and first-year graduate students in their learning to conduct social scientific research. Such training now becomes feasible because of the availability of powerful free software and a wide range of datasets in the public domain. Many journals now require authors to submit and deposit replication datasets. Many original data from surveys and archival research are downloadable from the internet. Students no longer have to be just passive consumers of social scientific research but instead can actively scrutinize published research, play with the data, and reproduce or fail to reproduce previous findings. This will convert students from passive consumers into active learners. As reproducing research findings becomes the norm rather than the exception, it will empower the students, lower the barrier to their entry into the academic community, and challenge the professors and other knowledge producers. The wide gap between teaching and research commonly observed in undergraduate courses in social sciences will be narrowed. Such changes are likely to make teaching more interesting for professors, render learning more fruitful for students, and enable both parties to become more successful in their endeavors.

This book consists of eight chapters. Chapter 1 introduces R, illustrating how to write and execute programs using the software. Chapter 2 goes through the process of, and various main tasks in, getting data ready for analysis in R. Chapter 3 provides a conceptual background on the logic of statistical inference and then demonstrates how to make statistical inference with respect to one continuous outcome variable using one- and two-sample t tests. Chapter 4 moves into analyzing the relationship between two continuous variables, focusing on covariance and correlation. Chapter 5 introduces regression analysis, covering its conceptual foundation, model specification, estimation, interpretation, and inference. Chapter 6 continues with regression analysis, delving into various diagnostics and sensitivity analyses. Chapters 4 through 6 follow the same approach, integrating conceptual and mathematical foundation, data preparation, statistical analysis, and results reporting within each chapter. Chapter 7 walks readers through the process of replicating two published analyses. Finally, Chapter 8, as an appendix, provides a brief introduction to analyzing discrete data, demonstrating the Chi-squared test of independence and logistic regression.

No textbook can be perfect; this one is no exception. The minimalist approach, emphasizing the accessibility of R, comes at a price. Many commonly used functions and features of R, such as writing functions and loops, are not covered. Similarly, by focusing on teaching the research process of how to use

R to address substantive questions, this book covers primarily explaining one continuous outcome variable and relevant statistical techniques, such as mean, difference of means, covariance, correlation, and cross-sectional regression. Hence, comprehensiveness in both programming and statistics is sacrificed, on purpose, for greater accessibility, clarity, and depth. The goal is to make this book accessible and useful for novices in both programming and data analysis.

In sum, this book integrates R programming, the logic and steps of statistical inference, and the process of empirical social scientific research in a highly accessible and structured fashion. It emphasizes learning to use R for essential data management, visualization, analysis, and replicating published research findings. By the end of this book, students will have learned how to do the following: (1) use R to import data, inspect data, identify dataset attributes, and manage observations, variables, and datasets; (2) use R to graph simple histograms, box plots, scatter plots, and research findings; (3) use R to summarize data, conduct one-sample t-test, test the difference-of-means between groups, compute covariance and correlation, estimate and interpret ordinary least square (OLS) regression, and diagnose and correct regression assumption violations; and (4) replicate research findings in published journal articles. *The principle behind this book is to teach students to learn as little R as possible but to do as much substantively driven data analysis at the beginner or intermediate level as possible.* The minimalist approach should dramatically reduce the learning cost but still prove adequate for meeting the practical research needs of senior undergraduate and beginning graduate students in the social sciences. Having completed this book, students can competently use R and statistical analysis to answer substantive questions regarding some substantively interesting continuous outcome variable in a cross-sectional design. It is my hope that, the newly acquired competence will motivate students to want to, rather than being forced to, learn more about R and statistics.

Using R for Data Analysis
in Social Sciences

Learn about R and Write
First Toy Programs

Chapter Objectives

In this first chapter, we will aim to achieve the following objectives:

1. Understand when to use R in a research project.
2. Learn about the basic background of R, software installation, and getting help.
3. Learn to set up a project folder for R programs and data files.
4. Learn to write and execute simple toy programs.
5. Learn to find and set the working directory for a project in R.
6. Learn to create a data vector.
7. Learn to calculate descriptive statistics and handle missing values.
8. Learn to convert a data vector into a data frame.
9. Learn to refer to a variable within a data frame.
10. Learn to install an add-on package, "stargazer," load it into R, and use it to get a descriptive statistics table.
11. Learn to graph the distribution of a variable.
12. Apply all the lessons learned to a real-world data example.
13. Learn about common coding errors and how to get help.

Materials in this chapter need about an hour and a half for a class of about 10 students to cover in a lab, including brief lecturing and hands-on practice. Larger classes or self-study could take longer.

When to Use R in a Research Project

To complete an empirical research project involves several stages, often starting with the identification of a research problem and ending with the report of findings and implications:

1. Identify a research problem
2. Survey the literature (Find out what is known about the problem)
3. Formulate a theoretical argument and some testable hypothesis
4. Measure concepts
5. Collect data
6. Prepare data
7. Analyze data
8. Report findings and implications

The tasks of identifying a significant and interesting research problem, surveying the extant literature, formulating a coherent theoretical argument and some testable hypothesis that explain the research puzzle, measuring concepts in the theory empirically, and collecting data for the empirical indicators of the concepts—tasks (1) to (5)—are generally dealt with in substantive and research design courses in a field. Those topics are beyond the scope of this little R book. Yet tasks (6) to (8) may all involve R as a research instrument. Specifically, using R for actual research projects is to analyze particular research problems, such as evaluating the impact of a policy or testing the impact of a causal factor (or an independent variable) on an outcome (or a dependent variable) of interest, as postulated by pre-specified theoretical expectations. How to accomplish tasks (6) to (8) will be illustrated in the following chapters.

A research project of this type presents at least two challenges, for which R will be useful. First, in practice, such a project involves a range of tasks, such as importing data into software, merging different datasets together, verifying data, creating new variables, recoding and renaming variables, visualizing data, running statistical estimation procedures, carrying out diagnostic tests, and so on. Second, an analyst needs to be able to reproduce his or her own analysis, including dataset construction and estimation results, even years later. The first challenge concerns the efficiency of an analysis, whereas the second concerns the reproducibility and integrity of the analysis.

To achieve both efficiency and reproducibility, experienced analysts always choose to write down their computing code in one or more programs so that the code can be submitted, revised, and resubmitted to reproduce an analysis speedily and whenever necessary. Hence, in this book, we will focus on how to write and submit R programs for specific tasks in a program editor, rather than the interactive use or menu-driven interface of R. For all practical purposes, the programming approach is much more efficient and consistent than the interactive or menu-driven approach.

Before we step into how to use R, we will need to clarify some related organizational and housekeeping issues. In this chapter, we will first offer a very brief introduction to R, then demonstrate how to install R, write and execute R programs, install and load add-on packages, and produce graphical and numerical output, and then turn to essential reference information about important symbols and common coding errors. Notably, each line of R code will likely appear three times: presented as a stand-alone command line preceded or followed by an explanation of its purpose and function, listed together with the output from its execution, and collated with all other program code in the chapter for the sake of convenient reference. We will end the chapter with a section about miscellaneous issues of interest to ambitious readers and a section on exercises.

Essentials about R

A One-Paragraph Introduction to R

R is a computer language and an environment for statistical computing and graphics with important advantages. Started by Robert Gentleman and Ross Ihaka of the University of Auckland in 1995, it is now maintained by the R core-development team of volunteer developers. R is referred to as a computer language because as a dialect of the S language developed in the late 1980s at AT&T's labs, R allows users to follow the algorithms, define and add new functions, and write new analytic methods, rather than merely supplying canned routines. R is also a coherent system which provides an environment with an integrated suite of software facilities for data storage, manipulation, analysis, and visualization. In addition, R is flexible. It runs on Windows, UNIX, and Mac OS X. It can be easily extended in terms of new functions and state-of-the-art statistical methods; the over 10,000 add-on packages by the end of January 2017 through the CRAN family of internet sites testify to this fact. Last but not least, R is free, as are its numerous add-on packages. Hence, R is popular among practitioners in many fields and scholars in many disciplines, including the social sciences.

Installation

As an open source software for statistical computing, R can be easily downloaded from the following site: http://www.r-project.org/. We may simply click on the highlighted download R link to reach a list of CRAN mirror sites. Clicking on any site we prefer directs us to the page for downloading the software for three different platforms: Linux, Windows, and Mac. R works slightly differently across the three platforms. For the purpose of this book, we will focus on the language and functionality specific to the Windows platform. Mac users may consult the Miscellaneous Q&A Section later in the chapter for some brief explanation.

R is being constantly updated to new versions by developers. It is worth noting that some R programs and packages used in this book could require 3.3.2 or newer. If the version of R on a machine is not up to date, one may simply uninstall the old version and install the latest version following the procedures described previously, or refer to the subsection on how to update R in the Miscellaneous Q&A Section.

How to Start A Project Folder and Write Our First R Program

Learn to Set up A Project Folder for Programs and Data Files

The first step in a project is to set up a project folder to hold relevant datasets, programs, and output files. We can think of a project folder as our home mailing address, and all the relevant datasets, programs, and output files as the mail and packages to be delivered to us. Without the mailing address, the packages and mail will not be delivered to the right place. Hence, a project folder allows us to easily find all the relevant files and avoid having them mingled and conflated with those files for other projects or purposes.

In Windows, we can create a project folder via the following steps: Open My Computer or File Explorer; right click on the root directory, such as C: or D:; click on New; click on New Folder or Folder; and type in a meaningful name for the new folder, such as Project.

Learn to Find and Set A Working Directory for A Project

When we open R, the default interface is the R Console page, which is based on the interactive mode. To create an R program, we should go to the R Editor page. To do so, we can open R, click on File on the menu bar, and then click on New script to open the R program editor. Now, click on the Save button on the menu bar or the Save option under File, and we will be prompted to enter a filename for an R program file that ends with .R. For an experiment, name the file session1.R (remember to end it with .R), and then save the file in the Project folder.

Learn to Write and Execute the Simplest Toy Program

Now is the time for us to learn to write an extremely simple R program and run it. R has a default working directory or folder (think of it as the post office address for mail and packages). We are interested in telling R to change the current default working directory to the Project folder. It is like directing our mail to be delivered to our own home address, rather than the post office address. The Project folder is where we keep our program and data files.

To do so, we first identify the working directory of the current R session, then change it to the Project folder, and finally verify that the change is successful.

In the program editor, first type in

```
getwd()
```

The getwd function lists the name of the current working directory.

Next, type in

```
setwd("C:/Project")
```

The setwd function changes the current working directory for the current R session. The argument of the function is inside the parentheses, between double quotation marks, and employs one forward slash; it specifies the path to the Project folder as the new current working directory for the current R session. This line of code makes it possible, during the rest of our R session, for us to refer to the files within the Project folder without specifying the path again. Finally, note that R is case sensitive. Hence, R will treat **Project** and **project** as two different folders. If there is a mismatch in spelling between the program code and the actual folder name, R will produce an error message. Also note that any mismatch in terms of quotation marks, colon, etc. will cause R to produce an error message.

In specifying the path, we may use one forward slash as above, or alternatively, two double back slashes as follows:

```
setwd("C:\\Project")
```

Please note the double back slashes. This is very important. If we copy the path from our computer File Explorer, the copied and pasted path will contain only one back slash. For R, we will need to add an extra back slash, or change it to one forward slash.

Finally, type in again

```
getwd()
```

This allows us to verify the task is done as instructed.

We save these three lines of code into a program file called session1.R. This three-line R program asks R to display the default working directory, then sets the Project folder as our new current working directory, and finally asks R to display the current working directory again.

Having the .R suffix in the program filename is a good practice for two reasons. It helps us see immediately that it is an R program file. When we open a program file in the R editor, all files with .R suffix will appear automatically in the list of files for us to choose to open. If the program file does not have the .R suffix and if we want to open it in the R program editor, it will not show up automatically in the list of files. We will have to choose "All Files (*.*)" from file type in the lower right corner in order to see all files in the folder.

```
getwd()
setwd("C:/Project")
getwd()
```

To execute this little program in R, we may choose one of the following two ways:

1. If we want to execute the program line by line, put the cursor anywhere in that line of code, then we can execute it in one of three ways: (a) hit two keys Ctrl+R on the keyboard together; (b) right click the mouse and then click on Run line or selection; (c) click on the third little icon (right next to the second save script icon) on the upper left corner, representing Run line or selection.
2. If we want to execute the whole program in one run, highlight the whole program in R editor, and then either right click the mouse and click on Run line or selection, or hit two keys Ctrl+R on the keyboard together.

When we execute the program above, we will get the following output in R:

```
getwd()

[1] "C:/Users/Quan Li/Box Sync/R Book/Rnw_oup_formal"

setwd("C:/Project")
getwd()

[1] "C:/Project"
```

Note that the first line of code getwd() shows that the default current working directory was "C:/Users/Quan Li/Box Sync/R Book/Rnw_oup_formal", in which I have kept my knitr .Rnw and LaTex files for writing this R book. Then, the second line of code asks R to set the current working directory to "C:/Project" instead. The third line of code shows that for the rest of this R session, files will be drawn from or saved to this new working directory unless otherwise specified via a different file path.

One essential point about programming is that one should document the purpose of a program as a whole and what each line of code does so that days, weeks, or months from now, we or any others who open up the program will be able to understand what the program does and how it does it. For this purpose, we insert comment lines that begin with the # sign into a program. The # sign tells R not to execute that line. Note that the first comment specifies the purpose, time, and software version used. After adding comment lines, the little toy R program above will now be complete and look like the following:

```
# First R toy program, today's date, R version 3.2.3
# show current working directory path
getwd()

# change the working directory for program to project folder
setwd("C:/Project")

# show current working directory path again to verify
getwd()
```

To demonstrate the general process graphically, Figure 1.1 presents four screenshots from R console and editor, which proceed from opening R (picture 1), to opening R editor (picture 2), to typing the three lines of code in R editor (picture 3), to running those three lines and producing output in R console (picture 4).

The biggest benefit of writing and saving a program is to reproduce the same output at any time so long as the functions of the software remain unchanged. For a reader unfamiliar with this approach of working with a software package, it might be useful to close R, open it again, and re-run the little program for replication and verification. Remember to save the program first before closing it; otherwise, we will lose all the changes since we last saved it. The ability to run the same program and produce the same result years after is one of the most important reasons why we prefer to program, rather than using the interactive mode via point and click.

Create, Describe, and Graph A Vector: A Simple Toy Example

Since R is an object-oriented programming language, it is useful to know something about how R works with data. A simplified view is that R relies on a variety of functions, which take in data as input and then produce desired output objects. In other words, R treats data as objects and operates on data objects through functions (which are themselves treated as objects as well), in order to manipulate data, create graphs, and conduct statistical analysis.

The most basic data object in R is a vector. A vector is a combination of elements, such as numbers, characters, or logical statements (like TRUE, FALSE). The elements within a single vector must be of the same type, i.e., numeric, character, or logical. In a simple example provided in the R manual, a vector named x consists of five numbers ordered as 10.4, 5.6, 3.1, 6.4, 21.7.

```
File  Edit  View  Misc  Packages  Windows  Help

R Console

R version 3.3.1 (2016-06-21) -- "Bug in Your Hair"
Copyright (C) 2016 The R Foundation for Statistical Computing
Platform: i386-w64-mingw32/i386 (32-bit)

R is free software and comes with ABSOLUTELY NO WARRANTY.
You are welcome to redistribute it under certain conditions.
Type 'license()' or 'licence()' for distribution details.

  Natural language support but running in an English locale

R is a collaborative project with many contributors.
Type 'contributors()' for more information and
'citation()' on how to cite R or R packages in publications.

Type 'demo()' for some demos, 'help()' for on-line help, or
'help.start()' for an HTML browser interface to help.
Type 'q()' to quit R.

[Previously saved workspace restored]

>
```

(a) picture 1

```
File  Edit  View  Misc  Packages  Windows  Help
Source R code...
New script
Open script...
Display file(s)...
Load Workspace...      (2016-06-21) -- "B$
Save Workspace...  Ctrl+S  )16 The R Foundatio$
Load History...            ·64-mingw32/i386 (3$
Save History...
Change dir...          re and comes with $
                       to redistribute it$
Print...          Ctrl+P   or 'licence()' fo$
Save to File...
Exit                   ge support but run$
```

(b) picture 2

Figure 1.1 How to Write First Toy Program in R.

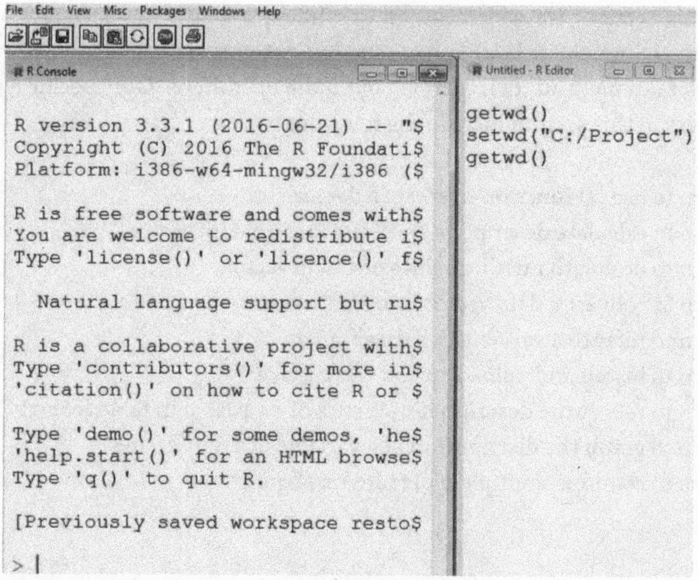

```
File  Edit  View  Misc  Packages  Windows  Help

R Console                                    R Untitled - R Editor

R version 3.3.1 (2016-06-21) -- "$       getwd()
Copyright (C) 2016 The R Foundati$       setwd("C:/Project")
Platform: i386-w64-mingw32/i386 ($       getwd()

R is free software and comes with$
You are welcome to redistribute i$
Type 'license()' or 'licence()' f$

    Natural language support but ru$

R is a collaborative project with$
Type 'contributors()' for more in$
'citation()' on how to cite R or $

Type 'demo()' for some demos, 'he$
'help.start()' for an HTML browse$
Type 'q()' to quit R.

[Previously saved workspace resto$

>
```

(c) picture 3

```
File  Edit  View  Misc  Packages  Windows  Help

R Console                                    R Untitled - R Editor

Copyright (C) 2016 The R Foundati$       getwd()
Platform: i386-w64-mingw32/i386 ($       setwd("C:/Project")
                                         getwd()
R is free software and comes with$
You are welcome to redistribute i$
Type 'license()' or 'licence()' f$

    Natural language support but ru$

R is a collaborative project with$
Type 'contributors()' for more in$
'citation()' on how to cite R or $

Type 'demo()' for some demos, 'he$
'help.start()' for an HTML browse$
Type 'q()' to quit R.

[Previously saved workspace resto$

> getwd()
[1] "C:/Users/quanli/Documents"
> setwd("C:/Project")
> getwd()
[1] "C:/Project"
```

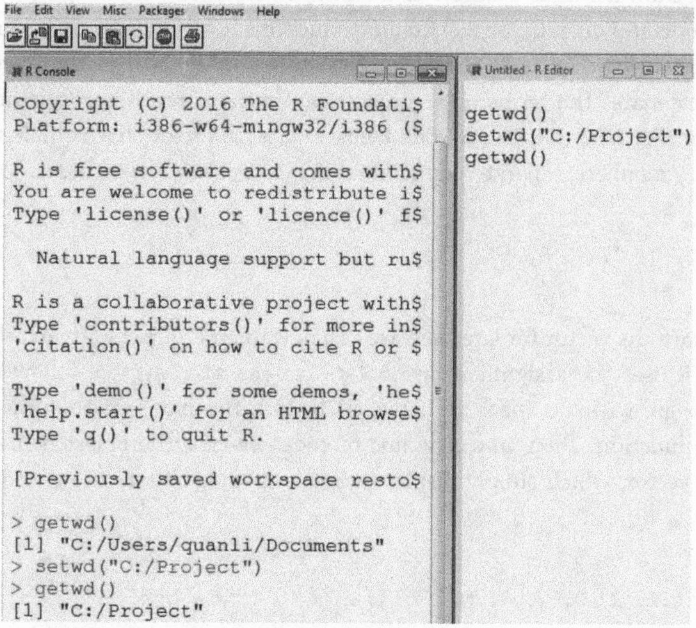

(d) picture 4

Figure 1.1 (Continued)

In this section, we will focus on expanding our first toy program around one artificial numeric data vector, carrying out various operations, turning it into a data frame, and then carrying out more operations. Our specific learning objectives in this section include the following:

1. Learn to use c() function to create a data vector
2. Learn to calculate descriptive statistics for this data vector
3. Learn to deal with missing values of a data vector
4. Learn to convert a data vector into a data frame
5. Learn to refer to a variable in a data frame
6. Learn to install and upload an add-on package
7. Learn to report the descriptive statistics of a variable in table format
8. Learn to graph the distribution of a variable in a data frame
9. Learn to combine multiple plots into one figure

Create A Vector Using c() Function

We will show a simple example of a numeric vector as a data object. To show how R operates on data, we will first introduce one function and one assignment operator for objects in R. The first function is c(). The c() function combines or concatenates the terms or arguments inside the parentheses together into a vector. For example, the R code below creates a vector that contains some arbitrary numbers, separated by commas, inside a pair of parentheses.

```
c(1, 2, 0, 2, 4, 5, 10, 1)
```

To save the vector for later use, we assign it to an R object with an arbitrary name. R uses the assignment symbol <- (a less than symbol followed by a minus sign, with no space in between) to link the name of the object and the c() function. Then, in a new line of code, we type the object name given to the vector, which simply displays what is in that object. The R code is as follows:

```
v1 <- c(1, 2, 0, 2, 4, 5, 10, 1)
v1
```

As noted, R is an object-oriented programming language. R can work with a variety of objects, such as "numeric," "logical," "character," "list," "matrix," "array," "factor," or "data.frame." Different objects have different attributes. Even though we will not go into details about all their differences in this introductory book, it is always a good idea to know what type of an object we have created. To identify the object type of v1, we simply apply the class() function.

```
class(v1)
```

Collecting these four lines of code, mingled with explanatory comment lines R ignores in execution, we produce the following R program:

```
# use c() function to create a vector object
c(1, 2, 0, 2, 4, 5, 10, 1)

# assign the c function output to an object named v1
v1 <- c(1, 2, 0, 2, 4, 5, 10, 1)

# call object v1 to see what is in it
v1

# identify object type of v1
class(v1)
```

Running this program in R produces the following output:

```
# use c() function to create a vector object
c(1, 2, 0, 2, 4, 5, 10, 1)

[1]  1  2  0  2  4  5 10  1

# assign the c function output to an object named v1
v1 <- c(1, 2, 0, 2, 4, 5, 10, 1)

# call object v1 to see what is in it
v1

[1]  1  2  0  2  4  5 10  1

# identify object type of v1
class(v1)

[1] "numeric"
```

Calculate Descriptive Statistics for A Vector

Now that we have created our first data vector in R, we can work with it to practice some useful R functions. For example, we can ask R to tell us how many observations are in v1, its sample mean, and its sample variance, as well as various other summary statistics regarding v1. Notice how we use comment lines to keep track of what we did for ourselves and to tell others who will see our code in the future what we did.

```
# find the number of observations in variable v1
length(v1)

# find v1's sample mean (two ways: mean function or formula)
mean(v1)
sum(v1)/length(v1)

# find v1's sample variance (variance function or formula)
var(v1)
sum((v1-mean(v1))^2)/(length(v1)-1)

# find v1's sample standard deviation (function
# or square root of sample variance)
sd(v1)
sqrt(var(v1))

# find v1's sample minimum and maximum using functions
max(v1)
min(v1)
```

Several issues on the code above are worth clarification. First, eight new functions are introduced, including length, mean, sum, var, sd, sqrt, min, and max. They identify the number of observations, mean, total sum, sample variance, sample standard deviation, minimum, and maximum of v1, respectively.

Second, the code employs some of the commonly used mathematical operators in R, including addition (+), subtraction (-), multiplication (*), division (/), and exponentiation (^). These are self-explanatory and should be memorized for future use.

Third, the code above shows alternative ways to compute sample mean, variance, and standard deviations. In other words, sample mean is computed as the sum of all observations of v1 divided by the number of observations, sample variance is calculated as the sum of squared deviations of v1 from its mean divided by (the number of observations minus one), and sample standard deviation is the square root of sample variance. More details about these will be discussed in Chapter 3.

Finally, parentheses are used to structure the order of mathematical operations. Always start with calculations inside parentheses. Also, perform exponentiation, multiplication, and division from left to right; then, perform addition and subtraction from left to right.

Executing the code above in R produces the following output:

```
# find total number of observations in variable v1
length(v1)

[1] 8

# find v1's sample mean (two ways: mean function or formula)
mean(v1)

[1] 3.125

sum(v1)/length(v1)

[1] 3.125

# find v1's sample variance (variance function or formula)
var(v1)

[1] 10.41071

sum((v1-mean(v1))^2)/(length(v1)-1)

[1] 10.41071

# find v1's sample standard deviation (function
# or square root of sample variance)
sd(v1)

[1] 3.226564

sqrt(var(v1))

[1] 3.226564

# find v1's sample minimum and maximum using functions
max(v1)

[1] 10

min(v1)

[1] 0
```

Handle Missing Values in Descriptive Statistics

The artificial variable v1 above does not have any missing value. However, missing values are common in real-world data. What happens when missing values are present? This question is relevant both when we compute descriptive statistics for a vector and when we want to know how many missing or non-missing values are in a vector.

Suppose we create a new variable called v2, which is identical to v1 except for that v2 has two missing values. In R, the default missing value is denoted by NA. Hence, we replace two observations in v1 with NA to generate v2.

```
# create v2 with missing values
v2 <- c(1, 2, 0, 2, NA, 5, 10, NA)
```

If we compute the mean of v2 with the mean() function without removing the missing values, we obtain the following output:

```
# compute mean of v2 without removing missing values
mean(v2)

[1] NA
```

Apparently, if there are missing values in a variable and R is not told to consider their presence when executing a function, then the output of that function will be NA. Hence, we need to tell R to ignore observations that are NA (missing values). We do so by inserting the na.rm=TRUE option inside the function, meaning that it is true to remove NA observations.

```
# compute mean of v2 after removing missing values
mean(v2, na.rm = TRUE)

[1] 3.333333
```

In actual data analysis, it is also important that we get correct information on the numbers of total, missing, and non-missing observations for a variable of interest. The length() function introduced earlier only identifies the total number of elements of a vector, including both missing and non-missing values. To identify the number of missing values in a variable, we need to use a new function, is.na(). The is.na() function produces a vector of logical values (TRUE or FALSE) for the vector listed in the function: TRUE if an element is a missing value; FALSE if it is not missing. Basically, we can think of the function as if it were asking whether each element in a vector is na or not. In contrast, to verify if an element of a vector is a non-missing value or not, we add the ! sign (meaning not) before the is.na() function. Applying is.na() and !is.na() to v2 gives us the following TRUE or FALSE output with respect to each element of v2. The R code and output are listed below. Note how for each element of v2, is.na() and !is.na() give us exactly opposite logical values.

```
# display output from is.na() function
is.na(v2)

[1] FALSE FALSE FALSE FALSE  TRUE FALSE FALSE  TRUE

# display output from !is.na() function
!is.na(v2)

[1]  TRUE  TRUE  TRUE  TRUE FALSE  TRUE  TRUE FALSE
```

To find how many missing values are in v2, we use the sum() function to count the total number of TRUE values in the output of is.na(). For the number of non-missing values, we apply !is.na() instead to count the number of TRUE values. Note how in the output below, the total number of observations = missing values + non-missing values.

```
# find total number of observations in v2
length(v2)

[1] 8

# find the number of missing values in v2
sum(is.na(v2))

[1] 2

# find the number of non-missing values in v2
sum(!is.na(v2))

[1] 6
```

Convert A Vector into A Data Frame

So far, we have been working with vectors like v1 and v2. In actual data analysis, we typically work with a dataset that has observations as rows and variables as columns. In R, we also work with this type of data object, called a data frame. A data frame in R is often displayed in matrix form, which is a two-dimensional data object consisting of rows by columns. For our purposes, we can think of a data frame as a typical dataset like in Excel, with rows indicating observations and columns indicating variables. Each column or variable of a data frame must be of the same data type (character, numeric, logical), but different columns or variables could be of different data types.

How do we convert a vector into a data frame in R? We simply apply the data.frame() function to v1, which will turn it into a data frame, and then assign the output from the function into a data frame arbitrarily named. The R code is as follows:

```
# convert data vector v1 into a data frame vd
vd <- data.frame(v1)
```

Recall that a data frame is a two-dimensional data object with rows by columns, just like a typical dataset with rows indicating observations and columns indicating variables. Hence, we can think of vd as a dataset containing one variable called v1 with eight observations.

We may also combine vectors v1 and v2 together into a data frame by applying the data.frame() function. By combining v1 and v2, the new data frame now consists of two variables, v1 and v2, and eight observations. The R code is as follows:

```
# combine vectors v1 and v2 into data frame vd of two
# variables v1 and v2
vd <- data.frame(v1, v2)
```

The R output for executing the code above and displaying the data frame content is as follows:

```
# convert data vector v1 into a data frame vd
vd <- data.frame(v1)

# display vd
vd

  v1
1  1
2  2
3  0
4  2
5  4
6  5
7 10
8  1

# combine vectors v1 and v2 into data frame vd of two
# variables v1 and v2
```

```
vd <- data.frame(v1, v2)

# display vd
vd

   v1 v2
1   1  1
2   2  2
3   0  0
4   2  2
5   4 NA
6   5  5
7  10 10
8   1 NA
```

Note that we first created a dataset or data frame vd with one variable and eight observations, and then we created another dataset vd that overwrote the previous dataset of the same name. We could have given the second one a different name to avoid overwriting the first one.

Now that we have created a dataset or data frame vd with two variables and eight observations, how do we refer to a variable in the data frame? R uses the $ sign to link a data frame and a variable in the data frame. Hence, vd$v1 refers to variable v1 in vd, and vd$v2 refers to variable v2 in vd.

Format Output into Table

An important part of presenting research findings is to format output into a table. The base R package, however, does not produce nicely formatted output. As noted earlier, one of the most important strengths of R is the availability of add-on packages R users provide for free through the CRAN family of internet sites. R is reported to have nearly 12,000 free add-on packages as of 2017. One free package, stargazer, allows us to present the statistical results in a formatted table.

To apply the package to our data frame vd, we will learn how to complete the following tasks: install a user-written package, load the package into R, and apply the stargazer() function to produce a table.

How to Install and Load an Add-on Package

To install the stargazer package, follow the steps in Figure 1.2: Open R in Windows, click on Packages on the menu bar, click on Install Packages from the options (picture 1), select a CRAN mirror site nearby and click OK (picture 2), select the package to install and click OK (picture 3), and a successful installation will be shown in R console (picture 4).

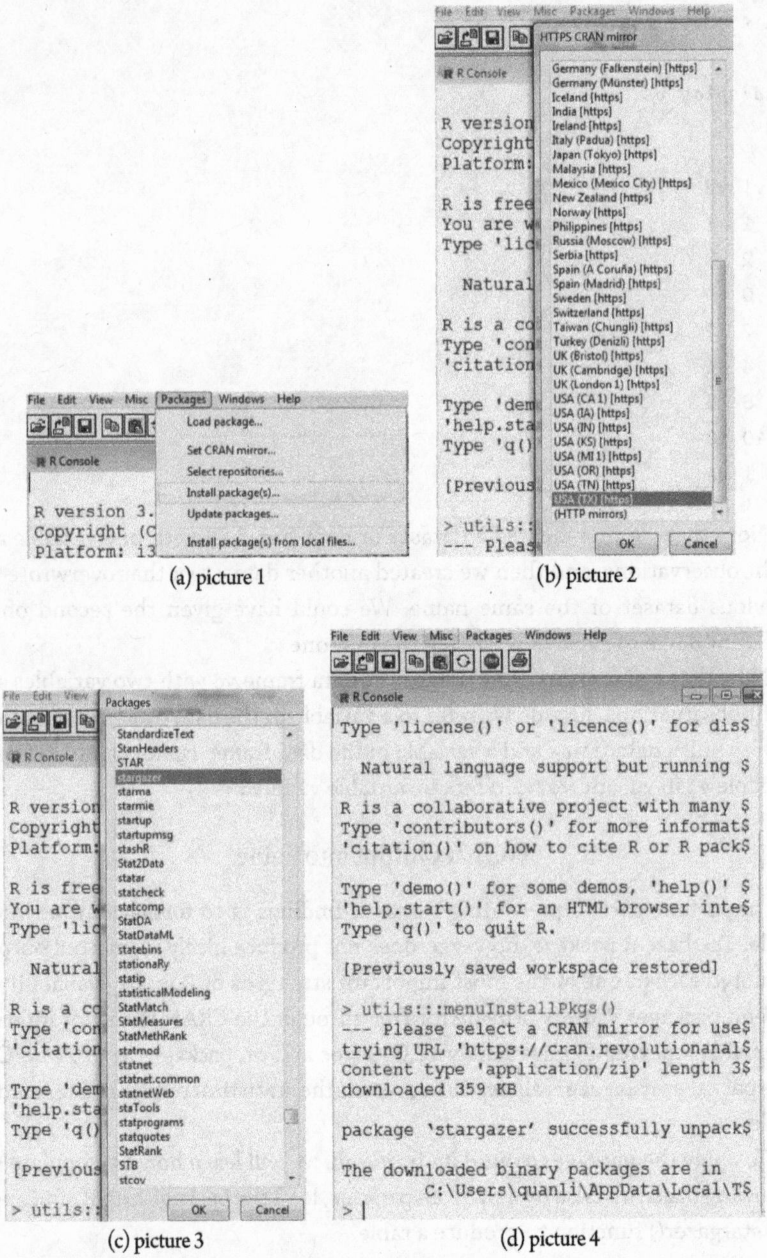

(a) picture 1

(b) picture 2

(c) picture 3

(d) picture 4

Figure 1.2 How to Install Add-on Package.

Note that an add-on package only needs to be installed once for future use. Hence, we do not have to include and run the installation command in our R program. However, in every R session, if we plan to use an add-on package, we will have to load it into R via the library() function. After loading, a citation of each package will also show up for users. The R code is as follows:

```
# install.packages('stargazer')
library(stargazer)
```

Before we move on, it needs to be emphasized that all add-on packages must be first installed before they can be loaded into R using the library() function. Yet all add-on packages only need to be installed once. Thus, in the rest of the chapter, before we use the library() function, we will always keep a line of code on package installation as a reminder that the package must be installed first, and yet we will always comment out that line of code since it only needs to be installed once.

Produce Descriptive Statistics Table

Now that we have loaded the stargazer package, we may produce a formatted table of descriptive statistics for variables in vd via the stargazer() function. The R code is as follows:

```
# produce formatted descriptive statistics of variables in
# data frame vd
stargazer(vd, type = "text")
```

Two issues are worth clarification. First, to get descriptive statistics for v1, we have to apply the stargazer() function to the data frame vd containing v1; if we apply the function to v1 alone, we will get a display of all its observations rather than its descriptive statistics (try it!). Second, the stargazer() function allows one to choose among three types of output formats: "latex" (default) for LaTeX code, "html" for HTML/CSS code, and "text" for ASCII text output. For users not familiar with the first two types, we specify type="text". The R output is as follows:

```
# install package first and for once only
# install.packages('stargazer')

# load stargazer into R
library(stargazer)

# produce formatted descriptive statistics of variable(s)
# in data frame vd
```

```
stargazer(vd, type = "text")
```

```
==================================
Statistic N Mean  St. Dev. Min Max
----------------------------------
v1        8 3.125 3.227     0  10
v2        6 3.333 3.670     0  10
----------------------------------
```

We may modify the code above to generate a variety of formatted output. The following code and their comment lines illustrate several possible variations.

```
# display dataset in a table format
stargazer(vd, type = "text", summary = FALSE, rownames = FALSE)
```

```
# add additional statistics to be reported median,
# interquartile range (25th and 75th percentile)
stargazer(vd, type = "text", median = TRUE, iqr = TRUE)
```

```
# use c() function to choose statistics to be reported
stargazer(vd, type = "text", summary.stat = c("n", "mean",
    "median", "sd"))
```

For example, select descriptive statistics of variables in vd may be presented as follows:

```
# produce formatted select descriptive statistics of
# variables in vd
stargazer(vd, type = "text", summary.stat = c("n", "mean",
    "sd", "min", "p25", "median", "p75", "max"))
```

```
========================================================
Statistic N Mean  St. Dev. Min Pctl(25) Median Pctl(75) Max
--------------------------------------------------------
v1        8 3.125 3.227     0    1        2      4.2     10
v2        6 3.333 3.670     0    1.2      2      4.2     10
--------------------------------------------------------
```

Graph the Distribution of A Variable

Visualizing the distribution of a variable of interest is an important part of data analysis. To illustrate, we will use several R functions to graph the distribution of variable v1 in dataset vd. How we graph vd$v1 depends on what type of variable we think it is, i.e., whether it is discrete or continuous. A discrete variable is one that only takes on a finite number of values, e.g., gender, age, and the number of children in a household. In contrast, a continuous variable is one that could take on an infinite number of possible values, even within a range, like weight, distance, and income.

If we treat v1 as a discrete variable, then we can use frequency table and bar chart to demonstrate its distribution. A frequency table displays data values of a variable and how often each value occurs. It is often first used to examine the distribution of a discrete variable. In R, the table() function computes the frequency count for each value of a variable. The R code and output are as follows:

```
# display the frequency count of v1
table(vd$v1)


 0  1  2  4  5 10
 1  2  2  1  1  1
```

The top row in output shows each value of vd$v1, and the second row the frequency count of each value.

A bar chart displays the distribution of a discrete variable in terms of the frequencies of its values or some other measures. In R, the barplot() function uses the frequency count output produced from the table() function to show a bar plot. Figure 1.3 is created using the code below:

```
# graph distribution of discrete variable vd$v1: bar chart
barplot(table(vd$v1))
```

If we treat vd$v1 as a continuous variable, then we are more interested in the center, symmetry or skewness, and outliers in the distribution of the variable. We can use boxplot and histogram to demonstrate its distribution. In R, the hist() function produces histogram, and the boxplot() function creates box plot. The R code for plotting vd$v1 is as follows:

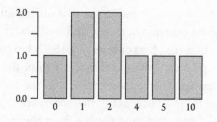

Figure 1.3 Distribution of Discrete Variable vd$v1: Bar Chart.

```
# graph distribution of continuous variable vd$v1: box
# plot and histogram
boxplot(vd$v1)
hist(vd$v1)
```

Sometimes, we are interested in placing the plots together into one figure for ease of comparison. To do so, we use the par() function to set graphical parameters, such as the number of rows and columns in a figure. If we want a figure of two plots side by side, that is, organized into one row and two columns, we specify mfrow=c(1,2) in the par() function, where the first value refers to the number of rows and the second the number of columns. Figure 1.4 is created using the code below:

```
# create a figure with two plots
# set graphical parameters for a figure of one row, two columns
par(mfrow = c(1, 2))

# graph distribution of continuous variable vd$v1: box
# plot and histogram
boxplot(vd$v1)
hist(vd$v1)
```

A box plot presents important attributes of a plotted variable: (1) the median, indicated by the dark horizontal line inside the box; (2) the first (25th) and third (75th) quartiles (i.e., interquartile range), represented by the lower and upper boundaries of the box, respectively; (3) the short horizontal lines outside the box, together with the dotted lines linking to the box, are called whiskers and represent the minimum and maximum values excluding outliers; (4) outliers (if any), denoted by dots that are 1.5 times larger than the upper quartile or 1.5 times less than the lower quartile. In Figure 1.4, the box plot shows that for vd$v1, the median value is 2, the 25th and 75th percentile values are 1 and 4.5, the minimum and maximum values are 0 and 5, and the outlier is 10. Overall, the box plot shows that the variable is centered within the interquartile range, yet it is not symmetrically distributed but skewed toward an outlier.

A histogram is also frequently used to show the distribution of a continuous variable in terms of its center, symmetry, and outliers. It puts values of the plotted variable into bins (i.e., bars or intervals). Each bin contains the number of times or frequency of data values contained within the bin. The area of a bin represents the frequency of occurrences within the bin. In Figure 1.4, the histogram shows that the 0–2 bin contains five observations, the bin from above 2 to 4 contains one observation, and the bin from above 4 to 6 contains one observation, and the bin from above 8 to 10 contains one observation. Overall,

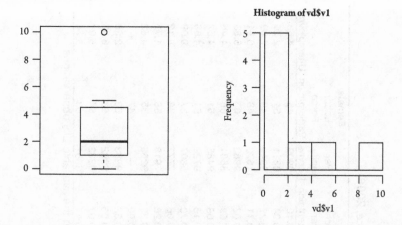

Figure 1.4 Distribution of Continuous Variable vd$v1: Boxplot and Histogram.

the histogram shows that the variable is single peaked but it is seriously skewed to the right.

R allows us to modify and polish these plots in many different ways. However, to make graphing accessible to beginners, we intentionally make the plots as simple as possible, without any additional details.

Simple Real-World Example: Data from Iversen and Soskice (2006)

In this section, we will apply the code from the simple toy example to a real-world data example, drawn from the following published article:

> Iversen, Torben, and David Soskice. 2006. "Electoral Institutions and the Politics of Coalitions: Why Some Democracies Redistribute More Than Others." *American Political Science Review* 100(2): 165–81.

In this article, Iversen and Soskice study the variations in government redistribution across democracies. They argue that proportional representation electoral systems enable center-left governments to dominate and produce more redistribution whereas majoritarian systems enable center-right governments to dominate and engage in less redistribution. Table A1 in their article provides country means for variables used in their statistical analysis, as shown in Table 1.1.

Next, we will demonstrate how to read data on several variables in that table into R, provide descriptive statistics, and show distribution plots for some key variables.

Table 1.1 Country Means for Variables Used in Regression Analysis (from Iverson and Soskice, 2006)

	Redistribution (reduction in Gini)	Inequality (wages)	Partisanship (right)	Voter Turnout	Union-ization	Veto Points	Electoral System (PR)	Left Frag-mentation	Right over-Representation	Per capita Income	Female Labor Force Participation	Unemploym
Australia	23.97	1.70	0.47	84	46	3	0	−0.39	0.10	10909	46	4.63
Austria	—	—	0.30	87	54	1	1	−0.18	0.04	8311	51	2.76
Belgium	35.56	1.64	0.36	88	48	1	1	−0.34	0.27	8949	43	7.89
Canada	21.26	1.82	0.36	68	30	2	0	0.18	−0.11	11670	48	6.91
Denmark	37.89	1.58	0.35	84	67	0	1	−0.40	0.07	9982	63	6.83
Finland	35.17	1.68	0.30	79	53	1	1	−0.18	0.09	8661	66	4.48
France	25.36	1.94	0.40	66	18	1	0	0.10	0.09	9485	51	4.57
Germany	18.70	1.70	0.39	81	34	4	1	−0.13	0.15	9729	51	4.86
Ireland	—	—	0.42	75	48	0	0	−0.33	0.70	5807	37	9.09
Italy	12.13	1.63	0.37	93	34	1	1	0.20	0.08	7777	38	8.12
Japan	—	—	0.78	71	31	1	0	0.22	0.28	7918	56	1.77
Netherlands	30.59	1.64	0.31	85	33	0	1	0.18	−0.36	9269	35	4.62
New Zealand	—	—	0.43	85	23	0	0	−0.40	0.98	—	47	—
Norway	27.52	1.50	0.15	80	54	0	1	−0.02	−0.32	9863	52	2.28
Sweden	37.89	1.58	0.17	84	67	0	1	−0.40	−0.03	9982	63	6.83
U.K.	22.67	1.78	0.52	76	42	0	0	0.08	0.07	9282	54	5.01
U.S.	17.60	2.07	0.40	56	23	5	0	0.00	−0.17	13651	53	5.74

Note: Time coverage is 1950–96 except for redistribution and inequality, which are restricted to the available LIS observations.

```
# create dataset from Iversen and Soskice

# assign c() function output to vector object country
country <- c("Australia","Austria","Belgium","Canada",
"Denmark","Finland","France","Germany","Ireland", "Italy",
"Japan","Netherlands","New Zealand","Norway","Sweden","U.K.",
"US")

# assign c() output to object gini.red for reduction in GINI
gini.red <- c(23.97,NA,35.56,21.26,37.89,35.17,25.36,18.7,NA,
              12.13,NA,30.59,NA,27.52,37.89,22.67,17.6)

# assign c() output to object wage.ineq for wage inequality
wage.ineq <- c(1.7,NA,1.64,1.82,1.58,1.68,1.94,1.7,NA,1.63,NA,
               1.64,NA,1.5,1.58,1.78,2.07)

# assign c() output to object pr for electoral system
pr <- c(0,1,1,0,1,1,0,1,0,1,0,1,0,1,1,0,0)

# use data.frame function to combine four vector objects
# assign data.frame function output to data frame is2006apsr
is2006apsr <- data.frame(country, gini.red, wage.ineq, pr)

# call data frame is2006apsr to display content
is2006apsr
```

	country	gini.red	wage.ineq	pr
1	Australia	23.97	1.70	0
2	Austria	NA	NA	1
3	Belgium	35.56	1.64	1
4	Canada	21.26	1.82	0
5	Denmark	37.89	1.58	1
6	Finland	35.17	1.68	1
7	France	25.36	1.94	0
8	Germany	18.70	1.70	1
9	Ireland	NA	NA	0
10	Italy	12.13	1.63	1
11	Japan	NA	NA	0
12	Netherlands	30.59	1.64	1
13	New Zealand	NA	NA	0
14	Norway	27.52	1.50	1
15	Sweden	37.89	1.58	1

| 16 | U.K. | 22.67 | 1.78 | 0 |
| 17 | US | 17.60 | 2.07 | 0 |

Now that the dataset is ready, we can compute the descriptive statistics for gini.red, wage.ineq, and pr, and present them in a formatted table, using the stargazer package. We will load the package and then apply the stargazer() function as in the R code below.

```
# produce formatted table of descriptive statistics
# install package first and for once only
# install.packages("stargazer")

# load stargazer into R
library(stargazer)

# produce descriptive statistics table of select variables
stargazer(is2006apsr, type="text", title="Summary Statistics",
        median=TRUE, covariate.labels=c("GINI reduction",
        "wage inequality","PR system"))
```

Several added features in the stargazer code need clarification. First, we add a title to the table with the title="" option. Second, the default summary statistics reported include n, mean, standard deviation, minimum, and maximum. We now also ask for the median value of each variable with median=TRUE. We may even request for the 25th and 75th percentiles for each variable with a similar option like iqr=TRUE. Third, instead of using abbreviated variable names, we now give each variable a more meaningful variable label in the table. This is reflected in the covariates.labels= option.

Table 1.2 reports the summary statistics for the three numeric variables. Note that we intentionally did not input all variables from Table A1 in Iversen and Soskice (2006), expecting that readers will enter the rest of the data themselves as a take-home assignment.

Table 1.2 **Statistics of Imported Data from Iversen and Soskice (2006)**

```
Descriptive Statistics
========================================================
Statistic        N    Mean   St. Dev.  Min   Median  Max
--------------------------------------------------------
GINI reduction   13  26.639   8.320   12.130  25.360 37.890
wage inequality  13   1.712   0.157    1.500   1.680  2.070
PR system        17   0.529   0.514     0       1      1
--------------------------------------------------------
```

Next, we will apply some graphing code to the wage.ineq variable in is2006 apsr. Since it is a continuous variable, we produce its box plot and histogram. Figure 1.5 is created using the R code below:

```
# create a figure with two plots
# set graphic parameters for figure of one row, two columns
par(mfrow=c(1,2))

# graph distribution of wage inequality
boxplot(is2006apsr$wage.ineq)
hist(is2006apsr$wage.ineq)
```

Finally, we provide a bar plot for the discrete electoral system variable pr, with a value of 1 indicating a proportional representation system and 0 indicating a majoritarian system. Figure 1.6 is created using the R code below:

```
# graph distribution of electoral system variable pr
barplot(table(is2006apsr$pr))
```

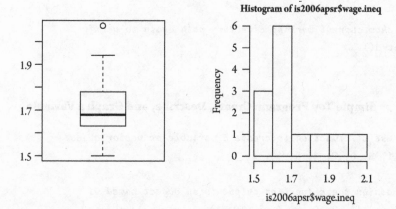

Figure 1.5 Distribution of Wage Inequality from Iversen and Soskice (2006).

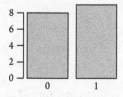

Figure 1.6 Distribution of PR and Majoritarian Systems from Iversen and Soskice (2006).

Chapter 1: R Program Code

By now, we have gone over individual lines of R code to accomplish different tasks. Could we compile them into one coherent R program? The answer is yes, and to do so is easy. Below we list all the R code used in this chapter, which one could copy and paste into R program editor and save them as one program file into our project folder. As noted earlier, the biggest advantage of keeping the R code in a permanent program file is that we can replicate at any time what we have produced. This benefit cannot be overemphasized.

First R Toy Program

```
# How to Start a Project Folder and Write First R Program
# show current working directory path
getwd()

# change working directory for program to this folder one
# could also use setwd('C:\\project')
setwd("C:/Project")

# show current working directory path again to verify
getwd()
```

Simple Toy Program: Create, Describe, and Graph a Variable

```
# use c() function to create a variable or vector object
c(1, 2, 0, 2, 4, 5, 10, 1)

# assign the c function output to an object named v1
v1 <- c(1, 2, 0, 2, 4, 5, 10, 1)

# call object v1 to see what is in it
v1

# identify object type of v1
class(v1)

# calculate descriptive statistics for v1:
# find total number of observations in variable v1
```

```
length(v1)

# find v1's sample mean (two ways: mean function or formula)
mean(v1)
sum(v1)/length(v1)

# find v1's sample variance (variance function or formula)
var(v1)
sum((v1-mean(v1))^2)/(length(v1)-1)

# find v1's sample standard deviation (function
# or square root of sample variance)
sd(v1)
sqrt(var(v1))

# find v1's sample minimum and maximum
max(v1)
min(v1)

# handle missing values in descriptive statistics:
# create variable v2 with missing values
v2 <- c(1, 2, 0, 2, NA, 5, 10, NA)

# compute mean of v2 without removing missing values
mean(v2)

# compute mean of v2 after removing missing values
mean(v2, na.rm=TRUE)

# display output from is.na() function
is.na(v2)

# display output from !is.na() function
!is.na(v2)

# find total number of observations in v2
length(v2)

# find the number of missing values in v2
sum(is.na(v2))
```

```
# find the number of non-missing values in v2
sum(!is.na(v2))

# convert vector v1 into a data frame vd with a variable v1
vd <- data.frame(v1)

# display vd
vd

# combine vectors v1 and v2 into data frame vd
# with two variables v1 and v2
vd <- data.frame(v1, v2)

# display vd
vd

# Format descriptive statistics output into table:
# install package first and for once only
# install.packages("stargazer")

# load stargazer into R
library(stargazer)

# produce descriptive statistics table for data frame vd
stargazer(vd, type="text")

# display dataset in a table format
stargazer(vd, type="text", summary=FALSE, rownames=FALSE)

# add additional statistics to be reported:
# median, interquartile range (25th and 75th percentile)
stargazer(vd, type="text", median=TRUE, iqr=TRUE)

# use c() function to choose statistics to be reported
stargazer(vd, type="text", summary.stat=c("n", "mean",
          "median", "sd"))

# produce select descriptive statistics table for vd
stargazer(vd, type="text", summary.stat=c("n", "mean", "sd",
          "min", "p25", "median", "p75", "max"))
```

```
# Graph the distribution of variable:
# display the frequency count of v1 in vd
table(vd$v1)


# graph distribution of discrete variable vd$v1: bar chart
barplot(table(vd$v1))


# graph distribution of continuous variable vd$v1:
# box plot and histogram
boxplot(vd$v1)
hist(vd$v1)


# create a figure with two plots
# set graphic parameters for figure of one row, two columns
par(mfrow=c(1,2))
# graph distribution of continuous variable vd$v1:
# box plot and histogram
boxplot(vd$v1)
hist(vd$v1)
```

Simple Real-World Example: Data from Iversen and Soskice (2006)

```
# create dataset from Iversen and Soskice

# assign c() function output to vector object country
country <- c("Australia","Austria","Belgium","Canada",
"Denmark","Finland","France","Germany","Ireland", "Italy",
"Japan","Netherlands","New Zealand","Norway","Sweden","U.K.",
"US")

# assign c() output to object gini.red for reduction in GINI
gini.red <- c(23.97,NA,35.56,21.26,37.89,35.17,25.36,18.7,NA,
              12.13,NA,30.59,NA,27.52,37.89,22.67,17.6)

# assign c() output to object wage.ineq for wage inequality
wage.ineq <- c(1.7,NA,1.64,1.82,1.58,1.68,1.94,1.7,NA,1.63,NA,
               1.64,NA,1.5,1.58,1.78,2.07)

# assign c() output to object pr for electoral system
pr <- c(0,1,1,0,1,1,0,1,0,1,0,1,0,1,1,0,0)
```

```
# use data.frame function to combine four vector objects
# assign data.frame function output to data frame is2006apsr
is2006apsr <- data.frame(country, gini.red, wage.ineq, pr)

# call data frame is2006apsr to display content
is2006apsr

# produce formatted table of descriptive statistics
# install package first and for once only
# install.packages("stargazer")

# load stargazer into R
library(stargazer)

# produce descriptive statistics table of select variables
stargazer(is2006apsr, type="text", title="Summary Statistics",
          median=TRUE, covariate.labels=c("GINI reduction",
          "wage inequality","PR system"))

# create a figure with two plots
# set graphic parameters for figure of one row, two columns
par(mfrow=c(1,2))

# graph distribution of wage inequality
boxplot(is2006apsr$wage.ineq)
hist(is2006apsr$wage.ineq)

# graph distribution of electoral system variable pr
barplot(table(is2006apsr$pr))
```

Troubleshoot and Get Help

One important principle to keep in mind in using R is that we will always have coding errors, serious or minor, such that troubleshooting and getting help is an indispensable part of using R. Knowing where to look for coding errors and where and how to get help is critical and can save one many hours. When a program fails to execute, it is common for a beginner to spend half an hour searching for a major error in their code, only to find that their error was due to a missing comma or parenthesis, a misspelled word, or a mix-up in the upper or lower case.

These occurrences are just too common to ignore. Here we provide information about common coding errors and useful resources for beginners in R.

Common Coding Errors for Beginners

When we create our first programs in R, we will definitely make errors. Learning to debug these errors is part of getting proficient with R. It is common to make programming errors in R, just like in any other software environment. The best suggestion is: Don't Panic!

It is useful to remember that there is more often than not a very simple reason for why we get an error message. R's error messages are not always clear or useful. We can always help ourselves by checking the following places to identify simple errors:

- Spelling: Go through the code to make sure spellings are correct.
- Case: R is sensitive to upper or lower case.
- Path: Is the file path correctly pointing to the right folder? Do we use double back slashes or one forward slash?
- Quotation: Should quotation marks be used? Are they symmetric (beginning and ending) ones?
- Parentheses: Are they matched? ...

How to Get Help

Using R involves continuous learning. So knowing how to get help is important. If we have questions about a particular function, say, library(), we can type in at the prompt either *help(library)* or *?library*, and R will direct us to the documentation page explaining this function.

```
> help(library)
>?library
```

More often, we need to seek help outside R itself. The last several years have witnessed an exponential increase in online communities and resources on the use of R. They are extremely valuable and useful, especially for beginner users. Here are a few possibilities.

- Rseek.org: a search engine that allows us to search for help on the official website, the CRAN, the archives of the mailing lists, and the documentation of R.
- http://www.r-bloggers.com/: R-bloggers is a blog aggregator that allows us to search for help through all articles by R-user bloggers.

- http://www.inside-r.org/: inside-R is a community site for R sponsored by Revolution Analytics that allows us to get help through searching blogs and asking questions.
- http://www.cookbook-r.com/: Cookbook for R, created by Winston Chang, provides useful information on various topics, including R basics, numbers, strings, formulas, data input and output, data manipulation, statistical analysis, graphs, scripts and functions, and tools for experiments.
- http://www.statmethods.net/: Quick-R, created by Rob Kabacoff and based on his popular book *R in Action*, provides useful information on the R code related to data input and management, basic and advanced statistics, and graphs.

Important Reference Information: Symbols, Operators, and Functions

In this section, we provide several tables to which we will refer later in the book. They concern important reference information, including symbols frequently used in R programs, common arithmetic and logical operators, and common mathematical and statistical functions. Table 1.3 provides a list of symbols frequently used in R. Table 1.4 provides a list of arithmetic operators. The order of operations follows the usual rules, with parentheses for grouping operations. Table 1.5 provides a list of logical operators. Table 1.6 provides a list of common statistical and mathematical functions. Note that these lists are by no means exhaustive.

Table 1.3 **Important Symbols in R**

Symbol	Description
<- or =	assignment symbol (assign function output from right to object on left)
#	comment character (indicating the code for own reference which R ignores)
$	symbol linking an R data object and a variable in the object
( )	parentheses for arguments of functions,
\\ or /	symbol for specifying path to folder or file (instead of default \ in Windows)
[]	square brackets for referencing entries in vectors, data frames, arrays, or lists

Table 1.4 **Arithmetic Operators**

Arithmetic	Description
+	addition
-	subtraction
*	multiplication
/	division
^	exponentiation (raising to a power)
%/%	integer part of quotient or division
%%	remainder part (modulo)

Table 1.5 **Logical Operators**

Logical	Description
<	less than
<=	less than or equal to
>	greater than
>=	greater than or equal to
==	exactly equal to
!=	not equal to
!x	not x
x|y	x or y
x&y	x and y
x%in%y	binary logical operator for whether x matches y or not

Summary

This first chapter provides an overview of the steps for completing a research project, offers a one-paragraph introduction to R, shows how to install R and its add-on packages, mentions how to get help, presents an example of how to write and execute a simple R program as an ice-breaker, then demonstrates how to create, describe, and graph a variable in R with a simple numerical example; next it illustrates how to report descriptive statistics in a table, and finally it concludes with applying the R code to a real-world data example from a published article. This chapter is worth spending a lot of time on to mull over the code and make it work in R as smoothly as possible. Starting from the next chapter, we will work with larger raw datasets used in applied research. In Chapter 2, we will focus on getting a dataset ready for statistical analysis.

Table 1.6 **Common Statistical and Mathematical Functions**

Function	Description	Example
length(x)	number of values in x	length(c(3, 1, 6, 0, 6)) = 5
max(x)	maximum value of x	max(c(3, 1, 6, 0, 6)) = 6
min(x)	minimum value of x	min(c(3, 1, 6, 0, 6)) = 0
mean(x)	arithmetic mean of x	mean(c(3, 1, 6, 0, 6)) = 3.2
median(x)	median of x	median(c(3, 1, 6, 0, 6)) = 3
quantile(x, c(.25,.75))	quartile values of x	quantile(c(3, 1, 6, 0, 6), c(0.25, 0.75)) = 1, 6
range(x)	range	range(c(3, 1, 6, 0, 6)) = (0,6)
sd(x)	sample standard deviation	sd(c(3, 1, 6, 0, 6)) = 2.774887
sum(x)	sum of x	sum(c(3, 1, 6, 0, 6)) = 16
var(x)	sample variance	var(c(3, 1, 6, 0, 6)) = 7.7
abs(x)	absolute value of x	*abs*(2 − 10) = 8
factorial(x)	factorial of x	*factorial*(10) = 3628800
exp(x)	antilog, e raiased to a power x	*exp*(2.302585) = 10
log(x)	natural log (base e) of x	*log*(10) = 2.302585
log10(x)	log (base 10) of x	log10(100) = 2
rank(x)	find ranks to values in vector x	rank(c(3, 1, 6)) = (2 1 3)
round(x,n)	rounding x to nth digit	*round*(*log*(10), 3) = 2.303
rnorm(n)	n random numbers from standard normal distribution	rnorm(2): −0.4959407, −1.4102038
sqrt(x)	square root of x	*sqrt*(10) = 3.162278

Before heading in Chapter 2, it is useful for us to address some miscellaneous questions many beginning R users often come across.

Miscellaneous Q&As for Ambitious Readers

This section supplements the materials already covered or introduces some special topics beyond the scope of the main text. For supplementary materials, students do not need to learn immediately the additional materials to move forward to the next chapter, but more ambitious students will find these materials help improve their proficiency with R. For special topics, students may consult the discussion here or other online materials.

How to Update R to a Newer Version

R is a constantly evolving and improving software, which makes it necessary to update R to its newer version. The steps to update R on Windows are rather easy. First, install an add-on package called "installr"; then execute the following R code.

```
# load package
library(installr)

# update R
updateR()
```

How to Use R on Mac

To use R on a Mac machine, we have to first install R for Mac, as noted in the installation section. Once R is installed, running it on Mac requires only slight modifications to the R code for Windows. The most obvious difference is how to refer to the path to a file.

To illustrate the difference, we may first create a Project folder on the Mac desktop by clicking on the *NewFolder* option under *File* on the upper left corner of the home screen. Then to obtain the path for the Project folder, we first click on the folder, then click *File* on the upper left corner of the screen, next click the *GetInfo* option, and then copy the path right after *where* : in the *Projectinfo* page for our R program. Now take our first toy program for Windows as an example. All we need to modify in that program for Mac is to replace the Windows path with the Mac path, as follows:

```
# First R practice program, July 2016, R version 3.2.3
# show current working directory path
getwd()

# change working directory for program to project folder
# first copy the path from getinfo
# and then add the project folder name
setwd("/Users/quanli/Desktop/Project")

# show current working directory path again to verify
getwd()
```

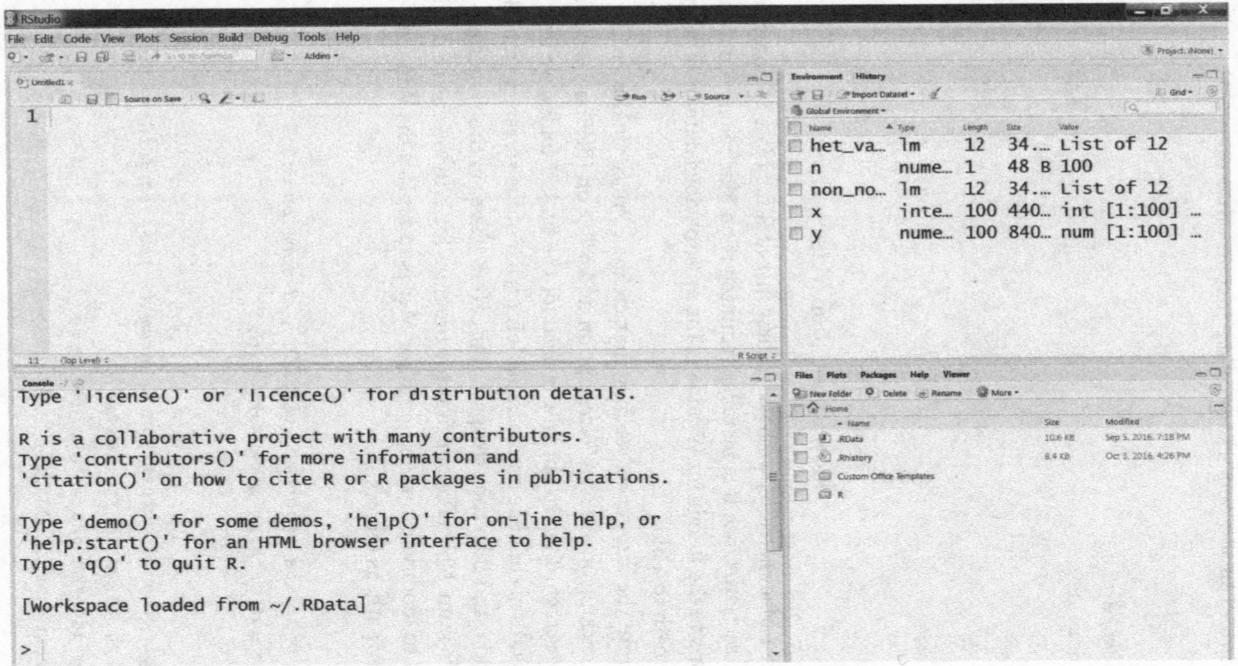
RStudio
File Edit Code View Plots Session Build Debug Tools Help
Addins
Project: (None)
Untitled1
Source on Save
Run
Source
1
(Top Level)
R Script
Environment History
Import Dataset
Global Environment
Grid
Name Type Length Size Value
het_va... lm 12 34.... List of 12
n nume... 1 48 B 100
non_no... lm 12 34.... List of 12
x inte... 100 440... int [1:100] ...
y nume... 100 840... num [1:100] ...
Console
Type 'license()' or 'licence()' for distribution details.
R is a collaborative project with many contributors.
Type 'contributors()' for more information and
'citation()' on how to cite R or R packages in publications.
Type 'demo()' for some demos, 'help()' for on-line help, or
'help.start()' for an HTML browser interface to help.
Type 'q()' to quit R.
[Workspace loaded from ~/.RData]
>
Files Plots Packages Help Viewer
New Folder Delete Rename More
Home
Name Size Modified
.RData 10.6 KB Sep 5, 2016, 7:18 PM
.Rhistory 8.4 KB Oct 3, 2016, 4:26 PM
Custom Office Templates
R

Figure 1.7 RStudio Screenshot.

We may write down this program in the R editor on Mac, which we can open by clicking on *NewDocument* option under *File*.

We can execute the R program on Mac in two ways. We can place the cursor in the line of code to be executed and then hold down two key strokes *Command* and *Return* at the same time. Alternatively, we can place the cursor in the line of code to be executed and then click *Edit* and *Execute* sequentially. To execute the entire program, we highlight the whole program and then apply either method above.

What Is RStudio, and How Do I Use It?

RStudio as an open source software provides an integrated development environment (IDE) for R. The software includes a console, syntax-highlighting editor, plotting, history, debugging, and workspace management. It certainly offers an analyst many more nice and convenient features than R does. For more information, one could visit https://www.rstudio.com/. The installation is straightforward and requires very little effort.

Figure 1.7 provides a screenshot of the RStudio interface, which is split into four panels. The upper left is the R script or program editor; the lower left is the R console for interactive use, with the version of R on top and the prompt below; the upper right is the workspace showing all active objects in the current session, as well as the history of commands used; the lower right is where tabs for files, plots, packages, help, and data viewer are located. Note that how these different panels are organized in the interface can be adjusted and re-organized. One can use RStudio just like R, but RStudio is easier to use (e.g., installing packages) and friendlier (e.g., seeing program and output at the same time).

How to Export R Output to a File

There are many ways to export R output. First, the simplest way to export all output from an R program into a text file is to employ the *sink*() function. The *sink*() function simply redirects output from the console to a file. We may insert the following two *sink*() function lines of code at the beginning and the end of the segment of an R program whose output we plan to export. We use v1 as an example below.

```
# change working directory for program to project folder
setwd("C:/Project")

# redirect and export console output to a file named output.txt
sink("output.txt")
```

```
# Simple Example: Create, Describe, and Graph a Variable
# use c() function to create a variable or vector object
c(1, 2, 0, 2, 4, 5, 10, 1)

# assign the c function output to an object named v1
v1 <- c(1, 2, 0, 2, 4, 5, 10, 1)

# call object v1 to see what is in it
v1

# restore output to the screen
sink()
```

Running this program and then opening output.txt, we will find the following output:

```
[1]  1  2  0  2  4  5 10  1
[1]  1  2  0  2  4  5 10  1
```

Two caveats are worth noting. The output between the two *sink()* functions is redirected to output.txt and thus, no longer shows up in the console. The file output.txt contains only the output from R functions but not the R code.

A second way to export R output is primarily to convert the select output into formatted statistical tables. As noted earlier, the stargazer package provides one way to export statistical output into a formatted table in the text or LaTeX format. Alternatively, we may send the computed statistics to a data object, use the write.table() function to export the data object to a tab- or comma-delimited file, and then format in Excel or Word. Furthermore, we use the *xtable*() function to create the LaTeX code for any statistical output object so that a nicely formatted table can be created in LaTeX.

A third way to export R output is to integrate the paper or report text, the R program code, and the R output into one file, via the *knitr* package plus *pandoc* for creating a Word file for the final paper or report, or via the *knitr* package plus *RStudio* for creating a .Rnw or .Rmd file that compiles into a pdf file of the final paper or report. This approach requires much greater investments in time and effort on the part of a user, but the final paper or report is typeset and professionally formatted. In fact, this R textbook was written as many chapter files in .Rnw format and then compiled into one book in pdf format.

How to Save a Graph into a File of pdf or Other Formats

To save a graph into a pdf file, we employ the *pdf* () function to first generate a graph called "graph1.pdf," and then shut down the graphing device with *dev.off* ()

function so that we may open the graph file to view it in another application such as Acrobat Reader.

```
# pdf() function creates a pdf file for subsequent graph
# function output
pdf("graph1.pdf")

# hist() function creates a histogram for variable v1
hist(v1)

# dev.off() returns back to screen
dev.off()
```

Note that because we did not tell R where to save the graph file, R will then save it in the working directory specified in the *setwd()* function earlier. Alternatively, we may specify the path to another folder in the *pdf()* function.

Sometimes we need to save a graph into other formats. To do so, we simply replace the pdf line of code with any one of the following:

```
# create image files of alternative formats
bmp("graph1.bmp")
jpeg("graph1.jpeg")
png("graph1.png")
postscript("graph1.ps")
```

Alternatively, one may simply copy and paste an image from R graph output into a Microsoft Word or PowerPoint file.

Why Do I See = Also Used as an Assignment Symbol Rather Than < —?

The composite symbol of less than and minus, <-, works as the assignment symbol in R; that is, the function output on the right of the composite symbol is assigned to an R object on the left of the symbol. Starting with version 1.4.0 in 2001, however, R also allows the equal sign, =, to serve as an assignment operator, but in this book, to be consistent, we will use <- throughout.

Other Than Vector and Data Frame, What Are Some Other Data Objects Often Used in R?

Two other data objects often used are array and list. We will discuss them in detail when we come across them in future sessions.

An array is a three-dimensional object with rows by columns by height, such as several matrices stacked on top of each other. Like in a matrix, all elements in an array must be of the same data type.

A list in R is a set of objects, which could be vectors, matrices, arrays, data frames, and other lists. A list allows us to gather these objects under one name.

How to Create a Box Plot of a Variable With Respect to Each Value of Another Variable

Often we would like to compare the distribution of a continuous variable across different groups (i.e., with respect to another variable). The R code is as follows:

```
# compare distribution of x1 across different groups of x2
boxplot(x1 ~ x2, data = filename)
```

Note that since we explicitly specify the data frame name with the data= option, we no longer need to use the $ sign to link the dataset to each variable.

Exercises

1. Create a homework project folder and then an R program file that is pointing to and saved in that folder.
2. Read the Soskice and Iversen (2006) article, identify the definitions of the variables in Table A1, and include variable definitions as comment lines in the program file.
3. Create a dataset of all the variables in Table 1.1.
4. Produce a table of summary statistics for the dataset as in the format of Table 1.2.
5. Reproduce Figure 1.5, and then discuss the distribution of the wage inequality variable.
6. Graph one by-group boxplot figure for wage inequality and electoral system, that is, one boxplot for the PR system and the other for the majoritarian system. Discuss the differences in the distribution of wage inequality between the two systems.
7. Save the R program, exit R, and then rerun the program in R to make sure the results can be replicated.

Get Data Ready: Import, Inspect, and Prepare Data

Chapter Objectives

In this chapter, we will begin to work with an original dataset used in actual data analysis. Working with an original dataset helps us to observe the whole process from importing data to reporting statistical results. For illustration purposes, we will focus on the following research question: Do countries that are more open to international trade grow faster economically and have higher income? To address this question empirically, we will first need to find a dataset that contains both measures of trade openness (i.e., $\frac{exports+imports}{GDP}$) and economic growth and then get data ready for statistical analysis. Getting data ready involves importing, inspecting, and managing data. Therefore, in this chapter, we will aim to achieve the following objectives:

1. Learn to read an original dataset into R and create a corresponding data object.
2. Learn to inspect imported data by viewing raw data in a spreadsheet format, identifying dataset attributes, and graphing select variables.
3. Learn to prepare data for analysis by managing datasets, observations, and variables.
4. Get familiar with a variety of logical and mathematical operators.

Preparation

Before we discuss how to accomplish these objectives, we must make sure that we are ready to move forward from Chapter 1. We have to be prepared in two important aspects. First, we have made adequate logistic preparations such as setting up a project folder, knowing how to write and execute a program in R, and locating and downloading necessary data and codebook files. Second, we have developed a conceptual roadmap for the different possible tasks that have to be completed in Chapter 2 and their interconnections. We will discuss each of these in detail.

Logistic Preparations

Before heading into Chapter 2, we should have completed the following tasks:

1. Set up a project folder to hold data, program, and output files.
2. Create a well-documented R program that resets the working directory to the project folder, and then save the program in the project folder.
3. Execute that program in R.
4. Obtain a codebook or readme file for a dataset to be read into R.
5. Download the dataset to be read into R and place it in the project folder.

While tasks (1) to (3)—are covered in the previous chapter, tasks (4) and (5)—are new. As a matter of principle and good practice, we should always obtain the codebook or readme file for any dataset we use. The codebook or readme file should include important information such as the format of a dataset, the sample information (e.g., year and country coverage), the unit of analysis (for example, country year, individual respondent, etc.), the number of variables, the number of observations, variable names, variable definitions and measurements, variable types, value labels if any, data sources, and sometimes, descriptive statistics for the variables (mean, maximum, minimum, variance or standard deviation, number of observations).

A codebook is important for three reasons. First, we can make sure a dataset suits our purpose in terms of variable and sample coverage. Second, we can choose the right command or function to import a dataset into R and verify whether it is read into R correctly or not. Finally, we can refer to the codebook when we prepare data for analysis. R does not do a very good job in handling variable labels. So we need the codebook to know what variables we have and how to manage them.

In social and behavioral sciences, raw data is often organized in a tabular or rectangular form, where each row is an observation and each column a variable. In this chapter, we will discuss how to import tabular data files in formats that are common in social and behavioral sciences, including comma- or tab-delimited text files, fixed-width text files, Excel files, Stata and SPSS files. But our first focus is to learn to import a commonly used original dataset on economic variables in the comma-delimited format, the Penn World Table Version 7.0 database.

The Penn World Table Version 7.0 database can be found at the following link: http://www.rug.nl/ggdc/productivity/pwt/pwt-releases/pwt-7.0. In the event that the link does not work because of site changes, readers may find it by googling it on the internet. The Penn World Table dataset was initially constructed by Alan Heston, Robert Summers, and Bettina Aten at the Center for International Comparisons of Production, Income and Prices at the University of Pennsylvania, and it has now been taken over by the University of California,

Davis and the University of Groningen. The dataset provides a large number of variables related to purchasing power parity and national income accounts converted to international prices for 189 countries and territories for the period 1950–2009, with 2005 as the reference year. It has been widely used by many scholars in social science disciplines. For our purposes, the dataset contains variables that measure trade openness and national income of many countries in different years.

On the website listed in the preceding paragraph, we will choose to download PWT7.0 data and readme files in one zipped file by clicking on "Complete Data Download." After downloading the zipped file, place it into the project folder. The next step depends on whether we are working with R in Windows or on a Mac machine. If we are using the Windows operating system, we need to download and install the 7zip freeware from this website: http://www.7-zip.org/, and then unzip the PWT7.0 zip file. After unzipping the PWT7.0 zip file in the project folder, we should see two files. One is pwt70_Vars_forWeb.xls, a readme or codebook file that defines variable names and labels; the other one is pwt70_w_country_names.csv, a comma-delimited data file that places variable names in the header row, observations in rows, and variables in columns. We will import the data file into R later.

Alternatively, if we are using a Mac machine, we do not need to download any additional software to unzip the file, but we do need to place the two files individually into the project folder. If we don't do this, R will give an error message when reading the data file because R is not able to find the data file inside the zip file.

Conceptual Overview of Chapter 2

Chapter 2 will help us learn how to import a dataset into R, how to inspect the imported data, and how to manage variables, observations, and datasets. Because Chapter 2 involves a large quantity of information, it can be difficult for us to see the big picture. As a result, we should develop a conceptual overview of how the different tasks, functions, and methods are related to each other in the overall scheme of things. For this purpose, Table 2.1 lists various data preparation tasks, add-on packages that need to be installed first, and relevant R functions and methods. For the sake of presenting a wholistic view, Table 2.1 includes not only the functions and methods discussed in the main text of Chapter 2 but also those covered in the Miscellaneous Q&A section.

Import Penn World Table 7.0 Dataset

Importing datasets into R is the first biggest hurdle for many beginners. It is not a trivial issue. Yet when a dataset is finally successfully read into R, sometimes

Table 2.1 **List of Data Preparation Tasks and Related R Functions**

Tasks	*Functions and Methods*
Import data	Add-on packages: foreign, Hmisc, readstata13, RODBC, gdata, haven, XLConnect
comma-delimited file	read.csv, read.table
tab-delimited file	read.table
Stata file	stata.get, read.dta, read.dta13
SPSS file	spss.get
SAS file	read.xport, read_sas
Excel file	odbcConnectExcel, sqlFetch, odbcClose, read.xls, readWorksheet
R data file	load
Inspect data	Add-on packages: None
view imported data	View, head, tail
learn dataset attributes	dim, names, str
plot select variables	hist, boxplot, qqnorm, par
edit imported data	fix
Manage datasets	Add-on packages: reshape2, DataCombine
sort data	order
select rows and columns	indexing method, logical operators, c
create a subset dataset	indexing method, operators, assignment, subset
merge datasets	merge
reshape data from long to wide	dcast
reshape data from wide to long	melt
Manage observations	Add-on packages: None
remove select observations	indexing method, operators, assignment
find and remove duplicates	duplicated, !duplicated
Manage variables	Add-on packages: Hmisc, car, reshape, pwt
create new variables	mathematical and logical operators, assignment, factor
show variable type	class
create leading and lagged variables	slide
create group-specific statistics	by, aggregate
rename variables	indexing method, names, assignment, rename
recode variable values	indexing method, assignment, recode
create variable labels	label

after much struggle, it can provide a great sense of achievement for students. To learn the importation of datasets into R, we will start with the comma-delimited file pwt70_w_country_names.csv.

Before importing the dataset, we must first finish a few tasks: (1) Install only once the add-on packages that will be used in the chapter. Assuming the packages have all been installed, the code install.packages() is currently commented out; otherwise, remove the comment symbol, run this line of code once, and then put the comment symbol back in. (2) Clean R's workspace—its temporary work area. (3) Set the current working directory to the project folder. It is a good practice to always start with these tasks at the beginning of a new program.

```
# install following packages only once, then comment out code
# install.packages(c('reshape2', 'DataCombine',
# 'Hmisc', 'haven', 'foreign', 'gdata', 'XLConnect',
# 'pwt', 'reshape', 'doBy'), dependencies=TRUE)

# remove all objects from workspace
rm(list = ls(all = TRUE))

# change working directory to point to project folder
setwd("C:/Project")
```

The ls() function returns a vector of the names of the objects in the current R session, with all=TRUE referring to all objects created. The rm() function removes all objects listed in the output of the ls() function. Hence, the line of code above tells R to remove all the objects from the workspace.

The setwd(), discussed extensively in the previous chapter, resets the current working directory in R. In the rest of the program, R will seek to find files in that directory without us specifying the pathname each time. In this case, we first created a folder named Project in the C drive, where the data files are stored.

To read the Penn World Table dataset into R and create a data object called pwt7, we will employ the following code:

```
# import comma-delimited file, create data object pwt7
pwt7 <- read.csv("pwt70_w_country_names.csv", header = TRUE,
    strip.white = TRUE, stringsAsFactors = FALSE,
    na.strings = c("NA", ""))
```

Since this code can be confusing to understand, we will provide a detailed discussion of each element in the code below.

1. The read.csv() function reads a comma-delimited data file into R. The arguments of the function are listed inside the parentheses.

2. The argument "pwt70_w_country_names.csv" represents the raw data file to be read into R, where .csv indicates that it is a comma-delimited file (a common file format option, which we can easily see in Excel when choosing to save a data file in Excel). Note that if we did not first specify setwd("C:/Project"), the first argument would have to be "C:/Project/pwt70_w_country_names.csv" instead. Be sure that the file name is surrounded by double quotation marks!

3. The argument header=TRUE is a logical statement, meaning that it is true that the first row contains variable names. If the raw data file does not have variable names in the first row, change the option to header=FALSE. We may simplify the argument to header=T or header=F.

4. The argument strip.white=TRUE removes any white space at the start and end of character fields. Spaces are often introduced accidentally during data entry. R treats the following three as different values: **"USA"** and **" USA"** or **"USA "** because of the absence or presence of white space before or after USA. We further illustrate this concept in the Miscellaneous Q&A section.

5. The argument stringsAsFactors = FALSE tells R to keep character variables as they are, rather than converting them to factors. We will explain what factors are later on.

6. The argument na.strings = c("NA","") tells R to treat the following two types of values as missing: "NA" which is R's default recognized coding of a missing value; blank space or empty string, denoted by the double quotation marks and without any white space in between. By default, R treats a blank cell in a column of character data as a character string of zero length rather than as missing. Finally, note how the c() function allows us to specify multiple symbols, all of which are coded as missing and separated by commas. Missing values are a common occurrence in social science data, with different software packages treating missing values a little bit differently. For R, NA is the default missing value code. If we find a dataset uses some other value or symbol to represent a missing value, we must tell R so that the data will be read into R correctly. For example, if datasets use . or −999 to represent missing values, we can tell R simply by specifying na.strings="." or na.strings="-999". Alternatively, we can use na.strings = c("NA", "", ".", "-999") instead.

7. The data output from the read.csv function is assigned via <- into a data object arbitrarily named as pwt7. The data object pwt7 is a data frame, which is a matrix style data object in R. Alternatively, a data frame can be thought of in simpler terms as a table in Excel. Once the new data object pwt7 is created, we can ask R to operate on it for analysis. If we only use the read.csv() function part of the code without assigning its output to a data object, R will merely display the dataset on the screen.

8. To read data into R smoothly, we need to follow R's rules for naming variables inside the raw dataset. A proper variable name can use letters, numbers, and dot or underline characters, but should never contain mathematical operators. Also, R does not like the presence of any blank space inside a variable name. Another factor worth considering is R's sensitivity to upper- and lower-case. For instance, name and Name are two different variables to R. Thus, it is common for an analyst to have to change some variable names in a raw dataset before reading it into R. In this type of situation, it is recommended that the analyst makes a copy of the original raw dataset and operates on the copied data file instead, leaving the original dataset intact.

It is important to note that the datasets we work with are often in various formats other than in a comma-delimited file. As one of its great strengths, R is extremely flexible and versatile in its ability to import datasets of various formats, as suggested by Table 2.1. As of right now, we will not engage the R code for importing datasets of different formats, but will learn that later in this chapter.

Inspect Imported Data
Eyeball Imported Dataset

After we import a dataset, it is both useful and important to take a direct look at the imported dataset itself. Examining the data provides an intuitive means for us to verify that the data has been imported correctly. Through quick glances, we can get a feel for the data, and spot check if observations have been imported correctly and whether variable names appear to be correct or not. There are many ways for us to look through and spot check an imported dataset.

The first method of eyeballing imported data is to open up a spreadsheet style viewer using the View() function. Note that the first letter of the function must be in uppercase.

```
# inspect dataset pwt7 in a spreadsheet style data viewer
View(pwt7)
```

Figure 2.1 shows that the dataset pwt7 is organized with observations in rows and variables in columns, a general principle worth remembering. The header row contains the variable names.

Another way of eyeballing the data is to use two functions, head() and tail(), to look at the first and last couple of observations, respectively. The option n= allows us to specify how many observations we choose to look at.

	country	isocode	year	POP	XRAT	Currency_Unit	ppp	tcgdp
1	Afghanistan	AFG	1950	8150.368	NA	NA NA	NA	NA
2	Afghanistan	AFG	1951	8284.473	NA	NA NA	NA	NA
3	Afghanistan	AFG	1952	8425.333	NA	NA NA	NA	NA
4	Afghanistan	AFG	1953	8573.217	NA	NA NA	NA	NA
5	Afghanistan	AFG	1954	8728.408	NA	NA NA	NA	NA
6	Afghanistan	AFG	1955	8891.209	1.680000e-02	Afghani	NA	NA
7	Afghanistan	AFG	1956	9061.938	2.000000e-02	Afghani	NA	NA
8	Afghanistan	AFG	1957	9240.934	2.000000e-02	Afghani	NA	NA
9	Afghanistan	AFG	1958	9428.556	2.000000e-02	Afghani	NA	NA
10	Afghanistan	AFG	1959	9624.606	2.000000e-02	Afghani	NA	NA

Figure 2.1 Using View() Function to View Raw Data.

```
# list first one observation in dataset pwt7
head(pwt7, n = 1)

# list last one observation in dataset pwt7
tail(pwt7, n = 1)
```

As an illustration, the R output for listing the last observation of pwt7 looks as follows:

```
# list last one observation in dataset pwt7
tail(pwt7, n = 1)

        country isocode year   POP    XRAT   Currency_Unit
11400 Zimbabwe     ZWE 2009 11383 1.4e+17 Zimbabwe Dollar
          ppp    tcgdp     cgdp    cgdp2     cda2       cc
11400 40289.96 1906.05 167.4471 174.4197 180.2302 81.78356
           cg       ci        p       p2       pc       pg
11400 7.759873 13.78792 2.87e-11 2.87e-11 2.91e-11 1.34e-11
           pi    openc     cgnp        y       y2
11400 3.55e-11 60.31122 94.11682 0.3670967 0.382383
        rgdpl   rgdpl2   rgdpch       kc       kg       ki
11400 142.5955 136.7233 142.564 86.89917 7.905525 14.74367
        openk rgdpeqa rgdpwok rgdpl2wok rgdpl2pe rgdpl2te
11400 83.74953 182.613      NA        NA       NA 314.1711
     rgdpl2th   rgdptt
11400      NA 151.4353
```

As shown in the output, the last observation in pwt7 (i.e., observation 11400) is a country called Zimbabwe in year 2009, with isocode ZWE, a population (POP) of 11383 (thousands), an exchange rate to US dollar (XRAT) being 1.4e+17, etc.

If we would like to see more observations at the beginning or end of the dataset, we can simply change the value after n=.

Identify Dataset Attributes: Dimension, Variable Names, and Dataset Structure

After a dataset has been read into R and we have visually inspected the imported data, we need to further verify that R imported the dataset correctly. We can get summary information about the dataset and then verify it against the information in the codebook. To do so, we introduce three functions, i.e., dim(), names(), and str(). They help us to learn about the dimensions of the dataset (its rows and columns, i.e., number of observations and number of variables), variable names, and the structure of the dataset, respectively.

```
# dimensions of pwt7: number of observations and number of
# variables
dim(pwt7)


# variable names in dataset pwt7
names(pwt7)


# structure of dataset pwt7
str(pwt7)
```

The R output looks as follows:

```
# dimensions of pwt7: number of observations and number of
# variables
dim(pwt7)

[1] 11400    37
```

The output of dim(pwt7) shows that the dataset includes 11,400 observations and 37 variables.

```
# variable names in dataset pwt7
names(pwt7)

 [1] "country"      "isocode"      "year"
 [4] "POP"          "XRAT"         "Currency_Unit"
 [7] "ppp"          "tcgdp"        "cgdp"
[10] "cgdp2"        "cda2"         "cc"
[13] "cg"           "ci"           "p"
[16] "p2"           "pc"           "pg"
[19] "pi"           "openc"        "cgnp"
[22] "y"            "y2"           "rgdpl"
[25] "rgdpl2"       "rgdpch"       "kc"
[28] "kg"           "ki"           "openk"
[31] "rgdpeqa"      "rgdpwok"      "rgdpl2wok"
[34] "rgdpl2pe"     "rgdpl2te"     "rgdpl2th"
[37] "rgdptt"
```

The output of the names(pwt7) function lists the names of all 37 variables of pwt7, which should be identical to those in the codebook. The numerical values inside the brackets correspond to the indexed column positions of the respective variables next to the brackets. For example, [1] means the variable country is in column 1, thus the variable year at the end of that row is in the 3rd column.

The 37th column contains the last variable rgdptt. This is the first time we have come across the use of square brackets in R. Since we will rely heavily on the use of brackets in this book, it is important to remember that R uses the square brackets [] to reference entries in vectors and data frames, an issue we will discuss extensively below.

```
# structure of dataset pwt7
str(pwt7)

'data.frame': 11400 obs. of  37 variables:
 $ country      : chr  "Afghanistan" "Afghanistan" "Afghanistan"
                       "Afghanistan" ...
 $ isocode      : chr  "AFG" "AFG" "AFG" "AFG" ...
 $ year         : int  1950 1951 1952 1953 1954 1955 1956 1957 1958
                       1959 ...
 $ POP          : num  8150 8284 8425 8573 8728 ...
 $ XRAT         : num  NA NA NA NA NA 0.0168 0.02 0.02 0.02 0.02 ...
 $ Currency_Unit: chr  NA NA NA NA ...
 $ ppp          : num  NA NA NA NA NA NA NA NA NA NA ...
 $ tcgdp        : num  NA NA NA NA NA NA NA NA NA NA ...
 $ cgdp         : num  NA NA NA NA NA NA NA NA NA NA ...
 $ cgdp2        : num  NA NA NA NA NA NA NA NA NA NA ...
 $ cda2         : num  NA NA NA NA NA NA NA NA NA NA ...
 $ cc           : num  NA NA NA NA NA NA NA NA NA NA ...
 $ cg           : num  NA NA NA NA NA NA NA NA NA NA ...
 $ ci           : num  NA NA NA NA NA NA NA NA NA NA ...
 $ p            : num  NA NA NA NA NA NA NA NA NA NA ...
 $ p2           : num  NA NA NA NA NA NA NA NA NA NA ...
 $ pc           : num  NA NA NA NA NA NA NA NA NA NA ...
 $ pg           : num  NA NA NA NA NA NA NA NA NA NA ...
 $ pi           : num  NA NA NA NA NA NA NA NA NA NA ...
 $ openc        : num  NA NA NA NA NA NA NA NA NA NA ...
 $ cgnp         : num  NA NA NA NA NA NA NA NA NA NA ...
 $ y            : num  NA NA NA NA NA NA NA NA NA NA ...
 $ y2           : num  NA NA NA NA NA NA NA NA NA NA ...
 $ rgdpl        : num  NA NA NA NA NA NA NA NA NA NA ...
 $ rgdpl2       : num  NA NA NA NA NA NA NA NA NA NA ...
 $ rgdpch       : num  NA NA NA NA NA NA NA NA NA NA ...
 $ kc           : num  NA NA NA NA NA NA NA NA NA NA ...
 $ kg           : num  NA NA NA NA NA NA NA NA NA NA ...
 $ ki           : num  NA NA NA NA NA NA NA NA NA NA ...
 $ openk        : num  NA NA NA NA NA NA NA NA NA NA ...
 $ rgdpeqa      : num  NA NA NA NA NA NA NA NA NA NA ...
 $ rgdpwok      : num  NA NA NA NA NA NA NA NA NA NA ...
 $ rgdpl2wok    : num  NA NA NA NA NA NA NA NA NA NA ...
 $ rgdpl2pe     : num  NA NA NA NA NA NA NA NA NA NA ...
```

```
$ rgdpl2te    : num  NA NA NA NA NA NA NA NA NA NA ...
$ rgdpl2th    : num  NA NA NA NA NA NA NA NA NA NA ...
$ rgdptt      : num  NA NA NA NA NA NA NA NA NA NA ...
```

The output of the str(pwt7) function provides a lot of information about the nature and structure of pwt7, showing its type as a data object (data.frame), its number of observations (11400 obs.), its number of variables (37), the name of each variable (right after each $ sign), the type of each variable (right after each colon: chr means character, int integer, num numeric), and the first few observations of each variable (right after each variable type). Notice how R treats some variables as character such as country, isocode, Currency_Unit (denoted as chr), some others as integer such as year (denoted as int), and still others as numeric (denoted as num). Also of note is how missing values are denoted as NA.

For specific definitions of the variables, please refer to the readme file downloaded earlier. For the purpose of this chapter, we will pay particular attention to three variables: country, year, and rgdpl. The variable country is a character string, containing the names of countries. The variable year is an integer variable, showing years. The variable rgdpl is a numeric variable for the real GDP per capita in international dollars, which is widely used as a measure of income per person in a country. Both country and year are id variables that allow us to uniquely identify each observation. The variable rgdpl is the focus of our discussion in this section.

Graph a Variable of Interest for Inspection

We may also graph the distributions of select variables of interest to inspect whether they are imported into R correctly. For example, we can use some code from the previous chapter to plot the distribution of rgdpl, as shown in Figure 2.2. Note how we first use the par() function to specify graphical parameters for a figure with plots arranged into various rows and columns. Recall that par(mfrow=c(2,2)) means to create a figure containing plots that are arranged into two rows and two columns.

```
# create a figure with three plots
# set graphic parameters for figure of two rows, two columns
par(mfrow=c(2,2))

# graph distribution of variable rgdpl in data frame pwt7
hist(pwt7$rgdpl)
boxplot(pwt7$rgdpl)
qqnorm(pwt7$rgdpl)
```

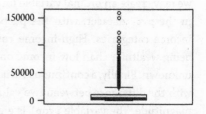

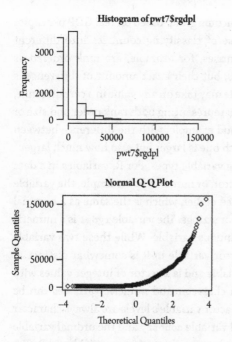

Figure 2.2 Distribution of Variable rgdpl.

Prepare Data I: Variable Types and Indexing

Preparing the imported data for analysis can be time-consuming and involves data manipulation and cleaning. Data management typically focuses on getting variables, observations, and datasets in order, with the end goal of getting a clean dataset ready for analysis. Before we go into the specifics of data management, we first need to learn some prerequisite information, primarily regarding variable types and the indexing method for referring to observations and variables.

Variable Types in R

R uses a variety of data objects, including scalar, vector, matrix, array, data frame, and list. For our purposes, we will focus on variables inside a data frame. Typically in statistics, variables are nominal, ordinal, or continuous. Nominal variables are categorical and their values are not ordered in any meaningful way. For example, in the pwt7 dataset, the variable country is nominal because its values are just country names and not rank ordered in terms of magnitude. Ordinal variables could also be categorical, but their values are rank ordered in terms of magnitude; yet ordinal variables do not carry any information about the amount of difference between values, unlike continuous variables. For example, we may create an ordinal variable for income group based on real GDP per capita in the pwt7 dataset, with the purpose of classifying countries into different income categories. High-income countries, for example, are rank ordered as being wealthier than low-income ones, but their exact amount of difference is unknown. Finally, a continuous variable may take on any value in a certain range, with the difference between two values representing both rank order and size of magnitude. The variable rgdpl is a good example, with the difference between its two values indicating not only which one is larger but also how much larger.

Now, R has its own ways of defining variable types. For R, variables in a data frame can be classified as character, factor, or numeric. For example, the variable country is a character variable, as noted earlier, which is the same as a nominal variable. Its values are country names or strings. The variable rgdpl is a numeric variable, which is the same as a continuous variable. While these two variable types are rather conventional, the factor variable in R is somewhat distinct. A factor variable in R is a categorical variable and is a vector of integer values with corresponding character values. Both character and numeric variables can be converted into factor variables, but a factor variable's levels are always character values. For example, both the nominal variable country and the ordinal variable income group discussed previously can be turned into factor variables in R. The most important use of the factor variable is that it can be used in statistical modeling directly. This even applies to a variable like country after it is converted into a factor variable. We will discuss the issue of variable types further in the next section.

Indexing

Knowing how R refers to the observations in a variable or the observations and variables in a dataset is critical. In this section, we will learn about indexing, which is the most basic method of reference in R, and we will rely on this referencing or indexing method throughout the book. In the indexing method, we place the position values or identifying conditions inside a pair of square brackets [] to reference entries in variables or data frames.

Referencing Observation in Variable

We will start with how to reference an observation in a variable. For illustration, we use the population variable in dataset pwt7, denoted as pwt7$POP, as an example. As shown in Figure 2.1, the variable's fifth observation equals 8728.408. We may refer to the fifth observation of pwt7$POP in two alternative methods, via either its position value or other unique identifying conditions.

For the first method, we specify the variable name, followed by a pair of square brackets and with the position value of its fifth observation (i.e., 5) placed inside.

To ask R to display the value of that observation, the R code and output are as follows:

```
# reference fifth observation of pwt7$POP
pwt7$POP[5]

[1] 8728.408
```

We may also refer to the fifth observation of pwt7$POP by specifying unique identifying conditions. For example, the observation is uniquely identified by relevant information for the country and year variables, i.e., Afghanistan in 1954. Hence, we may refer to that observation by placing the unique identifying information for country and year inside the square brackets. The R code and output are as follows:

```
# reference specific observation of pwt7$POP
pwt7$POP[pwt7$country == "Afghanistan" & pwt7$year == 1954]

[1] 8728.408
```

As expected, both referencing methods produce the same output value: 8728.408. The first method requires the position value of an observation in a variable, and the second method requires the corresponding values of the unique identifying variables. For the latter, note how two logical operators (double equal sign and &) are used; also note how the value of the character variable country must be surrounded by quotation marks, but not that of the numeric variable year.

Referencing Rows and Columns in Dataset

To reference entries in a data frame is different because a data frame has both rows and columns. Recall from Figure 2.1, the data frame pwt7 is a rectangle of data where rows represent observations and columns represent variables. Similar to the case with variable or vector, we also refer to a specific observation of a specific variable in a dataset in two alternative methods, via either relevant position values or unique identifying conditions.

Once again, take the fifth observation of the population variable in the pwt7 dataset as an example. We can refer to that entry in the context of a dataset rather than a variable. In the first method, we specify the data frame name (instead of a variable name), followed by a pair of square brackets, with the position values of the relevant row and column placed inside and separated by a comma. As shown in Figure 2.1, the fifth observation of the population variable lies in the intersection of the fifth observation and the fourth variable. The R code and output are as follows. Note how inside the square brackets, the two position values are observation first and variable second.

```
# reference fifth observation of fourth variable in pwt7
pwt7[5, 4]

[1] 8728.408
```

In the second method, we refer to a specific entry of a dataset by specifying unique row and column conditions separated by a comma. For example, the fifth observation and the fourth variable of pwt7 is uniquely identified by the relevant row information based on country and year and the relevant column information (POP). Hence, we may refer to that entry by placing the relevant row and column conditions inside the square brackets and separated by a comma. The R code and output are as follows. Note how the row condition comes first and the column condition second, with the column variable name surrounded by quotation marks. Please remember the row and column conditions must be separated by a comma.

```
# reference certain observation of certain variable in pwt7
pwt7[pwt7$country=="Afghanistan" & pwt7$year==1954, "POP"]

[1] 8728.408
```

As expected, both referencing methods produce the same output value: 8728.408. It is worth noting that even though the four lines of code produce the same output value, the first two lines concern how to reference an element in a vector, and the latter two lines concern how to reference an entry in a dataframe.

To generalize, dataframe[Select Rows, Select Columns] allows us to refer to specific rows and columns from any data frame, with position values or identifying conditions placed inside square brackets and separated by a comma. The index value or condition before the comma refers to specific rows or observations, and the index value or condition after the comma refers to specific columns or variables.

As an extension, if we leave an index position empty, it refers to all rows or columns. For example, pwt7[5,] refers to the fifth observation of all variables in pwt7; the empty index position after the comma tells R to include all variables. In contrast, pwt7[,4] refers to all observations of the fourth variable in pwt7; the empty index position before the comma tells R to include all observations. We may use various conditional expressions in these index positions so that we can refer to observations and variables in a dataset in a variety of ways. We will learn more about this issue in the next section. Needless to say, data management relies heavily on the indexing method.

Prepare Data II: Manage Datasets

Sort Observations

Before any data manipulation, it is a good practice to sort data according to a dataset's key ID variables. The key ID variables refer to those by which each observation of a dataset is uniquely identified. Take the pwt7 dataset as an example. Its key ID variables are country and year, which uniquely identify each row in the dataset. Thus we can sort pwt7 first by country and then by year within each country, both in ascending order. We can use the order() function, applied to all rows and all columns of pwt7. Note that in order to denote all columns, we need to leave a blank entry right after the comma inside the brackets.

```
# sort data first by country and then by year
pwt7 <- pwt7[order(pwt7$country, pwt7$year), ]
```

Now if necessary, we could also sort the dataset in descending order by year. In the code below, we add a minus sign in front of year to indicate descending order.

```
# sort data by country (ascending) and by year (descending)
pwt7 <- pwt7[order(pwt7$country, -pwt7$year),]
```

Select Observations and Variables

When we work with an original dataset in research, we often need to choose observations and variables for several purposes. First, we want to find out the values of certain observations that are of special interest to us. For example, using the Penn World Table data, we may want to know the value of GDP per capita for a certain country in a certain year. Second, we often do not need all the observations and all the variables, particularly if the original dataset is too large. Keeping all observations and variables can be unwieldy and costs computing time. Thus, we often choose select observations and variables to form a new dataset for analysis.

There are many ways to choose observations and variables in R. Here we illustrate how to use the most basic indexing method introduced earlier with several examples. The first example below demonstrates how to select the 100th and 102nd observations of all variables in pwt7.

```
# show select rows; example: observations 100 and 102
pwt7[c(100, 102), ]
```

Recall from Chapter 1 that the c() function combines the arguments inside the parentheses together into a vector. Also, note how the second index position after the comma is blank, which tells R to include all columns or variables for observations 100 and 102.

If we want to choose observations from 100 to 102, all we have to do is to replace the comma inside the c() function with a colon, which identifies continuous rows.

```
# show select rows; example: observations from 100 to 102
pwt7[c(100:102), ]
```

The second example concerns how to select all observations of certain variables in a data frame. The example below asks R to combine variables country, year, and rgdpl from pwt7 and show all their observations. In the first index value position inside the brackets, we use a blank entry to reference all rows or observations; in the second index value position, we use the c() function to select variables. The quotation marks, brackets, and commas help to tell R what to do.

```
# show select variables
pwt7[, c("country", "year", "rgdpl")]
```

The third example shows how we can combine the two examples above to select observations from 100 to 102 for three variables country, year, and rgdpl only.

```
# combine two selections: certain rows and certain columns
pwt7[c(100:102), c("country", "year", "rgdpl")]
```

Now let us see some more selection examples. If we want to show the value of real GDP per capita in purchasing power parity for Afghanistan since 2006, we can use the following code:

```
# show certain observations and certain variables that meet
# conditions: Afghanistan since 2006 for three variables
pwt7[pwt7$year>=2006 & pwt7$country=="Afghanistan",
c("country", "year", "rgdpl")]
```

We use >=, &, and == to specify the conditions for observations in terms of years and countries. Specifically, we use pwt7$year>=2006 to select years since 2006, pwt7$country=="Afghanistan" to select Afghanistan, and the & sign to specify that both conditions must be met for the observations. The R output looks like the following:

```
         country year     rgdpl
57 Afghanistan 2006   687.7274
58 Afghanistan 2007   736.4802
```

```
59 Afghanistan 2008 1009.8645
60 Afghanistan 2009 1170.9935
```

Now let us see a more complicated example. If we want to compare the values of GDP per capita of China and India for five different years, we can use the %in% as a logical operator to find those items from its left that match those to its right. In the code below, we choose years that equal to 1970, 1980, 1990, 2000, or 2009 and countries that are "India" or "China Version 1".

```
# select multiple countries and non-consecutive years
# for select variables
pwt7[pwt7$year %in% c(1970, 1980, 1990, 2000, 2009) &
    pwt7$country %in% c("India", "China Version 1"),
    c("country", "year", "rgdpl")]
```

The output looks like the following:

```
              country year      rgdpl
2121 China Version 1 1970   390.4169
2131 China Version 1 1980   640.2915
2141 China Version 1 1990  1262.7539
2151 China Version 1 2000  2888.3145
2160 China Version 1 2009  7008.1742
4641            India 1970   887.1750
4651            India 1980  1019.6258
4661            India 1990  1407.2194
4671            India 2000  1860.2439
4680            India 2009  3237.8371
```

Now if we are interested in all years between 1970 and 1990 instead, we just replace c(1970, 1980, 1990, 2000, 2009) with c(1970:1990).

It is worth noting that we can use a variety of logical operators to pick and choose rows or observations and columns or variables from a data frame. Recall from Table 1.5 some of the most common logical operators: < (less than), <= (less than or equal to), > (greater than), >= (greater than or equal to), == (equal to), != (not equal to), | (or), & (and).

Create New Dataset with Subset of Data

Now that we have learned how to select certain observations and variables, it is time to learn how to take those selections and create a second dataset. That turns out to be really simple. The following line of code tells R to choose all observations of three variables from pwt7 and assign them to a new dataset called pwt7new, which includes all observations but only three variables from pwt7.

```
# create a new dataset with three select variables
pwt7new <- pwt7[, c("country", "year", "rgdpl")]
```

If we use the same data frame name pwt7 for the new dataset, then the new dataset will overwrite the old dataset with the same name.

Merge Datasets

In applied data analysis, we often have to merge datasets because the variables we need come from different sources. Below we will provide an example of how to merge datasets in R through the use of the merge() function.

Suppose we use pwt7 to create two datasets in R, called pwt7.tmp1 and pwt7.tmp2, respectively, each with a different variable but two common merging ID variables (isocode and year).

```
# create two temporary pwt7 subsets for merging example
pwt7.tmp1 <- pwt7[, c("isocode", "year", "rgdpl")]
pwt7.tmp2 <- pwt7[, c("isocode", "year", "openk")]
```

To merge these two datasets, we can apply the merge() function and match merge observations from the two different datasets according to isocode and year.

```
# merge two datasets
pwt7.m <- merge(pwt7.tmp1, pwt7.tmp2, by = c("isocode",
    "year"), all = TRUE, sort = TRUE)
```

Inside the merge() function, we first specify the two datasets to be merged and then utilize the by= option and the c() function to specify the sorting ID variables according to which the two datasets are to be merged. Next, through the use of all=TRUE, we tell R that all extra unmatched observations from both datasets should be kept. Finally, the option sort=TRUE tells R that the merged dataset should be sorted by the sorting ID variables.

It is worth noting that this is a rather contrived example. A more practical example on merging datasets will be discussed later when we try to combine a dataset on group-specific statistics with the pwt7 dataset.

Two other functions—cbind() and rbind()—are sometimes used in combining datasets. Here we provide some generic examples. In the event that we want to combine horizontally two matrices with an equal number of rows but different columns, we can use the cbind() function without referring to any sorting ID.

In contrast, if we want to append vertically two datasets of an equal number of columns but different rows, we can use the rbind() function without using any sorting id. Note that in the R code below, data1 and data2 are just generic data frame names and do not refer to any specific data objects. Hence, executing these two lines of code without modification will produce an error message in R.

```
# combine datasets of equal observations, different variables
new.data <- cbind(data1, data2)


# append datasets of equal variables, different observations
new.data <- rbind(data1, data2)
```

Reshape Data Structure

We often need to reshape how a dataset is structured for analytical purposes. Suppose we are interested in comparing the values of GDP per capita, measured by rgdpl, between two countries over time. The most intuitive structure is to have their rgdpl values listed side by side for each year. This requires reorganzing the dataset structure. We will provide some examples by using some functions from the add-on package reshape2.

To illustrate how reshaping works, we first create a new dataset called pwt7.ip, which contains six years and three variables for two countries: India and Pakistan. It is organized by country and year and thus, is in a long form as displayed below. The R code and output are as follows:

```
# create a subset of pwt7 (India and Pakistan, three
# variables and six years)
pwt7.ip <- pwt7[pwt7$year %in% c(1950, 1960, 1970, 1980,
    1990, 2000) & pwt7$country %in% c("India", "Pakistan"),
    c("country", "year", "rgdpl")]


# display the long form dataset
pwt7.ip

        country year      rgdpl
4621      India 1950   594.1658
4631      India 1960   713.6806
4641      India 1970   887.1750
4651      India 1980  1019.6258
4661      India 1990  1407.2194
4671      India 2000  1860.2439
7681   Pakistan 1950   732.1559
```

```
7691 Pakistan 1960  732.4439
7701 Pakistan 1970 1148.8489
7711 Pakistan 1980 1453.3522
7721 Pakistan 1990 1933.9449
7731 Pakistan 2000 1858.5410
```

Next, we use the following R code to convert the newly created dataset long form pwt7.ip into a wide form. We first install and load the reshape2 package and then apply the dcast() function to reshape pwt7.ip. We expect that the rgdpl values of India and Pakistan will be arranged side by side for each year. We refer to this process as reshaping a dataset from a long form to a wide form.

```
# load reshape2 package
library(reshape2)

# reshape pwt7.ip from long to wide form
pwt7.ip2 <- dcast(pwt7.ip, year ~ country, value.var = "rgdpl")
```

The dcast() function turns a long form country-year dataset pwt7.ip into a wide form year dataset pwt7.ip2. Inside the dcast() function, we first specify the long dataset to be reshaped, then the variable to be retained as the sorting ID, followed by a tilde and the variable whose values will be used as the names of new columns (i.e., India and Pakistan), and end with the values of new variables (India and Pakistan) filled with the values of the variable specified in the value.var= option. The new dataset pwt7.ip2, as displayed below, is organized the way we expected.

```
# display the wide form dataset
pwt7.ip2

  year    India   Pakistan
1 1950   594.1658   732.1559
2 1960   713.6806   732.4439
3 1970   887.1750  1148.8489
4 1980  1019.6258  1453.3522
5 1990  1407.2194  1933.9449
6 2000  1860.2439  1858.5410
```

At this point, one may naturally ask how we can reshape a dataset from a wide form into a long form. To do so, we can apply the melt() function in reshape2. The R code and output below show how we can reshape the wide form pwt7.ip2 back into a long form.

```
# reshape a dataset from wide to long
melt(pwt7.ip2, id.vars = "year", variable.name = "country",
    value.name = "rgdpl")

   year  country      rgdpl
1  1950    India   594.1658
2  1960    India   713.6806
3  1970    India   887.1750
4  1980    India  1019.6258
5  1990    India  1407.2194
6  2000    India  1860.2439
7  1950 Pakistan   732.1559
8  1960 Pakistan   732.4439
9  1970 Pakistan  1148.8489
10 1980 Pakistan  1453.3522
11 1990 Pakistan  1933.9449
12 2000 Pakistan  1858.5410
```

Inside the melt() function, the option id.vars="year" specifies year is an ID variable; the option variable.name= specifies the name of a new variable that converts variable names from the wide form dataset into variable values in the long form dataset (wide-to-long); and the option value.name= specifies the name of a new variable that stores the values of the wide-to-long variables in the wide form dataset.

Prepare Data III: Manage Observations
Remove Select Observations

Sometimes we want to remove select observations that satisfy certain conditions. The easiest solution is to apply logical operators and the indexing method to a dataset. Take the dataset pwt7 as an example. In the dataset, there are two versions of GDP data for China, which are based on different price data, one official and the other non-official. Thus, for the same years for China, one set of observations is denoted by isocode "CHN", and another set by isocode "CH2". In data analysis, it is certainly inappropriate to include both sets of observations at the same time. The code below demonstrates a simple method to remove all the observations where isocode equals "CH2" and save the output into a new dataset, pwt7.nc.

```
# remove observations with isocode equal CH2
pwt7.nc <- pwt7[pwt7$isocode != "CH2", ]
```

To show the difference between the two datasets, pwt7 and pwt7.nc, we will apply the dim() function to both datasets and see that they have the same number of variables but that pwt7.nc has 60 fewer observations. We will further show that pwt7 has 60 years from 1950 to 2009 that meet the condition that isocode equals "CH2" and pwt7.nc has zero years that meet that condition.

```
# remove second set of China observations with isocode CH2
pwt7.nc <- pwt7[pwt7$isocode != "CH2", ]

# compare pwt7 and pwt7.nc
dim(pwt7)

[1] 11400    37

dim(pwt7.nc)

[1] 11340    37

# display the number of years under CH2
pwt7$year[pwt7$isocode == "CH2"]

 [1] 1950 1951 1952 1953 1954 1955 1956 1957 1958 1959 1960
[12] 1961 1962 1963 1964 1965 1966 1967 1968 1969 1970 1971
[23] 1972 1973 1974 1975 1976 1977 1978 1979 1980 1981 1982
[34] 1983 1984 1985 1986 1987 1988 1989 1990 1991 1992 1993
[45] 1994 1995 1996 1997 1998 1999 2000 2001 2002 2003 2004
[56] 2005 2006 2007 2008 2009

pwt7.nc$year[pwt7.nc$isocode == "CH2"]

integer(0)
```

Find and Remove Duplicate Observations

Datasets sometimes contain duplicate observations that must be removed. Below we will demonstrate how to remove duplicate observations based on some key sorting variables. For the sake of illustration, we will first create an artificial dataset with duplicate observations. Recall the dataset pwt7.ip listed in the previous section. Below we will employ the rbind() function to append all India observations from pwt7.ip to the dataset pwt7.ip itself, thus producing a dataset with one duplicate India observation for each year. The display of pwt7.dup shows the creation of duplicate observations is as expected.

```
# create dataset with duplicate India observations
pwt7.dup <- rbind(pwt7.ip, pwt7.ip[pwt7.ip$country=="India",])
```

```
# display data with duplicate observations
pwt7.dup
```

	country	year	rgdpl
4621	India	1950	594.1658
4631	India	1960	713.6806
4641	India	1970	887.1750
4651	India	1980	1019.6258
4661	India	1990	1407.2194
4671	India	2000	1860.2439
7681	Pakistan	1950	732.1559
7691	Pakistan	1960	732.4439
7701	Pakistan	1970	1148.8489
7711	Pakistan	1980	1453.3522
7721	Pakistan	1990	1933.9449
7731	Pakistan	2000	1858.5410
46211	India	1950	594.1658
46311	India	1960	713.6806
46411	India	1970	887.1750
46511	India	1980	1019.6258
46611	India	1990	1407.2194
46711	India	2000	1860.2439

Now we turn to apply the !duplicated() function to remove duplicate observations in pwt7.dup. The R code is as follows:

```
# remove duplicate observations
pwt7.dup[!duplicated(pwt7.dup[, c("country", "year")]), ]
```

The way the duplicated() function works is to assign a logical value TRUE or FALSE to each observation based on duplicate values for the key sorting variables: country and year. Since we have two key ID variables, we use the c() function to refer to them. We remove duplicate observations by asking R to select only observations that do *not* have duplicate values for country and year. In contrast to the duplicated() function, the !duplicated() function assigns TRUE to non-duplicated observations according to country and year. The R output is as follows:

	country	year	rgdpl
4621	India	1950	594.1658
4631	India	1960	713.6806
4641	India	1970	887.1750

```
4651      India 1980 1019.6258
4661      India 1990 1407.2194
4671      India 2000 1860.2439
7681 Pakistan 1950  732.1559
7691 Pakistan 1960  732.4439
7701 Pakistan 1970 1148.8489
7711 Pakistan 1980 1453.3522
7721 Pakistan 1990 1933.9449
7731 Pakistan 2000 1858.5410
```

If we are interested in saving the dataset without duplicate observations, we simply assign the output to a new data object.

Prepare Data IV: Manage Variables

Managing variables or columns of a data frame often involves the creation of new variables, renaming variables in terms of variable names, recoding variables in terms of variable values, and the creation of variable labels. This section relies heavily on the earlier discussion on variable types.

Create New Variables

In order to conduct data analysis to answer a research question, we often have to create new variables. Here we provide some examples on how to create numeric, character, and factor variables, how to construct leading, lagging, and growth rate variables, and how to compute a new variable representing group mean.

Numeric Variables: Real Investment Per Capita and Total Real Investment

We begin with some simple examples of numeric variables. Suppose we want to use pwt7 to create two new variables on investment: real investment per capita and total real investment in a country. For this task, the relevant variables include ki, rgdpl, and POP, which are defined in the readme file as follows:

• The variable ki is "Investment Share of PPP Converted GDP Per Capita at 2005 constant prices [rgdpl], in percent";
• The variable rgdpl is "PPP Converted GDP Per Capita (Laspeyres), derived from growth rates of c, g, i, at 2005 constant prices (2005 International dollar per person);
• The variable POP is "Population (in thousands)."

Therefore, real investment per capita (in 2005 international dollars) ought to be computed as $rgdpl * ki/100$, and total real investment (in 2005 international dollar) ought to be computed as $rgdpl * POP * 1000 * ki/100 = rgdpl * POP * ki * 10$.

The R code for creating these two variables is as follows:

```
# create real per capita investment in 2005 international $
pwt7$investpc <- pwt7$rgdpl*pwt7$ki/100

# create total real investment in 2005 international $
pwt7$invest <- pwt7$rgdpl*pwt7$POP*pwt7$ki*10
```

Character and Factor Variables: Income Group and Decade

We will demonstrate how to create character and factor variables. As noted earlier, the advantage of the factor variable is that it can be used directly in statistical modeling. Below we will demonstrate how to construct an income group variable, first as a character type and then converted into a factor one.

Suppose we want to create an income group variable that classifies countries into one of four categories: low-income, lower-middle-income, upper-middle-income, and high-income. The World Bank employs the following criteria based on 2012 Gross National Income: low-income is $1,035 or less; lower-middle-income is $1,036–$4,085; upper-middle-income is $4,086–$12,615; and high-income is $12,616 or more. For the sake of illustration, we will employ a similar set of cutoffs.

We will first show how to create a character variable using 1,000, 4,000, and 12,000 as the thresholds. We use the indexing method and various operators to specify conditions for each category of income group. For example, the new variable income.group is assigned a value of "low-income" if rgdpl is less than 1,000 (i.e., [pwt7$rgdpl<1000]). It is important to remember that the character value such as "low-income" needs to be placed inside double quotation marks.

```
# create a character variable income.group
pwt7$income.group <- NA
pwt7$income.group[pwt7$rgdpl<1000] <- "low-income"
pwt7$income.group[pwt7$rgdpl>1000&pwt7$rgdpl<4000]<-"low-middle"
pwt7$income.group[pwt7$rgdpl>4000&pwt7$rgdpl<12000]<-"up-middle"
pwt7$income.group[pwt7$rgdpl>12000] <- "high-income"
```

We can illustrate the variable type of income.group using the class() function. Recall that the class() function identifies the class of an R object, which could be "numeric," "logical," "character," "list," "matrix," "array," "factor," or "data.frame."

```
# show variable type using class() function
class(pwt7$income.group)

[1] "character"
```

We can convert this character variable into a factor type using the factor()
function.

```
# convert character variable into factor type
pwt7$income.group <- factor(pwt7$income.group,
    levels = c("low-income", "low-middle", "up-middle",
        "high-income"), ordered = TRUE)
```

The levels= and ordered=TRUE options inside the factor() function enable
the following assignment of integer values: 1=low-income, 2=lower-middle,
3=upper-middle, and 4=high-income, for the variable income.group.

Any character variable can be converted into a factor one using the factor()
function. As noted earlier, a character variable can not be used directly in a lot of
statistical modeling such as regression analysis, but a factor variable can be.

Again, we can confirm the variable type using the class() function. We can
also use the table() function to show the frequency count of observations in each
income category.

```
# show variable type again
class(pwt7$income.group)

[1] "ordered" "factor"

# show frequency count in each category
table(pwt7$income.group)
```

low-income	low-middle	up-middle	high-income
1613	2750	2421	1941

Next, we will show how to create a numeric variable to indicate income group
categories, check its variable type, and then convert it into a factor variable.

```
# create a numeric variable income.group2
pwt7$income.group2 <- NA
pwt7$income.group2[pwt7$rgdpl<1000] <- 1
pwt7$income.group2[pwt7$rgdpl>1000 & pwt7$rgdpl<4000] <- 2
pwt7$income.group2[pwt7$rgdpl>4000 & pwt7$rgdpl<12000] <- 3
pwt7$income.group2[pwt7$rgdpl>12000] <- 4
```

```
# show variable type using class() function
class(pwt7$income.group2)

[1] "numeric"
```

Note that when converting a numeric variable into a factor one, we use the labels= option in the factor() function, which will assign labels to the different levels of the numeric variable.

```
# convert numeric variable into factor variable
pwt7$income.group2 <- factor(pwt7$income.group2, labels =
    c("low-income", "low-middle", "up-middle", "high-income"))
```

Finally, we will illustrate how to create a decade factor variable to represent whether an observation is from the 1950s, 1960s, 1970s, 1980s, 1990s, or 2000s.

```
# create a character variable for decade
pwt7$decade <- NA
pwt7$decade[pwt7$year >= 1950 & pwt7$year <= 1959] <- "1950s"
pwt7$decade[pwt7$year >= 1960 & pwt7$year <= 1969] <- "1960s"
pwt7$decade[pwt7$year >= 1970 & pwt7$year <= 1979] <- "1970s"
pwt7$decade[pwt7$year >= 1980 & pwt7$year <= 1989] <- "1980s"
pwt7$decade[pwt7$year >= 1990 & pwt7$year <= 1999] <- "1990s"
pwt7$decade[pwt7$year >= 2000] <- "2000s"

# convert character variable into factor variable
pwt7$decade <- factor(pwt7$decade, levels = c("1950s", "1960s",
    "1970s", "1980s", "1990s", "2000s"), ordered = TRUE)

# show frequency count in each decade
table(pwt7$decade)


1950s 1960s 1970s 1980s 1990s 2000s
 1900  1900  1900  1900  1900  1900
```

Leading, Lagged, and Growth Rate Variables

We often need to create variables that lead or lag behind the current year or variables that represent annual growth rates. Take the annual economic growth rate of a country as an example. We often measure economic growth by dividing the annual change in GDP per capita with the level of GDP per capita in the previous year. We may denote economic growth in year t for country i as follows:

$$Growth_{t,i} = \frac{rgdpl_{t,i} - rgdpl_{t-1,i}}{rgdpl_{t-1,i}}$$

For example, country i's annual growth rate in 1990 is:

$$Growth_{1990,i} = \frac{rgdpl_{1990,i} - rgdpl_{1989,i}}{rgdpl_{1989,i}}.$$

In order to compute growth, we need to have the current year rgdpl and the one-year lagged rgdpl. The former is directly available as a variable, but the latter is not. To generate the one-year lagged rgdpl for each country, we apply the slide() function from the DataCombine package. The specific steps include: install the DataCombine package, load it into R, sort data in ascending order first by country and then by year, use the slide() function to create a new leading or lagged variable, assign the slide() function output to pwt7, and then compute the annual growth rate for rgdpl. The R code is as follows:

```
# create leading and lagging variables in a panel data
# load DataCombine package in order to use slide function
library(DataCombine)

# sort data first by country and then by year
pwt7 <- pwt7[order(pwt7$country, pwt7$year),]

# create a one-year leading variable for rgdpl
pwt7 <- slide(pwt7,Var="rgdpl", NewVar="rgdplead",
            GroupVar="country", slideBy=1)

# create a one-year lagged variable for rgdpl
pwt7 <- slide(pwt7, Var="rgdpl", NewVar="rgdplag",
            GroupVar="country", slideBy=-1)

# create annual growth rate for rgdpl
pwt7$growth <- (pwt7$rgdpl-pwt7$rgdplag)/pwt7$rgdplag
```

The arguments in the slide() function can be difficult to understand and thus, require clarification.

1. Specify the dataset used.
2. The option Var= identifies the variable whose leading or lagged version is created.

3. The option `NewVar=` specifies the name of the newly created leading or lagged variable.
4. The option `GroupVar=` identifies the cross-sectional group for which the leading or lagged variable is created.
5. The option `slideBy=` specifies by how many rows (time units like year) the new variable is to be lagged (-) or leading (+). For example, 1 indicates one-year leading whereas -1 means one year lagged.

Create a Group-Specific Variable: World Average Annual Growth

We often need to create by-group variables. World average economic growth rate is a good example of a by-group variable. It is an average of the growth rates of all countries by each year, which allows us to compare a country's own growth rate with that of the world economy. Below we will demonstrate how to create a by-group variable in R using the by() function.

```
# create world average annual growth using by() function
pwt7$growth.w <- by(pwt7$growth, pwt7$year, FUN=mean,
                    na.rm=TRUE)
```

The new variable indicating world average annual growth rate is called `growth.w`, assigned through the output of the by() function. The by() function first specifies the original variable `growth` that is used for computing group mean, then the group or index variable `year` for which the group mean is computed, followed by the `FUN=` option which specifies the statistic computed for each group. Since missing values are present in the `growth` variable, `na.rm=TRUE` must be specified to remove missing values in computation.

The by() function applies a function across subsets of data defined by the group variable. Hence, a variety of by-group statistics can be computed. For a list of such statistics, refer to Table 1.6.

Create and Merge More Group-Specific Statistics

We may also be interested in finding out the average economic growth rate for each income group during each decade. For this purpose we can use the aggregate() function as follows:

```
# compute by-group economic growth rates
aggregate(growth ~ decade + income.group, data=pwt7, FUN=mean)
```

Inside the aggregate() function, we first specify the variable whose values are to be aggregated, and then following a tilde, we must specify the group variables by which group statistics are to be computed. After that, we specify which dataset is to be used with data=, and which statistic is to be computed with FUN=. We may choose to compute different group-specific statistics from the list in Table 1.6. The R output is as follows:

	decade	income.group	growth
1	1950s	low-income	0.016622330
2	1960s	low-income	0.019106637
3	1970s	low-income	0.007661474
4	1980s	low-income	0.002613433
5	1990s	low-income	-0.004449034
6	2000s	low-income	0.015688352
7	1950s	low-middle	0.023500379
8	1960s	low-middle	0.026975806
9	1970s	low-middle	0.031768607
10	1980s	low-middle	0.008659334
11	1990s	low-middle	0.020114909
12	2000s	low-middle	0.035340001
13	1950s	up-middle	0.033518688
14	1960s	up-middle	0.048562439
15	1970s	up-middle	0.039638180
16	1980s	up-middle	0.010777898
17	1990s	up-middle	0.015921743
18	2000s	up-middle	0.038937086
19	1950s	high-income	0.019925973
20	1960s	high-income	0.036524799
21	1970s	high-income	0.035745528
22	1980s	high-income	0.021335852
23	1990s	high-income	0.019735372
24	2000s	high-income	0.026003399

The by() and aggregate() functions both produce summarizing information for groups. Yet they are different in several ways. First, the former works with any function such as mean or range, but the latter only works with a function that returns a single value such as mean. Second, the former may produce multiple by-group statistics at the same time, but the latter only one at a time. Finally, the output of the former is a list that requires as.data.frame((as.table(output))) to turn into a data frame, and the output of the latter is by default a data frame.

We may want to save the aggregate() output into a dataset by simply assigning it to a new data frame object called pwt7.ag. The R code is as follows:

```
# save by-group economic growth rates to a dataset
pwt7.ag <- aggregate(growth ~ decade + income.group,
                     data=pwt7, FUN=mean)
```

Often, though, we are interested in comparing a country's GDP per capita in a year with its income group's decade average. But the former lies in the dataset pwt7 whereas the latter is in pwt7.ag. We may merge the latter into the former by using the code discussed earlier. One complication in the process is that the variable growth in pwt7.ag is a group-specific statistic, whereas the variable growth in pwt7 is the value of GDP per capita for a country in a year. Hence, they measure different things even though they have the same variable name, as shown below.

```
# show variable names in pwt7.ag
names(pwt7.ag)

[1] "decade"        "income.group" "growth"
```

Therefore, we must first rename the growth variable in pwt7.ag, by using the code below, and then we merge the two datasets pwt7 and pwt7.ag according to two sorting ID variables income.group and decade. The R code is as follows:

```
# rename the growth variable in pwt7.ag
names(pwt7.ag)[names(pwt7.ag) == "growth"] <- "growth.di"

# merge pwt7.ag into pwt7
pwt7 <- merge(pwt7, pwt7.ag, by = c("decade", "income.group"),
    all = TRUE, sort = TRUE)
```

Often times, we need to create multiple group-specific statistics for multiple variables. The aggregate() function is limited for that purpose. The summaryBy() function in the doBy package can help produce multiple statistics for multiple variables over multiple groups at the same time. For example, if we are interested in producing both the mean and standard deviation for three variables—growth, openk, and POP—for each country in each decade, we may use the following R code. Inside summaryBy(), we first specify multiple variables whose group statistics need to be computed, and then after the tilde, specify multiple group variables; the statistics are specified via FUN=. For illustration, we save the output into a new dataset pwt7.cs and then display its last observation. Note how variable names in pwt7.cs combine original variable names and statistics computed.

```
# load package
library(doBy)

# generate multiple group-statistics for multiple
# variables
```

```
pwt7.cs <- summaryBy(growth + openk + POP ~ isocode + decade,
    FUN = c(mean, sd), data = pwt7, na.rm = TRUE)

# display last observation
tail(pwt7.cs, n = 1)

     isocode decade growth.mean openk.mean POP.mean
1140     ZWE  2000s -0.05472721   81.33989 11646.44
     growth.sd openk.sd  POP.sd
1140 0.05515508 4.734968 203.5446
```

Rename Variables

It often happens that the name of a variable from an original dataset is not what we would prefer to call it. Suppose we would like to refer to the POP variable in pwt7 as population instead. We may use the names() function, the square brackets, and the assignment symbol to do so.

```
# rename variable by changing column name of dataset with
# names() function and indexing brackets
names(pwt7)[names(pwt7) == "POP"] <- "population"
```

Running this line of code and names(pwt7) shows that the variable name POP is now changed to population.

```
# rename variable by changing column name of dataset with
# names() function and indexing brackets
names(pwt7)[names(pwt7) == "POP"] <- "population"

# confirm rename from output of names() function
names(pwt7)

 [1] "country"      "isocode"      "year"
 [4] "population"   "XRAT"         "Currency_Unit"
 [7] "ppp"          "tcgdp"        "cgdp"
[10] "cgdp2"        "cda2"         "cc"
[13] "cg"           "ci"           "p"
[16] "p2"           "pc"           "pg"
[19] "pi"           "openc"        "cgnp"
[22] "y"            "y2"           "rgdpl"
[25] "rgdpl2"       "rgdpch"       "kc"
[28] "kg"           "ki"           "openk"
```

```
[31]  "rgdpeqa"        "rgdpwok"          "rgdpl2wok"
[34]  "rgdpl2pe"       "rgdpl2te"         "rgdpl2th"
[37]  "rgdptt"         "income.group"     "income.group2"
[40]  "decade"         "rgdplead"         "rgdplag"
[43]  "growth"         "growth.w"
```

Recode Variable Values

Often we have to change how variable values are coded. Our first example will be how to recode certain values of two character variables in pwt7.

```
# recode variable value
pwt7$isocode[pwt7$isocode == "CH2"] <- "CHN"
pwt7$country[pwt7$country == "China Version 1"] <- "China"
```

The logic of this recoding approach is to assign the new values to select observations of a certain variable. The first line of code above selects the variable pwt7$isocode, and then, through the use of the indexing method, those observations where isocode equals CH2 are selected and assigned the value CHN. The double quotation marks must be used around the values in the case of a character variable. If we are recoding numeric variables, quotation marks are not necessary.

Now, recoding is particularly important for datasets in which missing values are assigned special numerical values such as –99 or –999. If we do not recode those special missing values into R's default missing value NA, they will be treated incorrectly as normal numerical values. Thus, we must recode them into R's default missing value NA. Hypothetically, if rgdpl used –999 as its missing value code, then we could use the following line of code to recode it.

```
# recode hypothetical missing value -999 in rgdpl
pwt7$rgdpl[pwt7$rgdpl == -999] <- NA
```

Create Variable Labels

We often use variable labels to keep track of variable definitions. R does not do as good a job with variable labels as other software packages like STATA or SAS. A remedy is to use the label() function from the Hmisc package that allows us to create meaningful labels or definitions for variables. Below we will show how to assign labels to certain variables in pwt7. We will first install the package Hmisc if we have not done so, or skip the step if we have, then load the package, and apply the label function to each variable to which we want to assign a meaningful label. Next, we assign a long label surrounded by double quotation marks to the output of the label function for each variable. Finally, we apply the label function to the whole dataset pwt7 to display the variable labels assigned. The R code, without output, is as follows:

```
# load Hmisc package
library(Hmisc)

# use label function to assign variable labels
label (pwt7$isocode) <- "Penn World Table country code"
label (pwt7$rgdpl) <- "PPP Converted GDP Per Capita (Laspeyres)
derived from growth rates of c, g, i, at 2005 constant prices"
label (pwt7$openk) <- "Openness at 2005 constant prices in
                        percent"
label (pwt7$pop) <- "Population (in thousands)"
label (pwt7$growth) <- "annual economic growth rate, based on
                        RGDPL"

# display labels of all variables
label(pwt7)
```

An important weakness of the label() function is that the assigned labels are only useful for functions from the Hmisc package. Still, it offers a good way to keep track of variable labels inside an R program.

Chapter 2 Program Code

Set Working Directory; Import and Inspect Data

```
# install packages only once, then comment out code
# install.packages(c("reshape2", "DataCombine", "Hmisc",
# "haven", "foreign", "gdata", "XLConnect", "pwt",
# "reshape", "doBy"), dependencies=TRUE)

# remove all objects from workspace
rm(list=ls(all=TRUE))

# change working directory to point to project folder
setwd("C:/Project")

# import comma-delimited file, create data object pwt7
pwt7 <- read.csv("pwt70_w_country_names.csv", header=TRUE,
                strip.white=TRUE, stringsAsFactors = FALSE,
```

```
                    na.strings=c("NA",""))

# Inspect Imported Data

# inspect dataset pwt7 in a spreadsheet style data viewer
View(pwt7)

# list first one observation in dataset pwt7
head(pwt7, n=1)

# list last one observation in dataset pwt7
tail(pwt7, n=1)

# dimensions of pwt7: number of observations and number of
# variables
dim(pwt7)

# variable names in dataset pwt7
names(pwt7)

# structure of dataset pwt7
str(pwt7)

# create a figure with three plots
# set graphic parameters for figure of two rows, two columns
par(mfrow=c(2,2))

# graph distribution of variable rgdpl in data frame pwt7
hist(pwt7$rgdpl)
boxplot(pwt7$rgdpl)
qqnorm(pwt7$rgdpl)
```

Manage Datasets, Observations, and Variables

```
# reference fifth observation of pwt7$POP
pwt7$POP[5]

# reference specific observation of pwt7$POP
pwt7$POP[pwt7$country=="Afghanistan" & pwt7$year==1954]

# reference fifth observation of fourth variable in pwt7
```

```
pwt7[5, 4]

# reference certain observation of certain variable in pwt7
pwt7[pwt7$country=="Afghanistan" & pwt7$year==1954, "POP"]

# sort data in ascending order by country and by year
pwt7 <- pwt7[order(pwt7$country, pwt7$year),]

# sort data by country (ascending) and by year (descending)
pwt7 <- pwt7[order(pwt7$country, -pwt7$year),]

# show select rows; example: observations 100 and 102
pwt7[c(100, 102),]

# show select rows; example: observations from 100 to 102
pwt7[c(100:102),]

# show select variables
pwt7[, c("country", "year", "rgdpl")]

# combine two selections: certain rows and certain columns
pwt7[c(100:102), c("country", "year", "rgdpl")]

# show certain observations and certain variables that meet
# conditions: Afghanistan since 2006 for three variables
pwt7[pwt7$year>=2006 & pwt7$country=="Afghanistan",
    c("country", "year", "rgdpl")]

# select multiple countries and non-consecutive years
# for select variables
pwt7[pwt7$year %in% c(1970, 1980, 1990, 2000, 2009) &
pwt7$country %in% c("India","China Version 1"),
c("country","year","rgdpl")]

# create a new dataset with three select variables
pwt7new <- pwt7[, c("country", "year", "rgdpl")]

# create two temporary pwt7 subsets for merging example
pwt7.tmp1 <- pwt7[,c("isocode", "year", "rgdpl")]
pwt7.tmp2 <- pwt7[,c("isocode", "year", "openk")]
```

```
# merge two datasets
pwt7.m<-merge(pwt7.tmp1, pwt7.tmp2, by=c("isocode","year"),
              all=TRUE, sort=TRUE)


# combine datasets of equal observations, different variables
new.data <- cbind(data1, data2)


# append datasets of equal variables, different observations
new.data <- rbind(data1, data2)


# create a subset of pwt7
# India and Pakistan, three variables and six years
pwt7.ip <- pwt7[pwt7$year %in% c(1950,1960,1970,1980,1990,2000)
        & pwt7$country %in% c("India","Pakistan"),
        c("country","year","rgdpl")]


# display the long form dataset
pwt7.ip


# load reshape2 package
library(reshape2)


# reshape pwt7.ip from long to wide form
pwt7.ip2 <- dcast(pwt7.ip, year~country, value.var="rgdpl")


# display the wide form dataset
pwt7.ip2


# reshape a dataset from wide to long
melt(pwt7.ip2, id.vars="year", variable.name="country",
     value.name="rgdpl")


# remove second set of China observations with isocode CH2
pwt7.nc <- pwt7[pwt7$isocode!="CH2",]


# compare pwt7 and pwt7.nc
dim(pwt7)
dim(pwt7.nc)


# display the number of years under CH2
pwt7$year[pwt7$isocode=="CH2"]
```

```
pwt7.nc$year[pwt7.nc$isocode=="CH2"]

# create dataset with duplicate India observations
pwt7.dup <- rbind(pwt7.ip, pwt7.ip[pwt7.ip$country=="India",])

# display data with duplicate observations
pwt7.dup

# remove duplicate observations
pwt7.dup[!duplicated(pwt7.dup[,c("country", "year")]),]

# create real per capita investment in 2005 international $
pwt7$investpc <- pwt7$rgdpl*pwt7$ki/100

# create total real investment in 2005 international $
pwt7$invest <- pwt7$rgdpl*pwt7$POP*pwt7$ki*10

# create a character variable income.group
pwt7$income.group <- NA
pwt7$income.group[pwt7$rgdpl<1000] <- "low-income"
pwt7$income.group[pwt7$rgdpl>1000&pwt7$rgdpl<4000]<-"low-middle"
pwt7$income.group[pwt7$rgdpl>4000&pwt7$rgdpl<12000]<-"up-middle"
pwt7$income.group[pwt7$rgdpl>12000] <- "high-income"

# show variable type using class() function
class(pwt7$income.group)

# convert character variable income.group into factor type
pwt7$income.group <- factor(pwt7$income.group,
           levels=c("low-income", "low-middle", "up-middle",
           "high-income"), ordered=TRUE)

# show variable type again
class(pwt7$income.group)

# show frequency count in each category
table(pwt7$income.group)

# create a numeric variable income.group2
pwt7$income.group2 <- NA
pwt7$income.group2[pwt7$rgdpl <1000] <- 1
```

```
pwt7$income.group2[pwt7$rgdpl>1000 & pwt7$rgdpl<4000] <- 2
pwt7$income.group2[pwt7$rgdpl>4000 & pwt7$rgdpl<12000] <- 3
pwt7$income.group2[pwt7$rgdpl > 12000] <- 4

# show variable type using class() function
class(pwt7$income.group2)

# convert numeric variable into factor variable
pwt7$income.group2 <- factor(pwt7$income.group2, labels=
    c("low-income", "low-middle", "up-middle", "high-income"))

# show variable type again
class(pwt7$income.group2)

# show frequency count within each category
table(pwt7$income.group2)

# create a character variable for decade
pwt7$decade <- NA
pwt7$decade[pwt7$year>=1950 & pwt7$year<=1959] <- "1950s"
pwt7$decade[pwt7$year>=1960 & pwt7$year<=1969] <- "1960s"
pwt7$decade[pwt7$year>=1970 & pwt7$year<=1979] <- "1970s"
pwt7$decade[pwt7$year>=1980 & pwt7$year<=1989] <- "1980s"
pwt7$decade[pwt7$year>=1990 & pwt7$year<=1999] <- "1990s"
pwt7$decade[pwt7$year>=2000] <- "2000s"

# convert character variable into factor variable
pwt7$decade <- factor(pwt7$decade, levels=c("1950s", "1960s",
            "1970s", "1980s", "1990s", "2000s"), ordered=TRUE)

# show frequency count in each decade
table(pwt7$decade)

# create leading and lagging variables in a panel dataset
# load DataCombine package in order to use slide function
library(DataCombine)

# sort data first by country and then by year
pwt7 <- pwt7[order(pwt7$country, pwt7$year),]

# create a one-year leading variable for rgdpl
```

```
pwt7 <- slide(pwt7,Var="rgdpl", NewVar="rgdplead",
            GroupVar="country", slideBy=1)


# create a one-year lagged variable for rgdpl
pwt7 <- slide(pwt7, Var="rgdpl", NewVar="rgdplag",
            GroupVar="country", slideBy=-1)



# create annual growth rate for rgdpl
pwt7$growth <- (pwt7$rgdpl-pwt7$rgdplag)/pwt7$rgdplag

#  create world average annual growth using by() function
pwt7$growth.w <- by(pwt7$growth, pwt7$year, FUN=mean,
                    na.rm=TRUE)

# compute by-group economic growth rates
aggregate(growth ~ decade + income.group, data=pwt7, FUN=mean)

# save by-group economic growth rates to a dataset
pwt7.ag <- aggregate(growth~decade+income.group, data=pwt7,
                    FUN=mean)

# rename the growth variable in pwt7.ag
names(pwt7.ag)[names(pwt7.ag)=="growth"] <- "growth.di"

# merge pwt7.ag into pwt7
pwt7 <- merge(pwt7, pwt7.ag, by=c("decade","income.group"),
            all=TRUE, sort=TRUE)

# load package
library(doBy)

# generate multiple group-statistics for multiple variables
pwt7.cs <- summaryBy(growth + openk + POP ~ isocode + decade,
                    FUN=c(mean, sd), data=pwt7, na.rm=TRUE)

# display last observation
tail(pwt7.cs, n=1)

# rename variable by changing column name of dataset
# with names() function and indexing brackets
```

```
names(pwt7)[names(pwt7)=="POP"] <- "population"

# confirm rename from output of names() function
names(pwt7)

# recode variable value
pwt7$isocode[pwt7$isocode=="CH2"] <- "CHN"
pwt7$country[pwt7$country=="China Version 1"] <- "China"

# recode hypothetical missing value -999 in rgdpl
pwt7$rgdpl[pwt7$rgdpl==-999] <- NA

# load Hmisc package
library(Hmisc)

# use label function to assign variable labels
label (pwt7$isocode) <- "Penn World Table country code"
label (pwt7$rgdpl) <- "PPP Converted GDP Per Capita (Laspeyres)
derived from growth rates of c, g, i, at 2005 constant prices"
label (pwt7$openk) <- "Openness at 2005 constant prices in
                        percent"
label (pwt7$pop) <- "Population (in thousands)"
label (pwt7$growth) <- "annual economic growth rate, based on
                        RGDPL"

# display labels of all variables
label(pwt7)
```

Summary

This chapter shows how to read an original raw dataset in the comma-delimited format into R, how to create a corresponding data object, how to inspect the imported data visually, how to obtain information on dataset attributes (dimensions, variable names, etc.), how to graph select variables, and how to manage variables, observations, and datasets in order to get data ready for analysis. Chapter 2 covers a large amount of materials that are necessary for using R to get ready for practical data analysis, even at the beginner's level. The large quantity of information, however, can make it difficult for us to see the big picture. Therefore, at this moment, it is useful to revisit Table 2.1 which provides a conceptual roadmap of the information in Chapter 2.

Now that we have learned how to prepare a dataset for analysis, it is time for us to learn how to use R to obtain descriptive statistics and make basic statistical inferences about an outcome variable of interest. These are the topics of Chapter 3. Yet before heading into Chapter 3, it is useful to address some miscellaneous questions that beginning R users often come up with.

Miscellaneous Q&As for Ambitious Readers

How do we Import Datasets of Other Formats into R?

The Penn World Table 7.0 dataset example illustrates how R imports a comma-delimited file. In practice, we will always come across datasets in many other formats. R is powerful in terms of data importation. Below we will present some sample code for importing datasets of several common formats. All the code below will assume we have executed setwd() function and specified where the datasets are stored.

(1) Tab-delimited file. The R code for a tab-delimited file is very similar to those for the comma-delimited file, except for how to denote that a file is tab-delimited.

```
dataframe.name <- read.table("filename.txt", header=TRUE,
                  sep="\t", na.strings=".", strip.white=TRUE,
                  stringsAsFactors=False)
```

The read.table() function imports a tab-delimited file called filename.txt, in which the header row contains variable names, the columns are separated by tabs, and the observation values denoted by "." are treated as missing. The output from the read.table function is assigned to a data object arbitrarily called dataframe.name.

We use the option sep="\t" to indicate the file is tab-delimited. The read.table function can also import the comma delimited file by specifying the option sep="," instead.

(2) Stata file. To import stata files into R, we may use one of the following several ways.

```
# install.packages("foreign")
# install.packages("Hmisc")
library(foreign)
library(Hmisc)
dataframe.name <- stata.get("filename.dta")
```

In the example above, we first use the library function to load into R two add-on packages, foreign and Hmisc. Note that the code assumes that the packages have been installed; if they have not been, we will get an error message when trying to load the packages. Then we use the stata.get function to read the stata file and create a data object called dataframe.name.

In a second way to import a stata file, we first use the library function to load into R the add-on package, foreign. Then we use the read.dta function to read the stata file, and create a data object dataframe.name.

```
library(foreign)
dataframe.name <- read.dta("filename.dta")
```

There are three important caveats to remember when we import stata files into R. First, many variable names in stata files contain underscores like in variable_name, which R does not like. We could use the option convert. underscore = TRUE to replace an underscore with a period. Second, many variables in stata files are often read into R as factor variables, which could be hard to work with for beginners. We could use the option convert.factors = FALSE to tell R to import numerical variables as numerical ones only. With these options added, the R code may appear as follows:

```
dataframe.name <- stata.get("filename.dta",
             convert.underscore=TRUE, convert.factors=FALSE)
dataframe.name <- read.dta("filename.dta",
             convert.underscore=TRUE, convert.factors=FALSE)
```

Finally, both stata.get and read.dta functions can not import files in the STATA13 format. A new package for importing Stata 13 data files is now available. The following code will allow us to do that.

```
# install.packages('readstata13')
library(readstata13)
dataframe.name <- read.dta13("filename.dta")
```

We first install and load the readstata13 package, then use the read.dta13 function to import the stata file, and assign it to a data object in R.

Stata files often contain very informative variable labels. Here is one way to preserve those variable labels in a separate file, which we refer to as "codebook" in the R code below.

```
dataframe.name <- read.dta("filename.dta")
var.labels <- attr(dataframe.name,"var.labels")
codebook <- data.frame(var.name=names(dataframe.name),
                  var.labels)
```

(3) SPSS file. Similar to stata files, we can use two alternative functions for importing SPSS files: read.spss in the foreign package, and spss.get in the Hmisc package. The latter is preferable because it automatically takes care of many options, making data importation smoother. The R code for the latter is as follows:

```
library(foreign)
library(Hmisc)
dataframe.name <- spss.get("filename.sav")
```

In many SPSS files, variables often come with value labels. If we want to keep the variables with those same levels defined by value labels, we can add an option to the argument of the function and use the following code instead.

```
dataframe.name <- spss.get("filename.sav",
                            use.value.labels=TRUE)
```

(4) SAS file. SAS files can be read into R using the foreign and haven packages among others. We can use the read.xport() function in the foreign package and the read_sas() function in the haven package to read two different SAS data formats, respectively.

```
library(foreign)
dataframe.name <- read.xport("filename.xport")
```

```
library(haven)
dataframe.name <- read_sas("filename.sas7bdat")
```

(5) Excel file. Most frequently students work with Excel spreadsheet files. The best data importing method, recommended in many books on R, is to export those files from within Excel to comma-delimited or tab-delimited files and then import them into R using the code described earlier. We encourage R beginners to follow this advice.

However, R does have the ability to directly communicate with Excel spreadsheets for data importation. The Excel file needs some preparation before we read it into R. For example, keep the variable names in the first row of the spreadsheet, and give the sheet to be read into R a worksheet name so that we can refer to it in R. Here is the R code:

```
# install.packages('RODBC')
library(RODBC)
channel <- odbcConnectExcel("filename.xls")
```

```
dataframe1 <- sqlFetch(channel, "worsheet1")
odbcClose(channel)
```

In the code, we first install and load the RODBC package into R; ignore the installation step if the package has been installed. The odbcConnectExcel() function reads an excel file called filename.xls, and returns an RODBC connection object called channel. Then the sqlFetch() function uses the channel object, imports the Excel worksheet labeled worksheet1, and assigns the output to an R data object called dataframe1. Finally, the odbcClose() function removes the RODBC connection object called channel.

Sometimes, we would like to import multiple worksheets from an Excel file. Suppose we have three worksheets, labeled worksheet1, worksheet2, and worksheet3. The code below shows how we can import the three worksheets into three R data objects called dataframe1, dataframe2, and dataframe3, respectively.

```
library(RODBC)
channel <- odbcConnectExcel("filename.xls")
dataframe1 <- sqlFetch(channel, "worsheet1")
dataframe2 <- sqlFetch(channel, "worsheet2")
dataframe3 <- sqlFetch(channel, "worsheet3")
odbcClose(channel)
```

A couple of other packages also can help import Excel files into R, including gdata and XLConnect. To use these packages, one may try the following code:

```
library(gdata)
dataframe <- read.xls("datafile.xls", sheet = 1)
```

```
library(XLConnet)
workbook <- loadWorkbook("datafile.xls")
dataframe <- readWorksheet(workbook, sheet = "Sheet1")
```

(6) R data format. If a data object is saved in R data format, it can be directly loaded into R using the load() function. The R code below shows how to save a data object in the workspace, and then load it into R.

```
save(data.object, file = "datafile.RData")
load("datafile.RData")
```

Can we Edit an Observation's Values in the Spreadsheet Viewer?

Recall that we used the View(pwt7) to open and eyeball the pwt7 data frame in a spreadsheet interface. In addition to View(pwt7), one can also use fix(pwt7) to view data. Yet while both can be used to view data, they are extremely different functions. View() just allows one to view data, but fix() allows one to not only view but also to edit and change values of a dataset within the spreadsheet viewer.

Could we use the Indexing Method to Indicate Variables?

We can use the indexing numbers to refer to variables in a dataset. To do so, we first use the names() function to find the indexing numbers for relevant variables, and then we can refer to them in other functions. The following is an example of how to choose country, year, and rgdpl from the pwt7 dataset. Note that based on the output for names() function, the number inside the brackets is the indexing number for the variable right next to it. In this case below, country is in the first column, year in the third column, and rgdpl in the 24th column. So the two lines of code produce the same output.

```
names(pwt7)

 [1] "country"     "isocode"        "year"
 [4] "population"  "XRAT"           "Currency_Unit"
 [7] "ppp"         "tcgdp"          "cgdp"
[10] "cgdp2"       "cda2"           "cc"
[13] "cg"          "ci"             "p"
[16] "p2"          "pc"             "pg"
[19] "pi"          "openc"          "cgnp"
[22] "y"           "y2"             "rgdpl"
[25] "rgdpl2"      "rgdpch"         "kc"
[28] "kg"          "ki"             "openk"
[31] "rgdpeqa"     "rgdpwok"        "rgdpl2wok"
[34] "rgdpl2pe"    "rgdpl2te"       "rgdpl2th"
[37] "rgdptt"      "income.group"   "income.group2"
[40] "decade"      "rgdplead"       "rgdplag"
[43] "growth"      "growth.w"
```

```
pwt7[, c(1, 3, 24)]
pwt7[, c("country", "year", "rgdpl")]
```

Does White Space Really Matter for Character Fields?

We use the following example to show whether R considers "USA" (without any white space) to be the same as " USA" (with one white space in front of USA).

```
# show that white space matters for character fields
# isTRUE tests if it is TRUE or FALSE that 'USA' is the
# same as ' USA'
isTRUE("USA" == " USA")
```

```
isTRUE("USA" == " USA")

[1] FALSE
```

The output shows that the statement that "USA" is the same as " USA" is FALSE.

Is there Another Way to get a Subset of a Dataset?

Earlier we showed how to use indexing to rows and columns as a way to select observations and variables in order to obtain a subset of pwt7. Another way to do this is to use the subset() function. Below is an example of using both indexing and subset to produce the same subset of pwt7.

```
# create a new dataset with five select variables
# excluding CH2 observations
pwt7.v1 <- pwt7[pwt7$isocode != "CH2", c("country", "isocode",
          "year","rgdpl","openk")]

# get the same result by using subset function
pwt7.v2 <- subset(pwt7, isocode != "CH2", c(country, isocode,
          year, rgdpl, openk))
```

Note that within the subset() function, we first specify the data frame name, then specify rows meeting conditions, then select the columns or variables using the c() function. Note that quotation marks are not needed inside the c() function within the subset() function.

We can also see a fuller expression of the same code below.

```
# a fuller expression of the same code
pwt7.v3 <- subset(pwt7, subset = (isocode != "CH2"), select =
    c("country", "isocode", "year", "rgdpl", "openk", "POP") )
```

Is there Another Way to Recode Variable Values?

An alternative way to recode variable values is to use the recode function from the car package. Since the package is an add-on, we have to install the car package first and then load it into R.

```
# install.packages('car')
library(car)
pwt7$isocode <- recode(pwt7$isocode, "'CH2'='CHN'")
```

Notice how we use single quotation marks around the strings, though single quotation marks are not necessary for numeric values.

How to Save Duplicate Observations Into a Different Dataset

Earlier we learned how to remove duplicate observations. Often it is necessary for us to know why duplicate observations exist and whether the observations that are duplicates according to the sorting variables also have duplicate values for other variables in the dataset. Hence, we often would like to send the duplicate observations to a separate dataset for examination. The following R code shows how to do that in two different ways.

```
# create a dataset of duplicated observations
pwt7.d <- pwt7[duplicated(pwt7[, c("isocode", "year")]), ]
```

An alternative way for inspecting duplicate observations is to assign a logical value TRUE or FALSE to each observation in the original dataset with TRUE indicating an observation has duplicated values for sorting variables, and assign the output to a new dataset. Then we can apply the View() function to directly view which observations are duplicates, and apply the table() function to get a frequency count of the number of duplicate observations in the dataset. The R code is listed below.

```
# assign a logical value TRUE or FALSE to each observation
# based on duplicate values for sorting variables, and
# assign the output to a data object
idx <- duplicated(pwt7[, c("isocode", "year")])

# directly view which observations are duplicates
View(idx)

# obtain a frequency count of the number of duplicate
# observations
table(idx)
```

Is there Another Way to Rename Variables?

The add-on package reshape provides a rename() function for us to easily rename variables.

```
# load the reshape package
library(reshape)

# apply the rename function to rename three variables and
# send output to pwt7
pwt7 <- rename(pwt7, c(POP = "population", openk = "trade",
    rgdpl = "rgdppc"))
```

Alternative Source of Penn World Table Data

We showed how to download the pwt7.0 dataset in a comma-delimited format earlier from the following link: www.rug.nl/ggdc/productivity/pwt/pwt-relea ses/pwt-7.0. Some scholars have put together an R package pwt, which contains six different earlier versions of Penn World Table data (pwt5.6, 6.1, 6.2, 7.0, and 7.1). So an easy way to access the pwt 7.0 dataset is to install the pwt package, upload the package in R, and then directly read the pwt7.0 dataset. The R code below shows how to upload the package and then read pwt7.0 in R.

```
library(pwt)
data(pwt7.0)
```

Exercises

For beginners who apply R to data analysis, the first biggest hurdle is reading data into R. The following set of exercises will focus on importing data sets to be used in this book.

1. Create a homework project folder and then an R program file that is pointing to and saved in that folder.
2. In Excel, save the Penn World Table 7 dataset as a tab-delimited file, then read the dataset into R, and produce a table of summary statistics.
3. Follow the instructions in Chapter 6, read the dataset used in Braithwaite (2006) into R, and produce a table of summary statistics.
4. Follow the instructions in Chapter 6, read the dataset used in Bénabou et al. (2015) into R, and produce a table of summary statistics.
5. Following the instructions in Chapter 8, read the dataset of the World Value Survey (WVS) Wave 6 into R, and produce a table of summary statistics.

3

One-Sample and Difference-of-Means Tests

Chapter Objectives

Starting from this chapter, we will learn how to use R to answer substantive questions using statistical inference. In this chapter, we will focus on questions one could ask regarding one continuous outcome variable of interest. A continuous variable can take on an infinite number of possible values within an interval such as income. Economic growth will be the variable used as an example throughout this chapter. Specifically, we will use statistical inferences to answer two substantive questions: What is the average economic growth rate in the world economy? Did the world economy grow faster in 1990 than in 1960? We will discuss in detail how to use statistical inference, sample data, and R to answer each of these two questions. The process learned here can be applied to similar questions about other continuous random variables of interest.

We will begin with a brief but important introduction to the logic of statistical inference and key concepts. We will then demonstrate how to get data ready for analysis in R. Next, for each research question, we will discuss statistical inference using two different methods: null hypothesis testing and confidence interval construction. We will emphasize both a coherent conceptual understanding of statistical inference and its implementation in R.

Our objectives in this chapter are as follows:

1. Learn to make conceptual preparation for statistical inference.
2. Learn to separate data preparation and analysis into different program files.
3. Learn to prepare data for analysis using R.
4. Learn to conduct null hypothesis testing using R.
5. Learn to construct confidence interval using R.
6. Learn to conduct statistical inference using one-sample t-test and the difference-of-means test.

Before we start the chapter, two issues are worth noting. First, there is some intentional repetition in our discussion of statistical inference among the first, third, and fourth sections of this chapter so that the coherence of the logic across different research problems can be clearly observed. At the same time, however, as we read from the first section, through the third section, to the fourth section, the discussion of statistical inference progresses from general to specific, from foundational to executable, and from simple to complex. The discussion gradually becomes in-depth and thorough, which ought to reduce the barrier to entry for beginners in both statistics and R.

Second, the mathematical representation of key concepts and test statistics is necessary and yet could be challenging for some readers. We can better comprehend the math material if in a second reading of the chapter, the math in the third and fourth sections is compared to the step-by-step R code in the miscellaneous section. The Miscellaneous Q&A section breaks down the R code for sample variance, standard deviation, t-test, and confidence interval construction in a step-by-step fashion. As a result, it illustrates clearly how each concept is implemented in computation by R.

Conceptual Preparation

Logic of Statistical Inference

The main use of statistical modeling is to help us answer substantive research questions by making statistical inferences regarding a population of subjects through the use of sample data. The notion of population refers to the universe of all subjects of interest to an analyst, and sample refers to a subset, ideally a randomly selected subset, of the population. When it is not feasible to collect data on the whole population of interest, statistical inference based on sample information becomes necessary. In a nutshell, we use sample data to compute sample statistics in order to estimate the attributes or parameters of the population and then draw inferences about them in a probabilistic manner.

What population attributes are we interested in? Table 3.1 illustrates some population parameters one could estimate and draw inferences about via corresponding sample statistics. In this chapter, we will study how to make inferences about a population mean and the difference between the population means of two groups; in the next chapters, we will learn about population correlation and regression coefficient.

Statistical inference informs us about population attributes based on sample data. That is, it informs us about the likelihood of sample statistics capturing population parameters. In other words, we use available sample information in the right column of Table 3.1 to guess unknown population attributes, referred to as parameters, in the left column of Table 3.1, in a probabilistic manner. The

Table 3.1 **Logic of Statistical Inference**

Target of Inference		Available Information for Inference
Unknown Population Parameter	probabilistic $\xleftarrow{\hspace{0.8cm}}$ inference	**Known Sample Statistics and Data**
1. population mean μ_Y	$\Leftarrow$	sample mean $\bar{y}$
2. difference in means of two populations $\mu_{Y_1} - \mu_{Y_2}$	$\Leftarrow$	difference in means of two samples $\bar{y}_1 - \bar{y}_2$
3. population variance σ^2	$\Leftarrow$	sample variance s^2
4. population correlation ρ	$\Leftarrow$	sample correlation r
5. population regression $Y = \beta_0 + \beta_k X_k + \varepsilon$	$\Leftarrow$	sample regression $y = b_0 + b_k x_k + e$

validity of statistical inference depends on whether a sample is randomly drawn from a population and whether the relevant assumptions about sample statistics and population parameters are satisfied.

Two Methods of Statistical Inference

We often use two methods to make statistical inferences from known sample information to unknown population parameters. The first method is to test a hypothesis regarding a hypothetical population parameter value in a probabilistic manner, and the second method involves constructing a confidence interval around the sample estimate to make a probabilistic prediction about an unknown population parameter. Hence, the two inferential methods are related but distinct.

Here we illustrate their conceptual differences and related concepts using an example, leaving more technical details for later sections. Assume a student named Joe, who is contemplating whether to take an introductory statistics course STAT101, is interested in the average student grade in this course to aid his decision. Also assume that on a 0–200 grading scale, the average course grade has a true population mean of 150 (just above C) and population standard deviation of 11, both of which are unknown to Joe. Since Joe does not have information on the grades of all students in the universe of past and future STAT101 classes, he cannot compute the true population average grade and thus, does not know it is 150. Joe, however, would like to know what the population average grade might be, based on some sample information. The undergraduate advisor in the department draws a random sample of 45 students based on records of past STAT101 classes and tells Joe that the sample has an average of 140 and standard deviation of 12. How can Joe use the available information to make an educated guess, or rather statistical inference, about the population average grade in STAT101?

In Joe's case, the task of statistical inference is to use the sample information (e.g., sample mean, sample standard deviation, and sample size) to infer about the population mean in a probabilistic manner. To make a long story short, the conceptual or mathematical foundation of Joe's inference is as follows. If resources permit us to collect repeated random samples from past records and obtain as many mean values as the number of samples, then we will find the following pattern: if the sample size is large enough, the plot of the many sample means follows a bell-shaped normal distribution curve, with the mean of the many sample means coinciding with the true population mean. This bell-shaped normal distribution curve is the probability distribution of the sample mean, which is called the sampling distribution of the sample mean. The property that if the sample size is large enough, the sampling distribution of the sample mean is approximately normal can be demonstrated mathematically. This property allows us to conduct hypothesis testing and construct a confidence interval about the population mean in a probabilistic manner. So even if Joe cannot obtain repeated samples himself, he can use the one sample provided by the advisor and the property of the sampling distribution of the sample mean to make statistical inferences.

Null Hypothesis Testing

The hypothesis testing method can be used to test whether the unknown population average grade equals some hypothetical value chosen by Joe, the analyst. Suppose Joe wants to test a null hypothesis that the unknown population mean equals 120 (Joe does not know the true population average grade is 150, but feeling challenged, he wonders whether it could be very low at 120 or D). Based on certain assumptions, Joe can construct a test statistic such as a Z- or t-statistic (depending on sample size and whether the population standard deviation is known). The Z- or t-test statistic, which will be discussed in detail later, has two similar features: (1) It measures the distance from the sample average grade to Joe's hypothetical population average grade in a standardized fashion, and (2) either test statistic follows some probability distribution – the standard normal distribution for the Z-statistic or the t-distribution for the t-statistic. Both distributions are bell-shaped, but somewhat different, which will be discussed later.

Using the computed value of the Z- or t-statistic and the probability distribution table for Z or t, Joe can find out the probability of making a Type I error, i.e., rejecting the null hypothesis when it is true. He can then make a comparison between the Type I error associated with his computed test statistic (i.e., the p value) and a commonly accepted Type I error rate, α, which is usually set at

5%. The decision rule in inference is as follows: If the p value is smaller than α, the null hypothesis (i.e., true population average grade equals 120) is rejected, and Joe can draw the conclusion that the true population mean is not 120; yet, if the p value is larger than α, the null hypothesis is not rejected, though Joe has no sufficient evidence to claim that the population average grade is indeed 120 (it might be 119, 121, 122, etc., none of which is explicitly tested). Therefore, generally speaking, the conclusion of null hypothesis testing is not very informative as to what the unknown population parameter value actually is.

We can summarize the process of null hypothesis testing more generally as follows:

1. Compute a sample estimate of an unknown population parameter of interest.
2. Specify a hypothetical population parameter value of interest in a null hypothesis.
3. Based on certain assumptions, construct a test statistic that measures the weighted distance between the sample estimate and the hypothetical population parameter.
4. Identify the Type I error (p value) associated with the computed test statistic.
5. Compare the computed Type I error rate with a commonly acceptable Type I error rate (α) and make a decision.

   • If the p value is smaller than α, reject the null hypothesis;
   • If the p value is larger than α, fail to reject the null hypothesis.

6. Discuss the substantive meaning of the statistical decision.

Apparently, the conclusion of null hypothesis testing depends on the choice of the hypothetical population parameter value, the choice of a test statistic, its assumptions being met or not, the sample size, and the choice of the acceptable Type I error threshold. Notably, one way to interpret the commonly accepted 5% level is that if Joe conducts such a test in 100 repeated random samples of the same size, he is willing to accept the mistake of incorrectly rejecting the null hypothesis 5 out of 100 times. Hence, inference based on hypothesis testing is probabilistic.

Confidence Interval Construction

The confidence interval method can be used to calculate a range of values that contains the unknown population mean at a confidence or probability level of Joe's choice. A commonly chosen confidence level is typically 95%, meaning that Joe is 95% confident that the calculated interval captures the unknown population mean. The computed 95% confidence interval may be interpreted as follows: If we compute such an interval repeatedly in 100 different random samples of the same size, we will capture the unknown population mean for about 95% of all 100 samples. In other words, the confidence interval Joe computes using the advisor's data may be one of the 95 confidence intervals capturing the unknown population mean, or may be one of the 5 confidence intervals failing to capture the unknown population mean. Hence, inference based on confidence interval is probabilistic in nature as well.

For Joe, the 95% confidence interval for the population average grade of STAT101 equals the known sample mean 140 plus or minus the 95% confidence level-associated margin of error, producing a range of values with upper and lower bounds. The margin of error is the product between a critical value and the standard error. The critical value is the 0.95 (confidence)-associated Z or t value in the Z or t distribution table. The standard error of the mean is the standard deviation of the probability distribution of the sample mean across repeated samples, measured here by standard deviation divided by the square root of sample size n.

In essence, the 95% confidence interval depends on the sample mean, the critical value determined by the chosen confidence level and the chosen probability distribution (Z or t), the standard error (determined by the standard deviation and sample size), and the sample size.

We can summarize the process of confidence interval construction more generally as follows:

1. Compute a sample estimate of an unknown population parameter of interest.
2. Choose a certain confidence level (e.g., 90%, 95%, or 99%) and find the corresponding critical value of a test statistic chosen based on certain assumptions.
3. Find the lower bound of the confidence interval, which equals the sample estimate minus the test statistic critical value multiplied by the standard error.
4. Find the upper bound of the confidence interval, which equals the sample estimate plus the test statistic critical value multiplied by the standard error.
5. Discuss the substantive meaning of the statistical result.

Relative to hypothesis testing, the confidence interval is more informative as it identifies a range of values that captures the population parameter at a pre-chosen confidence level. Notably, if we increase the confidence level, say, from 0.95 to 0.99, then the margin of error will rise and thus, the range as a whole will become wider. This means that a greater confidence level is associated with a less precise confidence interval.

Types of Errors, Sampling Distributions, and Statistical Inference

Statistical inference is vulnerable to two types of errors: Type I and Type II. The preceding discussion has primarily evolved around Type I error—rejecting the null hypothesis when it is true. Type I error is reflected by α—the acceptable Type I error rate—and the p value in hypothesis testing. If Type I error is the only concern, then analysts can merely minimize it to being near zero. That, unfortunately, is not feasible because of the presence of Type II error. Type II error is defined as the error of failing to reject the null hypothesis when it is false. In the context of the preceding example, Type I error means that Joe rejects the null hypothesis that the population average grade is 120 even though it is true; in contrast, Type II error means that Joe fails to reject the null hypothesis even though the population average grade is not 120. The two types of errors are inversely related to each other.

We will illustrate this relationship graphically below using a contrived example and, in the process, further clarify how statistical inference is made. Recall from our earlier discussion that if the sample size is large enough, the sampling distribution of the sample mean is a bell-shaped normal curve. As an illustration, Figure 3.1 plots two possible sampling distributions of the sample mean under two different *truth* conditions for Joe. If the null hypothesis is true, the center of the sampling distribution of the sample mean should fall on 120, the hypothetical population mean under the null hypothesis; the sampling distribution should look like the case on the left. However, if the null hypothesis is false and the population mean is actually 150, then the center of the sampling distribution of the sample mean should fall on 150 instead; the sampling distribution should then look like the case on the right.

The two possible sampling distributions end up overlapping with each other. In Figure 3.1, the vertical solid line in the middle of the figure denotes the Z test

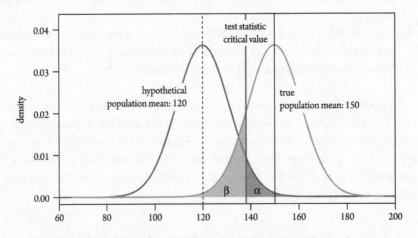

Figure 3.1 Types of Errors and Alternative Sampling Distributions.

critical value determined by Joe's choice of α at 5%, with respect to the null hypothesis of 120 (i.e., in the sampling distribution to the left). The area denoted by α is the acceptable Type I error when Joe tests the null hypothesis based on the sampling distribution on the left. The area denoted by β, located in the alternative sampling distribution, is the Type II error Joe incurs when he chooses a 5% Type I error cutoff α.

Several clarifications are in order. The first clarification concerns the decision rule in hypothesis testing. In Figure 3.1, based on the distribution on the left, if the computed Z-test statistic is larger than the Z-critical value (to the right of the critical value line and farther away from the hypothetical mean 120), then p value is smaller than α, and the null hypothesis is rejected; yet if the computed Z-test statistic is smaller than the Z-critical value (to the left of the line and thus, closer to the hypothetical mean 120), then p value is larger than α, and the null hypothesis is not rejected.

Second, the β area, which lies to the left of the critical value line, represents cases from the sampling distribution on the right centering on the true population mean 150, but for them, the null hypothesis is not rejected. Hence, the β area captures the error of failing to reject the null hypothesis even when it is false.

Third, one key point in Figure 3.1 is that the area indicating the size of α is inversely related to the area indicating the size of β. If we choose an α smaller than 5%, say, 1%, then the critical value line will shift toward the right, causing the area of α to shrink and the area of β to expand. This means that when we reduce the acceptable Type I error, we will at the same time increase Type II error.

Finally, the area β is unknown unless one knows the unknown population parameter value. In practice, researchers often estimate the size of β in the experimental design stage because they are interested in finding out the power of their test, i.e., $(1-\beta)$—the remaining area in the sampling distribution to the right in Figure 3.1. To do so, researchers often assume a population parameter value based on estimates from past experiments.

Data Preparation

For data preparation, we should have completed the following tasks:

1. Clean the workspace in R by removing all objects.
2. Create a project folder to hold the original Penn World Table data, program, and output files.
3. Create a well-documented R program to read the original dataset into R.

4. Inspect imported data to make sure the original data is imported into R properly.
5. Clean possible data problems.
6. Create a new dataset using a subset of the original dataset.
7. Create new variables for later use.
8. Install add-on packages needed.

Using what we learned in the previous two chapters, we must first use R to clean the workspace, set up our project folder, read data into R, inspect and clean imported data, install and load packages needed in this chapter, and prepare the data for analysis. All the tasks conducted below and related R code have been covered in the previous chapter. This chapter will use the following add-on packages: DataCombine, ggplot2, Rmisc, and stargazer; readers should use install.packages("DataCombine"), for example, to install these packages for once first. At the end of data preparation, we will have saved the cleaned dataset into a new R dataset "pwt7g" in the project folder.

```
# Data Cleaning and Management Program

# install following packages only once, then comment out code
# install.packages(c("DataCombine", "ggplot2", "Rmisc",
#                    "stargazer"), dependencies=TRUE)

# (1) before running program, remove all objects in workspace
rm(list=ls(all=TRUE))

# (2) change working directory to project folder
setwd("C:/Project")

# (3) import comma-delimited data file, create data object pwt7
pwt7 <- read.csv("pwt70_w_country_names.csv", header=TRUE,
                 strip.white=TRUE, stringsAsFactors = FALSE,
                 na.strings=c("NA",""))

# (4) inspect imported data using functions from last chapter
# inspect dataset pwt7 in a spreadsheet style data viewer
View(pwt7)

# list first one observation in dataset pwt7
head(pwt7, n=1)


# list last one observation in dataset pwt7
```

```
tail(pwt7, n=1)

# dimensions of pwt7: observations and variables
dim(pwt7)

# variable names in dataset pwt7
names(pwt7)

# structure of dataset pwt7
str(pwt7)

# (5) clean data
# sort data in ascending order by country and by year
pwt7 <- pwt7[order(pwt7$country, pwt7$year),]

# remove second set of China observations with isocode CH2
pwt7 <- pwt7[pwt7$isocode!="CH2",]

# create annual economic growth rate in a panel dataset
# load DataCombine package in order to use slide function
library(DataCombine)

# sort data in ascending order by country and by year
pwt7 <- pwt7[order(pwt7$country, pwt7$year),]

# create a one-year leading variable for rgdpl
pwt7 <- slide(pwt7, Var="rgdpl", NewVar="rgdplead",
              GroupVar="country", slideBy=1)

# create a one-year lagged variable for rgdpl
pwt7 <- slide(pwt7, Var="rgdpl", NewVar="rgdplag",
              GroupVar="country", slideBy=-1)

# create annual growth rate based on rgdpl
pwt7$growth <- (pwt7$rgdpl-pwt7$rgdplag)/pwt7$rgdplag

# create a new dataset: a subset of pwt7 with three variables
pwt7g <- pwt7[, c("country", "year", "rgdpl", "growth")]

# save R dataset
save(pwt7g, file="pwt7g.RData")
```

A best practice in managing work flow in data analysis is to save the R code above on data cleaning into one program file and then save the R code below on analysis into another program file.

To follow this best practice, we will now start a second program file focusing on analysis. We will begin the analysis program with the following R code:

```
# Data analysis program

# (1) before running program, remove all objects in workspace
rm(list=ls(all=TRUE))

# (2) change working directory to project folder
setwd("C:/Project")

# (3) load R data
load("pwt7g.RData")
```

What Is the Average Economic Growth Rate in the World Economy?

In the context of studying any substantive question, we first need to define what the population as the target of inference is and its relationship with the data we have available. Recall that the basic premise of valid statistical inference is random sampling, that is, each subject has an equal chance of being selected into a sample. This assumption is likely upheld in real probability samples, but most likely violated in convenience samples. In applied data analysis, we always have to take into consideration the consequences of any assumption violation, an issue addressed frequently later in the book.

In the present case, the question asks us to find the average economic growth rate in the population or universe of all countries. The available pwt7g dataset includes 190 countries from 1950 to 2009. We have to decide what kind of population we have in mind for our question. There are three possible scenarios.

In the first scenario, we may treat the pwt7g data coverage as a population. That is, we only care about the average economic growth rate among those covered by the dataset. If so, then the average growth rate based on the pwt7g dataset is a population parameter. In this scenario, since we already have population data, no statistical inference is necessary.

In the second scenario, for the question, we may be interested in a population consisting of all countries in a very general sense, covering those with available data already in the pwt7g dataset during 1950–2009, those with missing data in the pwt7g dataset during 1950–2009, and those from future years for the sake of prediction. In this scenario, the data we have resembles a convenience sample. Each country is not randomly selected into the sample, and the missingness or non-missingness of data for a country is most likely not random either.

In the third scenario, for the question, we may think of a population as the set of all countries that could have been produced by the economic, technological, and political processes that influence economic growth. In this scenario, the pwt7g dataset describes one realization of many possible populations that might have occurred by chance due to the underlying social processes; it is regarded as a random sample from some infinite hypothetical population or the superpopulation. Statistical inference goes from the observed data to the superpopulation. The real purpose of inference is to study the underlying data generation process.

Therefore, in the second and third scenarios, we use the average economic growth based on pwt7g to make inference about the average growth in the population. This process is called statistical inference. The first section has provided a brief introduction to the logic, methods, and key issues of statistical inference. In this section, we will further discuss statistical inference in greater technical details and demonstrate how to implement it in R.

Infer Population Mean from Sample Mean

Suppose a random variable Y, representing ECONOMIC GROWTH, has N number of elements or observations in the population. We are interested in knowing the mean of Y in the population, but it is not feasible to get data on all elements of the population. Thus, we draw a sample pwt7g of size n for a variable y, representing economic growth. In this case, we use the sample mean of y as an estimate of the population mean of Y. In this example, two issues are worth noting. First, upper case denotes population data whereas lower case denotes sample data. Second, the sample pwt7g is not randomly generated and yet, it probably has a good chance of being largely representative of the population.

The population mean of random variable Y is defined as its expected value or long-run average, denoted as:

$$\mu_Y = E(Y)$$

Alternatively, one could denote it as:

$$\mu = \frac{1}{N} \sum_{i=1}^{N} Y_i$$

where Y_i denotes observation i's value in Y, and i goes from observation 1 to the Nth observation in the population.

The corresponding sample mean of y is its arithmetic average within the sample, or the sum of all n measurements in the sample divided by the sample size, denoted as:

$$\bar{y} = \frac{1}{n} \sum_{i=1}^{n} y_i$$

Applied to the growth variable, we may rewrite the definitions of its population mean, denoted by μ_{Growth}, and sample mean, denoted by $\overline{growth}$, as follows:

$$\mu_{Growth} = \frac{1}{N} \sum_{i=1}^{N} Growth_i = \frac{sum\ of\ all\ observations\ in\ population}{population\ size\ N}$$

$$\overline{growth} = \frac{1}{n} \sum_{i=1}^{n} growth_i = \frac{sum\ of\ all\ observations\ in\ sample}{sample\ size\ n}$$

Based on the formula, we compute the sample mean $\overline{growth}$ as an estimate of μ_{Growth} (the average economic growth in the population), using pwt7g data in R:

```
# compute sample mean of growth
mean(pwt7g$growth, na.rm = TRUE)
```

[1] 0.02302498

Note that 0.023 is merely one estimate of the population mean based on one sample, thus it is not the value of the population mean. To get at the population mean, we may employ two methods of statistical inference: hypothesis testing and confidence interval. Before we discuss these inferential methods, we first must explain another important concept in describing a random variable: the dispersion of data points around the mean of a variable.

Aside: Population Standard Deviation, Sample Standard Deviation, and Standard Error

Variance and standard deviation are used to describe how data points are dispersed or vary around the mean of a random variable. In order for us to understand statistical inference, the notions of variance and standard deviation must be discussed because they influence both the process and the outcome of statistical inference. The relevance of standard deviation was mentioned in the first section and will be demonstrated in detail later.

Like the concept of mean, variance and standard deviation have both population and sample versions. The population variance of a continuous random variable Y is the expected value of the squared deviations from the population mean. The notion of deviation refers to the difference between the value of an observation and the mean. Each deviation is squared so that both negative and positive deviations are used to describe the dispersion of data around the mean.

$$\sigma^2 = Var(Y) = E[(Y - \mu)^2]$$

Alternatively, one could think of the population variance as the *long run average* of the *sum* of *squared deviations* from the *population mean* in the population.

$$\sigma^2 = \frac{1}{N} \sum_{i=1}^{N} (Y_i - \mu)^2$$

As usual, without population data, we have to obtain a sample estimate, denoted as s^2, of the population variance σ^2. This can be done using the following formula or estimator:

$$s^2 = \frac{1}{n-1} \sum_{i=1}^{n} (y_i - \bar{y})^2$$

The sample variance is the *sum* of *squared deviations* from the *sample mean*, divided by the *sample size n minus one*. Regarding this formula, a frequently asked question is why the sum of squared deviations from the sample mean must be divided by sample size n minus one, rather than n alone. The reason is simple. The sum of squared deviations from the sample mean divided by sample size n alone is a biased estimator of the population variance, with the bias being $\frac{n}{n-1}$. (In statistics, a sample statistic is called an unbiased estimator of the population parameter if the expected value of the sample statistic equals the population parameter.) Hence, the provided formula for s^2 is an unbiased estimator of the population variance σ^2.

To further illustrate the difference between population and sample variance, we will use the simplest artificial example possible. In a population, if we have three observations with values 1, 2, and 3, respectively, the population variance is simply the sum of three squared deviations from mean: $(1 - 2)^2 + (2 - 2)^2 + (3 - 2)^2 = 2$, divided by the population size 3. The population variance equals 0.67. Now, assume this is not a population but a sample instead. Then the sample variance will be: $\frac{2}{3-1} = 1$.

In R, the sample variance of economic growth s^2 is computed as follows:

```
# compute sample variance of growth
var(pwt7g$growth, na.rm = TRUE)

[1] 0.005638469
```

Note that the computed sample variance, 0.0056, is an estimate of the population variance σ^2 of the growth variable.

At this point, it is worth noting that the square root of the population variance of a variable is referred to as its population standard deviation, denoted as σ, and the square root of the sample variance of a variable is its sample standard deviation, denoted as s. The R code for computing the sample standard deviation s is as follows:

```
# compute sample standard deviation of growth
sd(pwt7g$growth, na.rm = TRUE)

[1] 0.07508974
```

The standard error of the mean, recall from the first section, is the standard deviation of the probability distribution of the sample mean across repeated samples. If we draw one sample, we will obtain one sample mean; then across many samples, we will obtain many sample means, one for each sample. These sample means will fluctuate around some unknown population mean μ. Hence, the standard error of the mean reflects the variability across repeated samples, whereas the standard deviation indicates the variability within a single sample. The smaller the standard error is, the more precisely the sample mean estimates the population mean. The standard error of the mean is measured by the population standard deviation σ divided by the square root of sample size n. As the sample size increases, the standard error decreases.

Next, we return to the question of how to make inference from sample mean to population mean with respect to the growth variable.

Hypothesis Test of Hypothetical Population Mean

Recall from the first section and the end of the third section that to get at the unknown population mean, we may employ two methods of statistical inference: null hypothesis testing and confidence interval construction. In this section, we will focus on the first method.

We know some countries grow rapidly in some years but slowly in other years, while other countries tend to grow slowly for a very long time. As a result, it is often difficult to guess what the average growth rate is in the population. Suppose scholars have reasons to believe and hypothesize that the average growth rate is 3% in the population. In contrast, our sample estimate is 0.023 or 2.3%. The question then becomes: Given the sampling error and noise, is 2.3% statistically the same as 3% or not? In other words, is their difference a statistical artifact or a fact?

This is a reasonable question. In the preceding example, the sample mean is 2.3%. In a different sample, the estimate may be 3.2%, or higher, or lower. So, the question implies the following: Is the difference between 2.3% and the hypothetical 3% due to random sampling error and noise, or due to a fundamental factual difference between the unknown population mean and the hypothetical population mean? We formulate these two possibilities into the following two hypotheses, where we use μ_{true} and μ_0 to denote the unknown and hypothetical population means, respectively.

Null hypothesis $H_0 : \mu_{true} = \mu_0 = 0.03$.
Alternative hypothesis $H_a : \mu_{true} \neq \mu_0 = 0.03$.

We will conduct a statistical test of the null hypothesis directly, but not the alternative hypothesis. The idea that sample mean is an unbiased estimator of population mean implies that the grand mean of all the sample means from many repeated samples will coincide with the unknown population mean. According to the central limit theorem, if the sample size is large enough, the sampling distribution of the sample mean will be approximately normal. These properties of the sample mean allow us to construct the following test statistic, called Z, to directly test the null hypothesis.

$$Z = \frac{\bar{y} - \mu_0}{\sigma/\sqrt{n}} = \frac{sample\ mean\ of\ growth\ -hypothetical\ population\ mean}{population\ standard\ deviation/square\ root\ of\ sample\ size}$$

Verbally, the Z statistic is the distance between the sample mean and the hypothetical population mean, measured in standard error units (based on population standard deviation σ). Hence, the Z statistic assumes that the value of the popoulation standard deviation is known.

When the sample size n is large enough, the Z statistic follows the standard normal probability distribution, denoted as N(0,1) (i.e., normally distributed, with the population mean equal to zero and variance equal to one). This feature allows us to use the computed Z statistic to identify the p value from the standard normal probability distribution table. The p value refers to the probability of finding a test statistic as large as the one we get if the null hypothesis is true (in the left of Figure 3.1), or the probability of making a Type I error (rejecting the null hypothesis when the null is true).

In hypothesis testing, we have to choose an acceptable Type I error cutoff (note that we do not choose to make Type I error zero because of its inverse relationship with Type II error). The convention is 5%, meaning that we are willing to reject the null hypothesis *incorrectly* for 5 out of 100 repeated random samples. As noted earlier in the first section, the decision rule for hypothesis testing is as follows: If the p value is larger than 5%, the null hypothesis will not be rejected; however, if the p value is smaller than 5%, the null hypothesis will be rejected.

The Type I error discussion earlier requires some further clarifications. First, it is not desirable to make Type I error go to zero because doing so will dramatically increase the Type II error—failing to reject the null when it is false. Second, the 5% rule for the acceptable Type I error threshold is merely a convention. Some other conventional cutoffs are 1% and 10%. There is some arbitrariness in these cutoffs, which casts doubt on the value and conclusion of null hypothesis testing.

A problem with the Z-test is that to compute it, we need to know the value of the population standard deviation σ. The irony is that if we knew the population standard deviation, then we already knew the population mean, and there is no point in testing the null hypothesis. Hence, without knowing the population standard deviation of growth, we have to find a substitute for it in order to test the null hypothesis. It turns out that if the substitute for σ is the sample standard deviation s, then the Z-test statistic turns into a t-test statistic, denoted as follows:

$$t = \frac{\bar{y} - \mu_0}{s/\sqrt{n}}$$

Verbally, the t-statistic is the distance between the sample mean and the hypothetical population mean, measured in standard error units (based on sample standard deviation). The t-statistic follows a t probability distribution with n – 1 degrees of freedom. The t distribution is like the normal distribution, except that it is flatter or has fatter tails because of greater uncertainty. The degree of freedom, often denoted as df in statistical output, is the sample size n minus the number of parameters estimated; hence, in this case, the degree of freedom is $(n-1)$.

We use the computed t-statistic to find the corresponding p value from the t probability distribution table, and then carry out the rest of the test just as in the Z-test. The R code for the t-test is as follows:

```
# conduct one sample mean t-test
t.test(pwt7g$growth, mu = 0.03)
```

The t.test() function tells R to conduct a t-test on the growth variable, assuming the population mean is 0.03 or 3% with option mu=0.03.

The R output shows that the t-statistic is -8.5529, with an extremely small p value. Since the p value is smaller than 0.05 or 5%, we reject the null hypothesis that the average economic growth in the population is 3%.

```
# conduct one sample mean t-test
t.test(pwt7g$growth, mu = 0.03)


One-Sample t-test

data:  pwt7g$growth
t = -8.5529, df = 8477, p-value < 2.2e-16
alternative hypothesis: true mean is not equal to 0.03
```

```
95 percent confidence interval:
 0.02142637 0.02462360
sample estimates:
 mean of x
 0.02302498
```

Confidence Interval for Predicting Unknown Population Mean

Recall from the first section and the end of the third section that to get at the unknown population mean, we may employ two methods of statistical inference: null hypothesis testing and confidence interval construction. In this section, we will focus on the second method.

A confidence interval is a range of values that contains the unknown population mean at a confidence level chosen by an analyst. The convention is to compute the 95% confidence interval, which means we are 95% confident (i.e., for about 95% of 100 repeated random samples) that the estimated range of values contains the population mean. The choice of 95% is based on the choice of the acceptable Type I error rate of 5%, that is, (1-0.05).

If we know the population standard deviation, then the 95% confidence interval for the population mean μ is:

$$\textit{sample mean} \pm \textit{margin of error} = \bar{y} \pm z_{0.05/2}\left(\frac{\sigma}{\sqrt{n}}\right)$$

In other words, the lower bound and the upper bound of the 95% confidence interval can be explicitly specified as follows:

$$\left[\bar{y} - z_{0.025}\left(\frac{\sigma}{\sqrt{n}}\right), \bar{y} + z_{0.025}\left(\frac{\sigma}{\sqrt{n}}\right)\right]$$

where $z_{0.05/2}$ is the Z-critical value corresponding to 0.95 from the standard normal distribution. Here, 0.05/2 indicates 0.025 Type I error on each side of the bell-shaped standard normal probability distribution.

As noted earlier, it is simply not possible to know the population standard deviation without knowing the population mean. This means that the population standard deviation is probably always unknown. Thus, in practice, we have to substitute the population standard deviation in the Z interval above with the sample standard deviation. As a result, we estimate a 95% t-based confidence interval instead. The formula for the 95% t-based confidence interval is as follows:

$$\left[\bar{y} - t_{0.025,n-1}\left(\frac{s}{\sqrt{n}}\right), \bar{y} + t_{0.025,n-1}\left(\frac{s}{\sqrt{n}}\right)\right]$$

As for estimation in R, it turns out that by default, the t.test() function reports the estimated 95% confidence interval, right below the null hypothesis testing result. The R output above shows that based on sample data pwt7g, we are about 95% confident that the average economic growth in the population of all countries is between 2.14% and 2.46%.

Obviously, a confidence interval is more informative than the null hypothesis testing. Hypothesis testing, relying on a hypothetical value of the population mean, does not help us to know where the unknown population mean is when we reject the null hypothesis. In contrast, confidence interval provides a range of estimates that contains the most probable values for the population mean at a pre-chosen confidence level.

Plot Mean and 95% Confidence Interval of Growth

In applied research, it has become common to present and communicate statistical findings graphically. In this section, we will demonstrate our findings on the mean and confidence interval of growth. We will introduce and employ the widely used ggplot2 package. The ggplot2 package, created by Hadley Wickham (2009) for R, has a consistent and compact syntax to describe and define statistical graphics. The idea is to build any plot from a few common elements: (1) dataset, (2) Aesthetics (aes), and (3) geometric objects (geom).

1. data: data frame only.
2. Aesthetic mappings (aes function): Define the roles of the variables in a graph, including xy-position, color, height, size, group, etc. For example, aes(x variable, y variable, color=z variable).
3. Geometric objects (geoms): type of graphics (abline, area, bar, boxplot, errorbar, history, line, point, polygon, etc.)

In a ggplot, data is summarized or transformed and then mapped onto a specific coordinate system. As an example, the histogram of growth in Figure 3.2 is based on the following R code:

```
# load ggplot2 package
library(ggplot2)

# plot a histogram of growth
ggplot(pwt7g, aes(growth*100)) + geom_histogram()
```

Figure 3.2 shows that growth is single-peaked and roughly normally distributed, with over half of the observations centering on growth rates that are positive but close to zero. At the tails of the plot appear to be some large positive and negative outliers.

Now we turn to plot the sample mean and 95% confidence interval of growth using the ggplot2 package. Since ggplot2 requires a data frame, we must produce

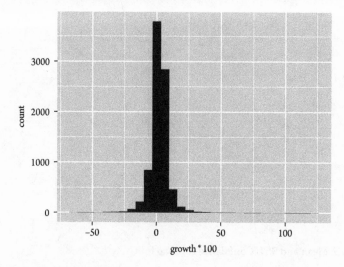

Figure 3.2 Histogram for Growth.

a dataset containing the sample mean and confidence interval as variables. We do so by using the Rmisc package. After installing the package once, we first load the Rmisc package, then apply the summarySE() function to compute the sample mean (denoted as growth), sample standard deviation (denoted as sd), standard error (denoted as se), and margin of error (denoted as ci), and then assign the output to a new data frame, growm.

```
# load Rmisc package to compute summary statistics
library(Rmisc)

# create a dataset of mean and confidence interval
growm <- summarySE(pwt7g, measurevar="growth", na.rm=TRUE)

# show class of new data object
class(growm)

[1] "data.frame"

# display the output of summarySE
growm

   .id    N    growth          sd           se          ci
1 <NA> 8478 0.02302498 0.07508974 0.0008155186 0.001598615
```

Next, we take the data frame growm, and graph the mean and 95% confidence interval of the growth variable from pwt7g. The R code and output for Figure 3.3 are as follows:

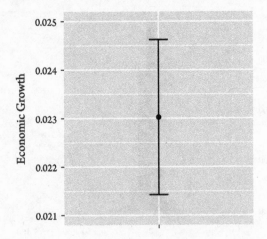

Figure 3.3 Mean and 95% Confidence Interval for Growth.

```
# load ggplot2 package
library(ggplot2)

# plot mean and 95% confidence interval
ggplot(growm, aes(x=factor(""), y=growth)) +
 geom_errorbar(aes(ymin=growth-ci, ymax=growth+ci), width=.1)+
 geom_point()+
 scale_x_discrete("")+
 scale_y_continuous(name="Economic Growth",
                    limits=c(0.021, 0.025),
                    breaks = scales::pretty_breaks(n=8))
```

Inside the ggplot() function, we specify the following components:

- data frame growm.
- Aesthetics. Inside the aes() function, (x=factor(""), y=growth)) means that x variable is an empty factor and y variable is growth.
- plus sign throughout indicating more details to be added.
- One geometric object: geom_errorbar(), marking the interval. An aes() function inside identifies the lower bound with growth-ci, the upper bound with growth+ci, and the width of the errorbar as 0.1.
- Another geometric object: geom_point(), indicating the data point of the y variable (the sample mean growth rate in this case).
- scale_x_discrete(""), leaving x-axis name, label, and tick blank.
- scale_y_continuous(), defining y-axis attributes, with variable name "Economic Growth", the range defined by limits=c(0.021, 0.025), and the number of breaks on the y-axis defined by breaks=.

Figure 3.3 demonstrates that the 95% confidence interval for growth lies roughly between 2.14% and 2.46%, with the sample mean at about 2.3%. Hence, the hypothetical population mean of 3% is outside this range, indicating that the null hypothesis ought to be rejected. At the same time, the width of the interval is narrow, suggesting that most likely, the average economic growth in the world is roughly a little over 2%. Figure 3.3 provides an informative answer to the research question asked at the beginning of this section.

Did the World Economy Grow More Quickly in 1990 than in 1960?

Did the world economy grow faster in 1990 than in 1960? The question asks us to find out whether the average economic growth in 1990 remained the same as in 1960 or not. The idea behind this question is to learn to use the difference between two samples (one for 1960, the other for 1990) to estimate and predict the difference between two populations (one for 1960, the other for 1990).

Infer Population Difference from Sample Difference

Suppose μ_{1960} and μ_{1990} represent the average economic growth rates in the populations of 1960 and 1990, respectively. The answer to the question is: $\mu_{1960} - \mu_{1990}$. Since we do not have the population data, we can only use the difference between the two sample means, i.e., $\bar{y}_{1960} - \bar{y}_{1990}$, based on the pwt7g data, to estimate the difference between the two population means.

Using the pwt7g data, we compute the following sample statistics:

```
# sample average growth rate in 1960
mean(pwt7g$growth[pwt7g$year==1960], na.rm = TRUE)
```

```
[1] 0.04171108
```

```
# sample average growth rate in 1990
mean(pwt7g$growth[pwt7g$year==1990], na.rm = TRUE)
```

```
[1] 0.0067163
```

```
# difference between sample means of 1960 and 1990
mean(pwt7g$growth[pwt7g$year==1960], na.rm = TRUE) -
  mean(pwt7g$growth[pwt7g$year==1990], na.rm = TRUE)
```

```
[1] 0.03499478
```

The sample average annualized growth rate is 0.0417 for 1960, and is 0.0067 for 1990. The difference between the two values is about 0.035. This fairly large and positive difference appears to indicate that the world economy was growing faster in 1960 than in 1990.

These values, however, are merely sample estimates and their difference. Again, to estimate the difference between the population means of two groups (i.e., $\mu_{population1} - \mu_{population2}$), we may employ two methods of statistical inference: null hypothesis testing and confidence interval construction. The choice of a test statistic depends on whether relevant assumptions are met or not. Thus, there are four possible scenarios and test statistics.

- Scenario 1: The populations are independent, normally distributed with a common variance σ^2.
- Scenario 2: The populations are independent, normally distributed with unequal variances.
- Scenario 3: The populations are dependent, normally distributed.
- Scenario 4: The populations are dependent and not normally distributed.

Hypothesis Test of Hypothetical Difference of Two Population Means

Suppose scholars are interested in identifying the difference in global economic growth between 1960 and 1990 to find an answer to conflicting theories regarding whether the world economy was growing at the same rate during those two periods. On one hand, the world economy should be growing faster in 1990 than in 1960 because of vast technological progress and increasing productivity. If so, then the difference in the average annualized growth rates between 1960 and 1990 should be negative. On the other hand, the world economy was going through some economic downturn and recession during the late 1980s and early 1990s, whereas there was a postwar economic boom in the world during the 1960s. If so, then the difference in the average annualized growth rates between 1960 and 1990 could be positive. To the extent that both arguments are equally valid theoretically, then the difference in the two population means reflects the net effect of these two competing forces.

As noted, based on the pwt7g data, their estimated difference is 0.035. The difference is notably large and positive. Now, the question is whether 0.035 results from random sampling error and noise and is in fact statistically not different from zero, or if we obtained 0.035 because the world economy was in fact growing faster in 1960 than in 1990. Again, like before, these two possibilities can be formulated into the following two hypotheses:

Null hypothesis $H_0 : \mu_{1960} - \mu_{1990} = 0$.
Alternative hypothesis $H_a : \mu_{1960} - \mu_{1990} \neq 0$.

Like before, we will construct a test statistic to test the null hypothesis directly. In principle, the logic of inference here remains the same as in previous sections. However, the research question in this problem involves some complications and as a result requires us to choose among several possible test statistics.

Two-Sample t-Test Under Scenario 1

This is often referred to as the two-sample pooled t-test. If we have two independent samples from two normal distributions with equal variances ($\sigma_{1960}^2 = \sigma_{1990}^2 = \sigma^2$), the test statistic for the null hypothesis is as follows:

$$t = \frac{(\bar{y}_{1960} - \bar{y}_{1990}) - (\mu_{1960} - \mu_{1990})}{s_p \sqrt{\dfrac{1}{n_{1960}} + \dfrac{1}{n_{1990}}}}$$

where s_p is the pooled sample standard deviation, computed as follows:

$$s_p = \sqrt{\frac{(n_{1960} - 1)s_{1960}^2 + (n_{1990} - 1)s_{1990}^2}{n_{1960} + n_{1990} - 2}}$$

The test statistic follows a t-distribution, with a degree of freedom ($n_{1960} + n_{1990} - 2$). Hence, the computed t-statistic, together with the degree of freedom, will allow us to identify the p value from the t probability distribution table. If the p value is larger than 0.05 or 5%, the null hypothesis will not be rejected; if the p value is smaller than 0.05 or 5%, the null hypothesis will be rejected.

The R code for the test is as follows:

```
# Difference-of-means test under scenario 1
t.test(pwt7g$growth[pwt7g$year==1960],
       pwt7g$growth[pwt7g$year==1990],
       var.equal=TRUE)
```

The t.test() function tells R to conduct a two-sample t-test, assuming the difference between the population means is zero. The option *var.equal = TRUE* assumes a common population variance. Note how we use the indexing method, introduced in Chapter 2, to tell R to compute the mean of growth for each of the two years. The R output is as follows:

```
Two-Sample t-test

data:  pwt7g$growth[pwt7g$year == 1960] and pwt7g$growth[pwt7g$year
  == 1990]
t = 3.4112, df = 237, p-value = 0.0007603
```

```
alternative hypothesis: true difference in means is not equal to 0
95 percent confidence interval:
 0.01478457 0.05520499
sample estimates:
 mean of x  mean of y
 0.04171108 0.00671630
```

The R output shows that the t-statistic is 3.41, with an extremely small p value. Since the p value is smaller than 0.05 or 5%, we reject the null hypothesis that the world economy was growing at the same rate in 1990 as in 1960. Thus, the difference between the two sample means is not due to random noise or sampling error, but results from the significant difference between the two population means.

Two-Sample t-Test Under Scenario 2

This is often referred to as Welch's two-sample t-test. If we have two independent samples from two normal distributions with unequal variances ($\sigma_{1960}^2 \neq \sigma_{1990}^2$), the test statistic for the null hypothesis is different from the one used above only with respect to in the denominator:

$$t = \frac{(\bar{y}_{1960} - \bar{y}_{1990}) - (\mu_{1960} - \mu_{1990})}{\sqrt{\dfrac{s_{1960}^2}{n_{1960}} + \dfrac{s_{1990}^2}{n_{1990}}}}$$

The test statistic follows approximately a t-distribution, with an adjusted degree of freedom df defined as follows:

$$df = \frac{\left(\dfrac{s_{1960}^2}{n_{1960}} + \dfrac{s_{1990}^2}{n_{1990}}\right)^2}{\dfrac{(s_{1960}^2/n_{1960})^2}{n_{1960}-1} + \dfrac{(s_{1990}^2/n_{1990})^2}{n_{1990}-1}}$$

The R code for the test is the same, except for one change in the option *var.equal* = *FALSE*, meaning that the population variances are no longer identical:

```
# Difference-of-means test under scenario 2
t.test(pwt7g$growth[pwt7g$year==1960],
       pwt7g$growth[pwt7g$year==1990],
       var.equal=FALSE)
```

The R output is as follows:

```
Welch Two-Sample t-test

data:  pwt7g$growth[pwt7g$year == 1960] and pwt7g$growth[pwt7g$year
  == 1990]
t = 3.819, df = 186.35, p-value = 0.0001824
alternative hypothesis: true difference in means is not equal to 0
95 percent confidence interval:
 0.01691751 0.05307206
sample estimates:
 mean of x  mean of y
0.04171108 0.00671630
```

In this test, the *t*-statistic is 3.819, which is about the same as before, with a relatively smaller degree of freedom. The *p* value remains extremely small. Since the *p* value is smaller than 0.05 or 5%, the null hypothesis that the world economy was growing at the same rate in 1990 as in 1960, will be rejected. Thus, the difference in the two sample means results from the significant difference of the population means of the two years, rather than random noise or sampling error.

Paired Two-Sample t-Test Under Scenario 3

This is often referred to as the paired two-sample *t*-test. A common assumption for the two test statistics above is that the two samples are independent of each other. For our dataset, however, whenever data is available, we observe most of the same countries in both 1960 and 1990. This is often referred to as a repeated measure design because the same country is observed repeatedly. Thus, many observations in 1990 are not independent of those in 1960. To control for this type of dependence among observations, we can use the following test statistic instead:

$$t = \frac{\bar{y}_{dif} - \mu_{dif}}{s_{dif}/\sqrt{n}}$$

where $\bar{y}_{dif}$ represents the sample average of the y_{dif} variable (growth difference within a country between 1960 and 1990), n represents the number of countries included in the computation, and s_{dif} is the sample standard deviation of the y_{dif} variable.

The R code for this test now adds *paired = TRUE* in the argument of the t.test() function. The R code and output are as follows:

```
# Difference-of-means test under scenario 3
t.test(pwt7g$growth[pwt7g$year==1960],
        pwt7g$growth[pwt7g$year==1990],
        var.equal=FALSE, paired=TRUE)
```

```
Paired t-test

data:  pwt7g$growth[pwt7g$year == 1960] and pwt7g$growth[pwt7g$year
  == 1990]
t = 2.7277, df = 73, p-value = 0.007983
alternative hypothesis: true difference in means is not equal to 0
95 percent confidence interval:
 0.005846337 0.037563117
sample estimates:
mean of the differences
           0.02170473
```

The R output shows a t-statistic of 2.73, under a much smaller degree of freedom, and with the p value being 0.008. Since it is still much smaller than the 5% Type I error threshold, the null hypothesis that the world economy was growing at the same rate in 1990 as in 1960 is rejected.

One important caveat for any paired test is that observations must be paired correctly between two groups. For example, Argentina in 1960 must match with Argentina in 1990. The t.test() function with paired=TRUE specified can do that so long as the number of observations for 1960 is the same for 1990 and the same country names are used and sorted in the same order.

However, if the two years (i.e., groups) have unequal numbers of countries, then running the code above will produce an error message. Hence, to conduct a paired difference-of-means test between two groups of unequal numbers of observations, some data management will be necessary. Since this issue is critically important, we will illustrate the process using the code below.

Suppose there are two datasets, g1960 and g1990. Each dataset contains two variables, country and growth, from two different years. They are then merged based on the variable country into one common dataset g. The R code for this process is shown below.

```
# generate two separate datasets
g1960 <- pwt7g[pwt7g$year==1960, c("growth", "country")]
g1990 <- pwt7g[pwt7g$year==1990, c("growth", "country")]

# merge two datasets by country
g <- merge(g1960, g1990, by="country")

# show variable names
names(g)

[1] "country"  "growth.x" "growth.y"
```

One detail worth noting is that since both datasets have the same variable named growth, to keep them separate in the merged dataset growth, the variable growth from g1960 is renamed as growth.x and the other one as growth.y. The R code and output for the paired t-test is as follows. As shown below, the results are exactly the same as those generated earlier.

```
# Difference-of-means test under scenario 3
t.test(g$growth.x, g$growth.y,
       var.equal=FALSE,
       paired=TRUE)
```

```
Paired t-test

data:  g$growth.x and g$growth.y
t = 2.7277, df = 73, p-value = 0.007983
alternative hypothesis: true difference in means is not equal to 0
95 percent confidence interval:
 0.005846337 0.037563117
sample estimates:
mean of the differences
              0.02170473
```

Wilcoxon Signed-Rank Test Under Scenario 4

When data in two populations are dependent and not normally distributed, we can use statistical tests that do not make any distributional assumption. Here we use the non-parametric Wilcoxon signed-rank test for the paired data. If data is not normally distributed, mean is no longer representative of the central tendency in the population. The Wilcoxon signed-rank test thus tests whether the medians from two populations are equal or not. Hence, in our example, the hypotheses are as follows:

Null hypothesis H_0: The difference in the population median growth rates of 1960 and 1990 is zero.

Alternative hypothesis H_a: The difference in the population median growth rates of 1960 and 1990 is not zero.

The statistical test here is to use the difference in the sample median growth rates of 1960 and 1990 to test the null hypothesis. To provide a context for the test, the R code and output for the sample median growth rates and their difference are as follows:

```
# compute median growth rates and their difference
median60 <- median(pwt7g$growth[pwt7g$year==1960], na.rm=TRUE)
```

```
median90 <- median(pwt7g$growth[pwt7g$year==1990], na.rm=TRUE)
dif <- median60 - median90

# display the results
median60

[1] 0.03793623

median90

[1] 0.01002076

dif

[1] 0.02791547
```

To test the null hypothesis, we must first sort the absolute values of the differences between growth rates from small to large, with the smallest difference assigned a rank of 1, the next smallest a rank of 2, and so on. Ties are assigned average ranks. We then add the ranks of all positive differences to get W+, and next add the ranks of all negative differences to get W−. The Wilcoxon signed-rank test statistic W is equal to the smaller one between the sum of positive ranks (W+) and the sum of negative ranks (W−).

If W+ and W− are not statistically different, then the null hypothesis is not rejected; if they are statistically different, however, the null hypothesis is rejected. The decision rule remains as before. That is, compare the p value (based on computed W) to the acceptable Type I error α (based on the critical value of W). The null hypothesis is rejected if the p value is smaller than α.

The R code and output for the test are as follows. Please note that we use two lines of R code to correspond to the two situations where the two groups have either equal or unequal numbers of observations.

```
# Non-parametric Wilcoxon signed-rank test under scenario 4
wilcox.test(pwt7g$growth[pwt7g$year==1960],
            pwt7g$growth[pwt7g$year==1990],
            paired=TRUE)


wilcox.test(g$growth.x, g$growth.y, paired=TRUE)
```

The results as shown are identical between the two situations in this example.

```
Wilcoxon signed-rank test with continuity correction

data:  pwt7g$growth[pwt7g$year == 1960] and pwt7g$growth[pwt7g$year
  == 1990]
```

```
V = 1977, p-value = 0.001508
alternative hypothesis: true location shift is not equal to 0

Wilcoxon signed-rank test with continuity correction

data: g$growth.x and g$growth.y
V = 1977, p-value = 0.001508
alternative hypothesis: true location shift is not equal to 0
```

The R output shows a p value of 0.0015, which is far smaller than the 0.05 threshold. Hence, we reject the null hypothesis that the world economy was growing at the same rate in 1990 as in 1960.

Summary Table of Alternative Difference-of-Means Tests

The difference-of-means tests are widely used in applied research. Since this section has covered a large number of tests, it is useful to display the different tests used, their underlying assumptions, and the corresponding R code together in one place. Table 3.2 does just that.

Note that the R code in Table 3.2 is in a generic form. To make sense of it, we should cross-reference the generic R code against the four specific scenarios concerning the difference in the average economic growth rate between 1960 and 1990. For the sake of convenience, the corresponding R code is repeated as follows:

Table 3.2 **Two-Sample Difference-of-Means Tests**

	Test	Assumptions	R Code
1.	Two-sample pooled t-test	populations independent, normally distributed, common variance	t.test(x1,x2,var.equal=TRUE)
2.	Welch's two-sample t-test	populations independent, normally distributed, unequal variances	t.test(x1,x2,var.equal=FALSE)
3.	Paired two-sample t-test	populations dependent, normally distributed, unequal variances	t.test(x1,x2,var.equal=FALSE, paired=TRUE)
4.	Wilcoxon signed-rank test	populations dependent and not normally distributed	wilcox.test(x1,x2,paired=TRUE)

```
# Difference-of-means test under scenario 1
t.test(pwt7g$growth[pwt7g$year==1960],
       pwt7g$growth[pwt7g$year==1990],
       var.equal=TRUE)


# Difference-of-means test under scenario 2
t.test(pwt7g$growth[pwt7g$year==1960],
       pwt7g$growth[pwt7g$year==1990],
       var.equal=FALSE)


# Difference-of-means test under scenario 3
t.test(pwt7g$growth[pwt7g$year==1960],
       pwt7g$growth[pwt7g$year==1990],
       var.equal=FALSE, paired=TRUE)


# generate two separate datasets
g1960 <- pwt7g[pwt7g$year==1960, c("growth", "country")]
g1990 <- pwt7g[pwt7g$year==1990, c("growth", "country")]


# merge two datasets by country
g <- merge(g1960, g1990, by="country")


# Difference-of-means test under scenario 3
t.test(g$growth.x, g$growth.y,
       var.equal=FALSE,
       paired=TRUE)


# Non-parametric Wilcoxon signed-rank test under scenario 4
wilcox.test(pwt7g$growth[pwt7g$year==1960],
            pwt7g$growth[pwt7g$year==1990],
            paired=TRUE)


wilcox.test(g$growth.x, g$growth.y,
            paired=TRUE)
```

Recall that in our example, the statistical results are consistent across the four tests. Robust test results are always reassuring. Yet as a matter of principle, when the results differ across different tests, we should identify which test meets the underlying assumptions most closely and choose that test accordingly.

Confidence Interval to Predict Difference of Two Population Means

A second method for making statistical inferences about the difference between two population means is to construct a confidence interval to predict that difference. If we choose the 95% confidence level, the constructed confidence interval means that we are 95% confident that the range of estimated differences based on the difference between two sample means captures the difference between two population means.

As before, without knowing the population mean, we do not know the population standard deviation. Therefore, we substitute the population standard deviation in the Z confidence interval formula with the sample standard deviation.

As implied by the logic in the first section the confidence interval here should be the difference in sample means plus or minus the t critical value times the standard error. However, depending on what assumptions we make, as in hypothesis testing, the constructed confidence interval varies.

For scenario 1, if we assume a common population variance for 1960 and 1990, then the confidence interval formula is as follows:

$$(\bar{y}_{1960} - \bar{y}_{1990}) \pm (t_{\alpha/2, n_{1960}+n_{1990}-2}) s_p \sqrt{\frac{1}{n_{1960}} + \frac{1}{n_{1990}}}$$

where $(t_{\alpha/2, n_{1960}+n_{1990}-2})$ refers to the t critical value that corresponds to the acceptable Type I error α (split into two tails of the distribution), with degree of freedom equal to $(n_{1960} + n_{1990} - 2)$; the standard error is $s_p \sqrt{\frac{1}{n_{1960}} + \frac{1}{n_{1990}}}$.

For scenario 2, if we assume unequal population variances for 1960 and 1990, then the confidence interval is as follows:

$$\bar{y}_{1960} - \bar{y}_{1990} \pm t_{\alpha/2, df} \sqrt{\frac{s_{1960}^2}{n_{1960}} + \frac{s_{1990}^2}{n_{1990}}}$$

where the degree of freedom df is defined earlier in the two-sample t-test under scenario 2, and the standard error is $\sqrt{\frac{s_{1960}^2}{n_{1960}} + \frac{s_{1990}^2}{n_{1990}}}$.

For scenario 3, if we assume a repeated measure design for two populations with unequal variances, the paired t confidence interval is as follows:

$$\bar{y}_{dif} \pm t_{\alpha/2, df=n} \left(\frac{s_{dif}}{\sqrt{n}} \right)$$

where $\bar{y}_{dif}$ represents the sample average of the y_{dif} variable (growth difference within a country between 1960 and 1990), n represents the number of countries included in the computation, and s_{dif} is the sample standard deviation of the y_{dif} variable.

It is important to remember that the t.test() function's default setting is to report the 95% confidence interval estimates. The output from the hypothesis testing section shows that based on the sample data pwt7g, we are 95% confident that the difference in growth rates between the populations of 1960 and 1990 is

- between 1.48% and 5.52% under scenario 1 (assuming populations are independent, normally distributed with a common variance).
- between 1.69% and 5.31% under scenario 2 (assuming populations are independent, normally distributed with unequal variances).
- between 0.58% and 3.76% under scenario 3 (assuming populations are dependent, normally distributed with unequal variances).

Plot Means and 95% Confidence Intervals of Growth in 1960 and 1990

In this section, we will demonstrate how to plot the means and 95% confidence intervals of growth for two separate years. To do so, we can take the code for Figure 3.3 and modify it slightly. Like before, we first load the Rmisc package, and then apply the summarySE() function to the growth variable in pwt7g. The summarySE() function computes the mean (labeled as growth), standard deviation (labeled as sd), standard error (labeled as se), and margin of error (labeled as ci), and after making all these computations, assigns the output to a separate data frame called growm2 for graphing. The only change we have made to the summarySE() function is through adding the groupvars=" option, which tells R to compute statistics for each group of the variable specified in the option. Since we focus on 1960 and 1990, we save only statistics from those two years to growm2. The R code and output are as follows:

```
# plot group means and confidence intervals
# load Rmisc package to compute summary statistics
library(Rmisc)

# create dataset of mean and confidence interval
growm2 <- summarySE(pwt7g, measurevar="growth",
                    groupvars="year", na.rm=TRUE)

# keep only data from 1960 and 1990
growm2 <- growm2[growm2$year==1960|growm2$year==1990,]

# display the output of summarySE
growm2

   year   N    growth         sd          se         ci
11 1960  74 0.04171108 0.05839089 0.006787803 0.01352807
41 1990 165 0.00671630 0.07907184 0.006155734 0.01215471
```

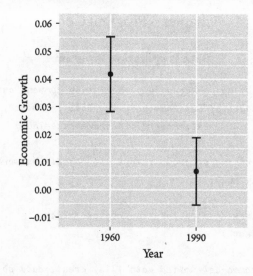

Figure 3.4 Mean and 95% Confidence Interval for Growth: 1960 and 1990.

Figure 3.4 compares the means and 95% confidence intervals of growth between two different years. The R code remains largely the same as that for Figure 3.3. One main change is the conversion of year into a factor variable, thus allowing only 1960 and 1990 to be plotted. The ggplot code is also modified to accommodate the new plot by year. The spcific code modifications include: specify x=year instead in aes(), add scale_x_discrete(name="Year") to treat the x variable as discrete and name it as "Year", and revise the values in limits= for the scale of y.

```
# load ggplot2 package
library(ggplot2)

# convert year variable into a factor variable
growm2$year <- as.factor(growm2$year)

# plot mean and 95% confidence interval
ggplot(growm2, aes(x=year, y=growth)) +
 geom_errorbar(aes(ymin=growth-ci, ymax=growth+ci), width=.1)+
 geom_point()+
 scale_x_discrete(name="Year")+
 scale_y_continuous(name="Economic Growth",
                    limits=c(-0.01, 0.06),
                    breaks = scales::pretty_breaks(n=7))
```

Chapter 3 Program Code

Data Preparation Program

```
# install following packages only once, then comment out code
# install.packages(c("DataCombine", "ggplot2", "Rmisc",
#                     "stargazer"), dependencies=TRUE)


# (1) before running program, remove all objects in workspace
rm(list=ls(all=TRUE))


# (2) change working directory to project folder
setwd("C:/Project")


# (3) import comma-deliimited data file, create data object pwt7
pwt7 <- read.csv("pwt70_w_country_names.csv", header=TRUE,
                 strip.white=TRUE, stringsAsFactors = FALSE,
                 na.strings=c("NA",""))


# (4) inspect imported data using functions from last chapter
# inspect dataset pwt7 in a spreadsheet style data viewer
View(pwt7)


# list first one observation in dataset pwt7
head(pwt7, n=1)


# list last one observation in dataset pwt7
tail(pwt7, n=1)


# dimensions of pwt7: observations and variables
dim(pwt7)


# variable names in dataset pwt7
names(pwt7)


# structure of dataset pwt7
str(pwt7)


# (5) clean data
# sort data in ascending order by country and by year
pwt7 <- pwt7[order(pwt7$country, pwt7$year),]
```

```
# remove second set of China observations with isocode CH2
pwt7 <- pwt7[pwt7$isocode!="CH2",]

# create annual economic growth rate in a panel dataset
# load DataCombine package in order to use slide function
library(DataCombine)

# sort data in ascending order by country and by year
pwt7 <- pwt7[order(pwt7$country, pwt7$year),]

# create a one-year leading variable for rgdpl
pwt7 <- slide(pwt7, Var="rgdpl", NewVar="rgdplead",
              GroupVar="country", slideBy=1)

# create a one-year lagged variable for rgdpl
pwt7 <- slide(pwt7, Var="rgdpl", NewVar="rgdplag",
              GroupVar="country", slideBy=-1)

# create annual growth rate based on rgdpl
pwt7$growth <- (pwt7$rgdpl-pwt7$rgdplag)/pwt7$rgdplag

# create a new dataset: a subset of pwt7 with three variables
pwt7g <- pwt7[, c("country", "year", "rgdpl", "growth")]

# save R dataset
save(pwt7g, file="pwt7g.RData")
```

Data Analysis Program

```
# (1) before running program, remove all objects in workspace
rm(list=ls(all=TRUE))

# (2) change working directory to project folder
setwd("C:/Project")

# (3) load R data
load("pwt7g.RData")

# compute sample mean of growth
mean(pwt7g$growth, na.rm = TRUE)

# compute sample variance of growth
```

```r
var(pwt7g$growth, na.rm = TRUE)

# compute sample standard deviation of growth
sd(pwt7g$growth, na.rm = TRUE)

# one-sample mean $t$-test and confidence interval
t.test(pwt7g$growth, mu=0.03)

# Plot mean and 95% confidence interval of growth
# load ggplot2 package
library(ggplot2)

# plot a histogram of growth
ggplot(pwt7g, aes(growth*100)) + geom_histogram()

# load Rmisc package to compute summary statistics
library(Rmisc)

# create a dataset of mean and confidence interval
growm <- summarySE(pwt7g, measurevar="growth", na.rm=TRUE)

# show class of new data object
class(growm)

# display the output of summarySE
growm

# load ggplot2 package
library(ggplot2)

# plot mean and 95% confidence interval
ggplot(growm, aes(x=factor(""), y=growth)) +
 geom_errorbar(aes(ymin=growth-ci, ymax=growth+ci), width=.1)+
 geom_point()+
 scale_x_discrete("")+
 scale_y_continuous(name="Economic Growth",
                    limits=c(0.021, 0.025),
                    breaks = scales::pretty_breaks(n=8))

# Two-sample t-test and confidence interval
# sample average growth rate in 1960
```

```
mean(pwt7g$growth[pwt7g$year==1960], na.rm = TRUE)

# sample average growth rate in 1990
mean(pwt7g$growth[pwt7g$year==1990], na.rm = TRUE)

# difference between sample means of 1960 and 1990
mean(pwt7g$growth[pwt7g$year==1960], na.rm = TRUE) -
  mean(pwt7g$growth[pwt7g$year==1990], na.rm = TRUE)

# difference of means test under scenario 1
t.test(pwt7g$growth[pwt7g$year==1960],
       pwt7g$growth[pwt7g$year==1990],
       var.equal=TRUE)

# difference of means test under scenario 2
t.test(pwt7g$growth[pwt7g$year==1960],
       pwt7g$growth[pwt7g$year==1990],
       var.equal=FALSE)

# difference of means test under scenario 3
t.test(pwt7g$growth[pwt7g$year==1960],
       pwt7g$growth[pwt7g$year==1990],
       var.equal=FALSE, paired=TRUE)

# generate two separate datasets
g1960 <- pwt7g[pwt7g$year==1960, c("growth", "country")]
g1990 <- pwt7g[pwt7g$year==1990, c("growth", "country")]

# merge two datasets by country
g <- merge(g1960, g1990, by="country")

# difference-of-means test under scenario 3
t.test(g$growth.x, g$growth.y,
       var.equal=FALSE,
       paired=TRUE)

# compute median growth rates and their difference
median60 <- median(pwt7g$growth[pwt7g$year==1960], na.rm=TRUE)
median90 <- median(pwt7g$growth[pwt7g$year==1990], na.rm=TRUE)
dif <- median60 - median90
```

```
# display the results
median60
median90
dif


# non-parametric Wilcoxon signed-rank test under scenario 4
wilcox.test(pwt7g$growth[pwt7g$year==1960],
            pwt7g$growth[pwt7g$year==1990],
            paired=TRUE)


wilcox.test(g$growth.x, g$growth.y, paired=TRUE)


# plot group means and confidence intervals
# load Rmisc package to compute summary statistics
library(Rmisc)


# create dataset of mean and confidence interval
growm2 <- summarySE(pwt7g, measurevar="growth",
                    groupvars="year", na.rm=TRUE)


# keep only data from 1960 and 1990
growm2 <- growm2[growm2$year==1960|growm2$year==1990,]


# display the output of summarySE
growm2


# load ggplot2 package
library(ggplot2)


# convert year variable into a factor variable
growm2$year<-as.factor(growm2$year)


# plot mean and 95% confidence interval
ggplot(growm2, aes(x=year, y=growth)) +
 geom_errorbar(aes(ymin=growth-ci, ymax=growth+ci), width=.1)+
 geom_point()+
 scale_x_discrete(name="Year")+
 scale_y_continuous(name="Economic Growth",
                    limits=c(-0.01, 0.06),
                    breaks = scales::pretty_breaks(n=7))
```

Summary

This chapter has demonstrated the types of questions one could ask about a continuous random variable of interest and answer using statistical inference. It provides conceptual preparation for understanding statistical inference, demonstrates how to get data ready for analysis in R, and then illustrates how to conduct two types of statistical inferences—null hypothesis testing and confidence interval construction—regarding the population attributes of a continuous random variable, using sample data. Both one-sample t-test and the difference-of-means tests are presented. Two key points in this chapter are worth noting. First, statistical inference is primarily concerned about figuring out population attributes using sample data. Hence, it is not the same as causal inference. Second, statistical inference can help to answer various questions of substantive interest. This chapter focuses on statistical inferences regarding one variable. In applied research, the most interesting statistical inferences usually revolve around the relationship between variables, which is the focus of the next chapter. Before heading into Chapter 4, it is useful, as usual, for us to address some miscellaneous questions beginning R users often have about the materials in Chapter 3.

Miscellaneous Q&As for Ambitious Readers
How do we Calculate Sample Variance and Standard Deviation in a Step-by-Step Manner?

```
# step-by-step calculation of sample mean, variance and
# standard deviation
# find number of non-missing values of growth: n
n <- sum(!is.na(pwt7g$growth))

# find sample mean of growth: m1
m1 <- mean(pwt7g$growth, na.rm=TRUE)

# find squared deviation of growth for each observation: d2
d2 <- (pwt7g$growth-m1)^2

# find sum of squared deviations of growth: s3
s3 <- sum(d2, na.rm=TRUE)

# find sample variance of growth: var2
var2 <- s3/(n-1)

# find sample standard deviation of growth: std2
```

```
std2 <- sqrt(var2)

# display computed results
cbind(n, s3, m1,var2, std2)

          n      s3        m1        var2       std2
[1,] 8478 47.7973 0.02302498 0.005638469 0.07508974

# calculate the mean of growth by formula
sum(pwt7g$growth, na.rm=TRUE)/n

[1] 0.02302498

# calculate sample variance using formula
sum((pwt7g$growth - mean(pwt7g$growth, na.rm=TRUE))^2,
    na.rm=TRUE)/(n-1)

[1] 0.005638469

# calculate sample standard deviation using formula
sqrt(sum((pwt7g$growth - mean(pwt7g$growth, na.rm=TRUE))^2,
        na.rm=TRUE)/(n-1))

[1] 0.07508974
```

How do we Conduct a One-Sample *t*-Test Step by Step?

```
# find the number of non-missing values for growth
n <- sum(!is.na(pwt7g$growth))

# find the sample mean of growth
m1 <- mean(pwt7g$growth, na.rm=TRUE)

# find sample variance and standard deviation of growth
d2 <- (pwt7g$growth-m1)^2
s3 <- sum(d2, na.rm=TRUE)
var2 <- s3/(n-1)
std2 <- sqrt(var2)

# find t statistic for null hypothesis (population mean=0.03)
t <- (m1-0.03)/(std2/sqrt(n))

# display computed results
```

```
cbind(n, m1, std2, t)
```

```
          n         m1        std2          t
[1,] 8478 0.02302498 0.07508974 -8.552863
```

```
# confirm results above using t.test function
t.test(pwt7g$growth, mu=0.03)
```

```
One-Sample t-test
```

```
data:  pwt7g$growth
t = -8.5529, df = 8477, p-value < 2.2e-16
alternative hypothesis: true mean is not equal to 0.03
95 percent confidence interval:
 0.02142637 0.02462360
sample estimates:
 mean of x
0.02302498
```

How do we Construct a Confidence Interval Step by Step?

```
# step-by-step calculation for 95% confidence interval
# find quantile t distribution critical value for 95% CI
t.c <- qt(0.975, n-1)
```

```
## calculate the lower and upper bounds
m1-t.c*(std2/sqrt(n))
```

```
[1] 0.02142637
```

```
m1+t.c*(std2/sqrt(n))
```

```
[1] 0.0246236
```

```
# confirm results above using t.test function for 95%
t.test(pwt7g$growth, mu=0.03, conf.level=0.95)
```

```
One-Sample t-test
```

```
data:  pwt7g$growth
t = -8.5529, df = 8477, p-value < 2.2e-16
```

```
alternative hypothesis: true mean is not equal to 0.03
95 percent confidence interval:
 0.02142637 0.02462360
sample estimates:
 mean of x
0.02302498
```

```
# step-by-step calculation for 99% confidence interval
# find quantile t distribution critical value for 99% CI
t.c <- qt(0.995, n-1)

## calculate the lower and upper bounds
m1-t.c*(std2/sqrt(n))

[1] 0.02092387

m1+t.c*(std2/sqrt(n))

[1] 0.02512609

# confirm results above using t.test function
t.test(pwt7g$growth, mu=0.03, conf.level=0.99)


One-Sample t-test

data:  pwt7g$growth
t = -8.5529, df = 8477, p-value < 2.2e-16
alternative hypothesis: true mean is not equal to 0.03
99 percent confidence interval:
 0.02092387 0.02512609
sample estimates:
 mean of x
0.02302498
```

How do we Compute a Difference-of-Means Test and Confidence Interval Step by Step?

```
# scenario 2: difference-of-means t-test
mean70 <- mean(pwt7g$growth[pwt7g$year==1970], na.rm=TRUE)


mean80 <- mean(pwt7g$growth[pwt7g$year==1980], na.rm=TRUE)
```

```
n70 <- sum(!is.na(pwt7g$growth[pwt7g$year==1970]))

n80 <- sum(!is.na(pwt7g$growth[pwt7g$year==1980]))

se70 <- sd(pwt7g$growth[pwt7g$year==1970], na.rm=TRUE)/
        sqrt(n70)

se80 <- sd(pwt7g$growth[pwt7g$year==1980], na.rm=TRUE)/
        sqrt(n80)

mean_dif <- (mean70-mean80)

se_dif <- sqrt(se70^2 + se80^2)

t_dif <- mean_dif/se_dif

revised_df <- ((se70^2/n70 + se80^2/n80)^2)/
  (((1/(n70-1))*(se70^2/n70)^2) + ((1/(n80-1))*(se80^2/n80)^2))

# display computed results
round(cbind(mean70, mean80, se70, se80, mean_dif, se_dif,
            t_dif, revised_df),4)

     mean70 mean80  se70   se80 mean_dif se_dif  t_dif
[1,] 0.0421 -0.001 0.007 0.0067   0.0431 0.0097 4.4505
     revised_df
[1,]   234.2231

# 95% confidence interval of difference of means
# difference of means plus or minus
# (95% t-critical*standard error of difference of means)
mean_dif + qt(c(0.025, 0.975), revised_df)*se_dif

[1] 0.02401343 0.06216152

round(c(mean_dif + qt(c(0.025, 0.975), revised_df)*se_dif), 4)

[1] 0.0240 0.0622


# confirm results above using t.test function
t.test(pwt7g$growth[pwt7g$year==1970],
       pwt7g$growth[pwt7g$year==1980],
```

```
        var.equal=FALSE)


Welch Two-Sample t-test

data: pwt7g$growth[pwt7g$year == 1970] and pwt7g$growth[pwt7g$year
  == 1980]
t = 4.4505, df = 256.18, p-value = 1.279e-05
alternative hypothesis: true difference in means is not equal to 0
95 percent confidence interval:
 0.02402192 0.06215303
sample estimates:
  mean of x    mean of y
 0.042080218 -0.001007259
```

How do we Test whether Two Populations have Equal Variances?

The choice among various difference-of-means tests depends partially on the assumption that two populations have a common variance. In the chapter, we did not discuss how to test whether this assumption holds or not. Here we offer an F test for whether the variances of growth are the same between 1960 and 1990.

Null hypothesis H_0 : $\sigma^2_{1960} = \sigma^2_{1990}$, i.e., $\dfrac{\sigma^2_{1960}}{\sigma^2_{1990}} = 1$

Alternative hypothesis H_a : $\sigma^2_{1960} \neq \sigma^2_{1990}$

The test statistic for the null hypothesis is: $F = \dfrac{S^2_{1960}}{S^2_{1990}}$

We reject the null hypothesis if the p value for the F test statistic is smaller than the acceptable Type I error, 0.05.

The R code and output below indicate that the p value is much smaller than 0.05. Hence, we reject the null hypothesis that growth in 1960 and growth in 1990 are of equal variance.

```
# F test of whether two populations have equal variances
var.test(pwt7g$growth[pwt7g$year==1960],
         pwt7g$growth[pwt7g$year==1990])


F test to compare two variances

data: pwt7g$growth[pwt7g$year == 1960] and pwt7g$growth[pwt7g$year
  == 1990]
F = 0.54531, num df = 73, denom df = 164, p-value =
0.003916
alternative hypothesis: true ratio of variances is not equal to 1
95 percent confidence interval:
```

```
 0.3738551 0.8195392
sample estimates:
ratio of variances
        0.5453139
```

```
# step-by-step calculation of F test
var(pwt7g$growth[pwt7g$year==1960], na.rm=TRUE)

[1] 0.003409496

var(pwt7g$growth[pwt7g$year==1990], na.rm=TRUE)

[1] 0.006252355

F.ratio <- var(pwt7g$growth[pwt7g$year==1960], na.rm=TRUE)/
           var(pwt7g$growth[pwt7g$year==1990], na.rm=TRUE)

F.ratio

[1] 0.5453139
```

What is Statistical Power?

Type II error refers to the probability of failing to reject a null hypothesis when it is false. Then, statistical power refers to the probability of rejecting the null hypothesis when it is false. Figure 3.1 shows that the size of Type II error is measured by the area of β in the alternative sampling distribution when the null hypothesis is false and the alternative hypothesis is true. In the context of Figure 3.1, the statistical power of the test refers to $1 - \beta$, which equals the remaining area of the alternative sampling distribution under the alternative hypothesis. Power analysis is important for experimental studies, particularly in medicine and epidemiology.

What are the Differences Between Two-Tailed and One-Tailed Tests?

This question is most relevant to hypothesis testing. For simplicity, we will use two-tailed tests for all hypothesis testing in this book, except in Figure 3.1, where a one-tailed test is illustrated. The best way to illustrate their differences is to re-analyze the two-tailed t-test in earlier in the section as a one-tailed test.

Null hypothesis $H_0 : \mu_{true} = \mu_0 = 0.03$.
Two-sided alternative hypothesis $H_a : \mu_{true} \neq \mu_0 = 0.03$.

One-sided null hypothesis $H_0 : \mu_{true} \leqslant \mu_0 = 0.03$.
One-sided alternative hypothesis $H_a : \mu_{true} > \mu_0 = 0.03$.

One-sided null hypothesis $H_0 : \mu_{true} \geqslant \mu_0 = 0.03$.
One-sided alternative hypothesis $H_a : \mu_{true} < \mu_0 = 0.03$.

Three pairs of null and alternative hypotheses are specified. The first pair is for a two-tailed test. The second and third pairs are for one-tailed tests, with different conditions in the null hypotheses tested.

Regardless of whether a test is one-tailed or two-tailed, the test statistic remains the same, with a degree of freedom $(n - 1)$:

$$t = \frac{\bar{y} - \mu_0}{s/\sqrt{n}}$$

The choice of the acceptable Type I error threshold also remains the same: $\alpha = 0.05$.

With the computed t-statistic and degree of freedom, the p value will be identified from a t-distribution table, as before. However, the size of the p value will differ, depending on the nature of the null hypothesis.

Two-tailed p value: $\mu_{true} = \mu_0 = 0.03$.
Left-tailed p value: $\mu_{true} \leqslant \mu_0 = 0.03$.
Right-tailed p value: $\mu_{true} \geqslant \mu_0 = 0.03$

The decision rule remains the same as well.

We illustrate how two-tailed and one-tailed tests can differ, using the following R code.

```
# conduct two-tailed and one-tailed one-sample-mean t-tests
t.test(pwt7g$growth, mu=0.03)
t.test(pwt7g$growth, mu=0.03, alternative = "greater")
t.test(pwt7g$growth, mu=0.03, alternative = "less")
```

The first line of code is the default two-tailed test, and the last two lines of code are for the respective one-sided null hypotheses specified via the alternative= option. This option refers to what is specified in the alternative hypothesis, which is opposite to what is in the null hypothesis. The R output is as follows:

```
# conduct two-tailed and one-tailed one-sample-mean t-tests
t.test(pwt7g$growth, mu=0.03)


One-Sample t-test
```

```
data:  pwt7g$growth
t = -8.5529, df = 8477, p-value < 2.2e-16
alternative hypothesis: true mean is not equal to 0.03
95 percent confidence interval:
 0.02142637 0.02462360
sample estimates:
 mean of x
0.02302498


t.test(pwt7g$growth, mu=0.03, alternative = "greater")


One-Sample t-test

data:  pwt7g$growth
t = -8.5529, df = 8477, p-value = 1
alternative hypothesis: true mean is greater than 0.03
95 percent confidence interval:
 0.02168343        Inf
sample estimates:
 mean of x
0.02302498


t.test(pwt7g$growth, mu=0.03, alternative = "less")


One-Sample t-test

data:  pwt7g$growth
t = -8.5529, df = 8477, p-value < 2.2e-16
alternative hypothesis: true mean is less than 0.03
95 percent confidence interval:
      -Inf 0.02436654
sample estimates:
 mean of x
0.02302498
```

The R output shows that the t-statistic is -8.5529, with a degree of freedom of 8477, for all three tests. In the two-tailed test, the p value is smaller than 0.05 and thus, the null hypothesis $\mu_{true} = 0.03$ is rejected. In the first one-tailed test of $\mu_{true} \leqslant 0.03$, the p value is reported as 1, much larger than 0.05, and thus, the null hypothesis is not rejected. In the second one-tailed test of $\mu_{true} \geqslant 0.03$, the p value is smaller than 0.05 and thus, the null hypothesis is rejected.

Finally, note that when a one-tailed test is applied, the analyst is essentially assuming that the other half of the sampling distribution under the null hypothesis is theoretically irrelevant or impossible. Thus, in a two-tailed test, the $\alpha = 0.05$ is split into 0.025 on each side of the distribution. Yet, in a one-tailed test, the $\alpha = 0.05$ is applied to only one side of the distribution.

Exercises

1. Based on the example in the chapter, start with an appropriate research question regarding wage inequality in the Soskice and Iversen (2006) article, and then conduct a one-sample t-test to answer the question using both null hypothesis testing and confidence interval. Be sure to discuss the procedures clearly and interpret the substantive meaning of the findings for the question.

2. Now start with a different research question regarding the difference in wage inequality between the proportional and majoritarian systems in the Soskice and Iversen (2006) article. Conduct a difference-of-means test to answer the question using both null hypothesis testing and confidence interval. Be sure to discuss the procedures clearly and interpret the substantive meaning of the findings for the question asked.

3. Find out the population difference in GDP per capita between rich and poor countries, using the Penn World Table data, and discuss the finding.

4. Based on the example in the chapter, start with an appropriate research question and conduct a one-sample t-test for the dependent variable in Braithwaite (2006) in Chapter 7. Discuss the substantive meaning of the findings for the question asked.

5. Now start with an appropriate research question and conduct a difference-of-means test for the dependent variable in Braithwaite (2006). For example, one could ask about the difference in the spread of military conflict between conflicts involving territorial claims and those involving other issues, or between conflicts in natural resource rich countries and others. Discuss the substantive meaning of the findings for the question asked.

6. Use the difference-of-means tests and the data from Benabou et al. (2015) in Chapter 7 to evaluate if male and female respondents differ in their attitudes toward the importance of child independence.

Covariance and Correlation

Chapter Objectives

In this chapter, we will use R to make statistical inferences about the relationship between continuous variables. Recall that a continuous variable can take an infinite number of possible values within an interval such as economic growth or height. We will learn to compute and understand covariance and correlation between two continuous variables, which sets the stage for regression analysis in the next chapter. In this chapter, we will focus on the following substantive question: Are trade openness and economic growth correlated?

Our objectives in this chapter are as follows:

1. Learn to separate data preparation and analysis into different program files.
2. Learn to prepare data for analysis.
3. Learn to visualize the relationship between two variables using scatter plot.
4. Learn about covariance and correlation coefficient, both sample and population versions.
5. Learn to make statistical inferences from sample coefficient estimate to population parameter.
6. Learn to compute and visualize correlation across different levels of a group variable.

As usual, before we move into the main materials, we will need to get data and software ready for analysis.

Data and Software Preparations

For data preparation, we should have completed the following tasks:

1. Set up a project folder to hold pwt7 data, program, and output files.
2. Create a well-documented R program to import pwt7 into R.
3. Inspect imported data.

4. Create a new dataset using a subset of pwt7 data.
5. Install add-on packages needed.
6. Create new variables for later use.

Recall from the previous chapters that a folder named Project has been created to hold data, program, and output files. The R code below, largely borrowed from the previous chapters, demonstrates how we should begin with a clean workspace, reset the working directory, import pwt7 data into R, briefly inspect imported data, create a new dataset arbitrarily named pwt7g using a subset of pwt7, install and load needed add-on packages, create the variable of interest growth, drop the observations before 1960 to control for the influence of the immediate post-WWII recovery, and save the produced dataset as an R dataset.

For software preparation for this chapter, we will need to install the following add-on packages in R first and for once: DataCombine, ggplot2, dplyr, broom, and gridExtra. We can install them before going through the chapter, and simply load them later using the library() function.

As noted in the previous chapter, a best practice in managing the workflow in data analysis is to use separate program files for data preparation and analysis. Hence, we will save the R code below on data preparation as one program file and then the R code for analysis as another program file.

```
# Data Preparation Program

# install following packages only once, then comment out code
# install.packages(c("DataCombine","ggplot2","dplyr","broom",
#                 "gridExtra","stargazer"), dependencies=TRUE)

# before running program, remove all objects in workspace
rm(list=ls(all=TRUE))

# change working directory to project folder
setwd("C:/Project")

# import comma-delimited data file, create data object pwt7
pwt7 <- read.csv("pwt70_w_country_names.csv", header=TRUE,
                strip.white=TRUE, stringsAsFactors = FALSE,
                na.strings=c("NA",""))

# create annual economic growth rate in a panel dataset
# load DataCombine package in order to use slide function
library(DataCombine)
```

```
# sort data in ascending order by country and by year
pwt7 <- pwt7[order(pwt7$country, pwt7$year),]

# create a one-year leading variable for rgdpl
pwt7 <- slide(pwt7, Var="rgdpl", NewVar="rgdplead",
              GroupVar="country", slideBy=1)

# create a one-year lagged variable for rgdpl
pwt7 <- slide(pwt7, Var="rgdpl", NewVar="rgdplag",
              GroupVar="country", slideBy=-1)

# create annual growth rate based on rgdpl
pwt7$growth <- (pwt7$rgdpl-pwt7$rgdplag)*100/pwt7$rgdplag

# create a new dataset of pwt7 with six variables
pwt7g <- pwt7[, c("isocode", "country", "year", "rgdpl",
                  "openk", "growth")]

# remove second set of China observations with isocode CH2
pwt7 <- pwt7[pwt7$isocode!="CH2",]

# drop pre-1960 observations
pwt7g<- pwt7g[pwt7g$year>=1960,]

# check variables in and class of pwt7g
names(pwt7g)

[1] "isocode" "country" "year"    "rgdpl"   "openk"
[6] "growth"

class(pwt7g)

[1] "data.frame"

# save R dataset
save(pwt7g, file="pwt7g.RData")
```

Using the R program above and the original pwt7 dataset, we have created a new R dataset pwt7g that contains six variables: isocode, country, year, rgdpl, openk, and growth. Note that openk is a country's total trade as a percentage share of its real GDP (in 2005 international dollar), and growth is a country's annual economic growth rate based on rgdpl (i.e., a country's real GDP per capita, in 2005 international dollar).

We will now start a second program file focusing on analysis, using the following R code:

```
# Data Analysis Program

# before running program, remove all objects in workspace
rm(list=ls(all=TRUE))

# change working directory to project folder
setwd("C:/Project")

# load R data
load("pwt7g.RData")

# compute descriptive statstics for growth and openk
summary(pwt7g$growth)

    Min.  1st Qu.  Median    Mean  3rd Qu.    Max.
-65.2500  -0.7268  2.3230  2.3040  5.2390  122.2000
    NA's
    1556

summary(pwt7g$openk)

   Min. 1st Qu.  Median    Mean 3rd Qu.    Max.    NA's
  1.035  39.560  63.840  73.590  96.620  443.200    1441
```

We use the summary() function to produce summary statistics for growth and openk for future references. As shown, the average growth rate is 2.3%, ranging from −65% to 122%; the average trade openness is about 74%, ranging from 1% to 443%. Both variables have huge variations. The median for growth is 2.32%, roughly equally to the average growth rate, suggesting that the distribution of the variable is not very skewed. In contrast, the median for openk is roughly 64%, much smaller than the mean, indicating that the variable is right skewed.

Visualize the Relationship Between Trade and Growth Using Scatter Plot

The first step in examining the relationship between any two continuous variables is to visualize their relationship using a scatter plot. How do we

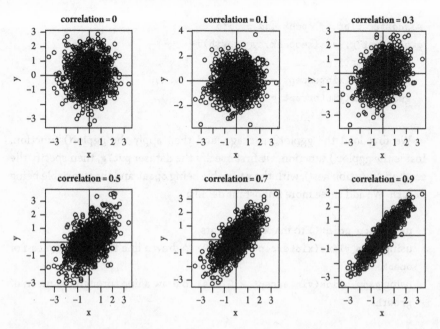

Figure 4.1 Simulated Positive Correlations of Two Random Variables.

interpret the pattern in a scatter plot? To do so, we must know what a strong or weak relationship looks like graphically. For illustration, Figure 4.1 presents six simulated correlations of varying strength between two random variables, denoted as x and y. Both variables have mean 0 and variance of 1, and each simulation is based on a random sample of 1,000 observations.

Each plot in Figure 4.1 is divided into four quadrants by two lines through the mean values of x and y, respectively. In the first plot, correlation is zero, and the data points are distributed roughly equally in the four quadrants. As the correlation between x and y rises to 0.1, 0.3, 0.5, 0.7, till 0.9 across the rest of the plots, increasingly more data points become concentrated in the upper right and lower left quadrants. In the upper right quadrant, the differences between any data point and the mean values of x and y, respectively, are always positive; in the lower left quadrants, both differences are always negative. This pattern indicates a positive association between x and y. Alternatively, if two variables are negatively correlated, we should find more data points lying in the upper left and lower right quadrants instead.

Given this background information, we turn to the scatter plot of trade openness and economic growth created using the R code below.

```
# load ggplot2 package
library(ggplot2)
```

```
# scatter plot of openk and growth
ggplot(pwt7g, aes(x=openk, y=growth))+
  geom_point() +
  geom_vline(xintercept = 73.59) +
  geom_hline(yintercept = 2.304)
```

We first load the ggplot2 package, and then apply the ggplot() function. Inside the ggplot() function, we first specify the dataset pwt7g, then specify the aesthetic function aes(), with the x variable being openk and the y variable being growth. We add three more important details:

- using geom_point() to mark data points,
- using geom_vline(xintercept = 73.59) to draw a line through the mean of openk
- using geom_hline(yintercept = 2.304) to draw a line through the mean of growth.

Note that if there are missing values in data, the option geom_point() will lead to a warning message in the output to the effect that certain rows containing missing values in geom_point() are removed.

Figure 4.2 shows the scatter plot between growth and openk for the whole sample in pwt7g. Comparing this figure with Figure 4.1, we may conclude that there is no clear, strong, positive or negative correlation between the two variables. But a significant number of observations appear to have extremely

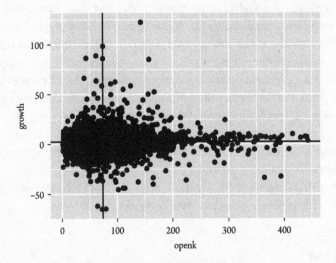

Figure 4.2 Scatter Plot of Trade Openness and Economic Growth.

large trade openness values and yet low growth rates, which is related to the right-skewed distribution of trade openness.

Are Trade Openness and Economic Growth Correlated?

The correlation coefficient is probably the most commonly used, basic statistic for describing the relationship between two continuous variables. In order to answer the research question posed above, we will estimate, test, and predict the correlation coefficient between two variables in the population. Specifically, we will estimate the size and direction of the correlation between growth and trade openness, test whether they are correlated in the population or not, and identify the strength of the correlation in the population. Before we discuss the correlation coefficient, however, we must first learn about its essential building bloc—covariance—and how to estimate it in R.

Conceptual Preparation: Population and Sample Covariance

The concept of covariance is critical to correlation and regression analysis. In Chapter 3, we discussed the notion of variance, in population and sample versions. Covariance, which is similar to variance but based on two variables, measures how two variables are linearly related. A positive covariance indicates a positive linear relationship between two variables, and a negative value indicates a negative linear relationship. Like variance, covariance also has both population and sample versions.

Take trade openness and growth as an example. The population covariance between trade and growth is defined as the *sum* of the *products* of their *deviations* from respective *population mean* values (μ_{growth} and μ_{trade}), divided by the *population size N*.

$$\sigma_{trade,growth} = \frac{1}{N} \sum_{i=1}^{N} (trade_i - \mu_{trade})(growth_i - \mu_{growth})$$

As before, typically, data are not available for the whole population, so computing the sample covariance as an estimate of the population variance is necessary. The sample covariance between trade and growth is defined as the *sum* of the *products* of their *deviations* from respective *sample mean* values ($\overline{growth}$ and $\overline{trade}$), divided by the *sample size n minus one*. It is an estimate of the population covariance, based on sample data.

$$S_{trade,growth} = \frac{1}{n-1} \sum_{i=1}^{n} (trade_i - \overline{trade})(growth_i - \overline{growth})$$

To further illustrate the numerical operation for a sample covariance, we will use the pwt7g data as an example. To calculate the sample covariance between two variables, we first find the deviation from the mean for each variable and then compute the product between the two deviations, for each observation. This procedure is shown for the Afghanistan 1971 observation below, which is the first observation with non-missing values for openk and growth, with openk being 16.54 and growth being 2.35. Their mean values—denoted as mean_o and mean_g—come from the data preparation section of this chapter.

isocode	year	openk	mean_o	deviation_o	growth	mean_g	deviation_g	product
AFG	1971	16.54	73.59	(16.54–73.59)	2.35	2.304	(2.35–2.304)	(16.54–73.59)(2.35–2.304)
AFG	1971	16.54	73.59	−57.05	2.35	2.304	0.046	−2.6243

For this observation, the product of deviations is -2.6243. Next, we compute the product of deviations for each observation, sum the products across all observations, and then divide the total sum by the sample size minus one. The final value is the sample covariance between openk and growth.

Three issues require clarification. First, we can understand this procedure more clearly in the context of Figure 4.2. The Afghanistan 1971 observation in our example lies in the upper left quadrant of Figure 4.2, with a positive deviation from the mean value of growth and a negative deviation from the mean value of openk. This is an example of below-average trade openness and above-average growth rate. As a result, for this observation, the product of deviations is negative.

In Figure 4.2, the products of deviations are positive for all observations in the upper right and lower left quadrants, and the product of deviations are negative for all observations in the upper left and lower right quadrants.

When all the products are added and summed together and then divided by (n-1), the computed sample covariance is merely an average of all the products. Depending on the relative size of the positive and negative products, the final computed value could be positive, negative, or even zero, indicating the direction of the sample correlation between two variables.

The second notable issue is that covariance is not unit free, as shown by its formula. It just so happens that in our example, both openk and growth are measured in percent. In many other applications, however, the unit of measurement of a variable influences the size of covariance. For example, population, measured in thousands or in millions, will produce covariance values that are dramatically but artificially different. Thus, it is inappropriate to compare covariance values as a way to compare the strength of correlation between two different pairs of variables.

The third notable issue is that covariance is sensitive to outliers in data. Observations that have very large deviations from the mean values of openk and growth produce very large products of deviations. For illustration, readers may refer to the Anscombe's quartet example in the Miscellaneous Q&A section.

The R code and output for computing sample covariance is as follows:

```
# sample covariance, only non-missing observations
cov(pwt7g$growth, pwt7g$openk, use = "complete.obs")

[1] 17.41489
```

The cov() function includes two variables in its argument and some option. Since both variables have missing values, the use="complete.obs" option is added to ensure only complete observations are used in computation; that is, missing values are deleted casewise. Without this option, the presence of missing values will produce NA when we run the cov() function, which interested readers can replicate on their own.

Based on the output, the sample covariance between the two variables is 17.42 in the post-1960 data of pwt7g. It is positive, meaning that the linear correlation between the two variables is positive. As noted, the sample covariance cannot tell us how strong the relationship is. For that information, we now turn to the correlation coefficient.

Sample Correlation Estimate and Population Correlation Parameter

We start with the Pearson correlation coefficient in the population and then show how to make inferences about it using its sample version. The correlation coefficient between trade and growth in the population, denoted by $\rho_{trade,growth}$, is defined as follows:

$$\rho_{trade,growth} = \frac{\sigma_{trade,growth}}{\sigma_{trade}\sigma_{growth}}$$

where $\sigma_{trade,growth}$ represents the covariance, and σ_{trade} and σ_{growth} represent the respective standard deviations. Verbally, the population correlation coefficient is the population covariance between two variables divided by the product of their population standard deviations.

As a result, the Pearson correlation coefficient is unit free, bounded between -1 (perfect negative linear correlation) and $+1$ (perfect positive linear correlation), with zero meaning no correlation and values approaching positive or negative one indicating stronger positive or negative linear correlations. The denominator in the formula helps to standardize the covariance so the strength of correlation between any two pairs of variables can be compared. It is also worth noting that the correlation coefficient applies to continuous random variables, and captures the linear, but not any non-linear, relationship between two variables. On this point, please refer to the Anscombe's quartet example in the Miscellaneous Q&A section.

Since we do not know the population mean and population standard deviation of either variable, we cannot know directly the value of the population correlation coefficient. As a result, we have to estimate it using sample data. The sample correlation coefficient, denoted by r, is defined as follows:

$$r = \frac{\frac{1}{n-1}\sum_{i=1}^{n}(trade_i - \overline{trade})(growth_i - \overline{growth})}{\sqrt{\frac{1}{n-1}\sum_{i=1}^{n}(trade_i - \overline{trade})^2}\sqrt{\frac{1}{n-1}\sum_{i=1}^{n}(growth_i - \overline{growth})^2}} = \frac{S_{trade,growth}}{S_{trade}S_{growth}}$$

The sample correlation coefficient is the sample covariance between two variables, divided by the product of their sample standard deviations. The R code for computing sample correlation coefficient is as follows:

```
# sample correlation coefficient, non-missing observations
cor(pwt7g$openk, pwt7g$growth, use="complete.obs")
```

```
[1] 0.04632766
```

The cor() function first specifies the two variables in its argument. Since both variables have missing values, the use="complete.obs" tells R to use only complete observations; missing values are deleted casewise.

As shown, the sample correlation coefficient between trade openness and economic growth is 0.0463. Recall that correlation coefficient ranges from -1 to $+1$, so the sample correlation between trade openness and economic growth is not strong at all, though it is not absolutely zero. One may also compare the strength of the sample correlation against the simulated pattern in Figure 4.1 to get an intuitive sense of how weak the correlation is.

For the sake of statistical inference, we must answer two questions. First, what is our choice between the following two different conclusions: (1) The sample correlation 0.0463 is not zero only because of random noise and sampling error and thus, the population correlation should be zero; (2) the sample correlation 0.0463 is statistically different from zero even after accounting for random noise and sampling error and thus, the population correlation should not be zero. This question will be addressed via hypothesis testing. Second, if the population correlation between trade and growth is not zero, what would be its most probable values? This question will be addressed via confidence interval construction.

Hypothesis Test of Hypothetical Population Correlation Coefficient

To answer our question raised above, we specify the following hypothesis:

Null hypothesis H_0 : $\rho_{trade,growth} = 0$. Trade openness and economic growth are not correlated in the population.

Alternative hypothesis $H_a : \rho_{trade,growth} \neq 0$. Trade openness and economic growth are correlated in the population.

To test the null hypothesis directly, we construct a test statistic, denoted as t. In the test statistic, r is the sample correlation coefficient, ρ is the hypothetical population parameter (which is zero), and n is the sample size. It is essentially the sample correlation r minus the hypothetical population correlation, divided by the standard error of r. The test statistic assumes that the two variables are normally distributed and linearly related.

$$t = \frac{r - \rho}{\sqrt{\frac{1 - r^2}{n - 2}}} = r\sqrt{\frac{n - 2}{1 - r^2}}$$

The R code and output for this test is as follows:

```
# making inferences over population correlation between
# openness and growth
cor.test(pwt7g$openk, pwt7g$growth, use = "complete.obs",
    "two.sided", "pearson")


Pearson's product-moment correlation

data:  pwt7g$openk and pwt7g$growth
t = 4.1331, df = 7942, p-value = 3.616e-05
alternative hypothesis: true correlation is not equal to 0
95 percent confidence interval:
 0.0243617 0.0682489
sample estimates:
        cor
0.04632766
```

The cor.test() function produces the statistical results. Inside the function, we first identify the two variables, and then with the use= option, specify that we will use all observations with no missing values, apply a two-tailed test, and adopt the Pearson correlation coefficient. Test statistics other than Pearson will be discussed briefly in the Miscellaneous Q&A section.

The reported test statistic is 4.13, producing an extremely small p value. Since the p value is much smaller than our acceptable Type I error rate α, which is commonly set at 0.05, we reject the null hypothesis that trade openness and economic growth are not correlated in the population. Hence, the positive sample correlation 0.0463 indicates that trade openness and economic growth are most likely positively correlated in the population. Still, a test of the null hypothesis does not tell us what the population correlation might be, which is the task of confidence interval construction.

Confidence Interval to Predict Population Correlation Coefficient

As before, the second method of statistical inference is to identify a range of estimates around the sample point estimate to predict the population correlation coefficient with 95% confidence. The computation of a confidence interval for the population correlation ρ is complicated because the sampling distribution of the sample correlation r is not normally distributed, that is, not bell-shaped. Thus, we have to take three steps to find the confidence interval for ρ. We first convert the sample correlation r to a z-score, then compute a confidence interval in terms of the z-score, and finally convert the confidence interval for z back to r. The technical details are skipped here.

As for computation, the same R code above also computes the confidence interval for the population correlation coefficient ρ between trade openness and growth. The output shows that the 95% confidence interval between trade openness and growth ranges between 0.024 and 0.068. These are not very high correlation values. While we are 95% confident that it is not zero in the population, the correlation is not large in size.

Does the Correlation between Trade and Growth Change over Time?

So far, we have focused on estimating the correlation coefficient for the whole sample period. One important practical issue of interest is whether this correlation is stable over time or not. Since we have data from 1960 to 2009, it should make sense that we double check whether the weak positive correlation changes over time.

This exercise will also give us an opportunity to introduce a very new but powerful package, dplyr, which provides many useful tools for efficient data manipulation. The package has five main manipulation functions:

- filter (for selecting rows);
- select (for selecting columns);
- arrange (for reordering rows);
- mutate (for adding new columns, based on other columns);
- summarize (for calculating any function within groups).

Another important feature of dplyr is that it allows us to chain or pipe commands using the operator %>% so that we can carry out operations sequentially, making the code easier to read and understand.

```
# annual sample correlations
# load package
```

```
library(dplyr)

# compute correlation coefficient for each year
# export output as a data frame to table1
table1 <- pwt7g %>%
  group_by(year) %>%
  summarize(corgo=cor(growth,openk, use="complete.obs"))%>%
  as.data.frame()
```

The data manipulation using dplyr follows a similar routine. The first argument is the data frame, pwt7g, which is chained to the next function, group_by(), through the %>% operator; the group_by(year) function groups pwt7g according to year, which is then chained to the next function, summarize(), through %>%; the summarize() function aggregates observations in each group according to the function specified in its argument, here through the cor() function discussed above, and naming the computed annual correlation as a variable corgo; the summarize() function is then chained to the as.data.frame() function that converts the output into a data frame. We then assign the final output to a data object called table1.

The R code and output below displays the sample correlation by year in table1, and then confirms the result for one year (2008) using the cor() function.

```
# display sample correlation by year
table1

   year      corgo
1  1960 -0.088669908
2  1961  0.013570047
3  1962  0.155394480
4  1963 -0.126845100
5  1964  0.164527138
6  1965 -0.309755328
7  1966  0.041406036
8  1967 -0.037983087
9  1968  0.219300797
10 1969 -0.001400059
11 1970  0.023754436
12 1971 -0.026237572
13 1972  0.153047244
14 1973  0.094684106
15 1974  0.158732122
16 1975 -0.079402962
```

```
17 1976   0.203832421
18 1977  -0.013028741
19 1978   0.119185248
20 1979   0.170675717
21 1980   0.039425137
22 1981  -0.005525857
23 1982  -0.054230981
24 1983   0.106302936
25 1984   0.097567637
26 1985  -0.087326184
27 1986   0.028679741
28 1987   0.144654601
29 1988   0.065212147
30 1989   0.125164070
31 1990   0.192614279
32 1991   0.095125813
33 1992   0.129421630
34 1993   0.023612018
35 1994  -0.023980665
36 1995  -0.068519368
37 1996   0.146776367
38 1997   0.043386123
39 1998   0.023136850
40 1999   0.043088089
41 2000  -0.028514080
42 2001   0.016959188
43 2002   0.022778702
44 2003  -0.017663575
45 2004   0.127992120
46 2005   0.005788010
47 2006   0.102126573
48 2007   0.089562647
49 2008  -0.010133645
50 2009  -0.198994731

# compare with example of single-year calculation
cor(pwt7g$openk[pwt7g$year==2008],
    pwt7g$growth[pwt7g$year==2008],
    use="complete.obs")

[1] -0.01013364
```

To facilitate our comparison of many values over time, we use the qplot()
and ggplot() functions in the ggplot2 package to produce two plots—one scatter
plot, the other line plot—to demonstrate the change of the sample correlation
coefficient over time. Then we use the grid.arrange() function from the gridExtra
package to join and display the two plots together.

```
# load packages
library(ggplot2)
library(gridExtra)

# produce annual sample correlation plot objects
corgo1 <- qplot(year, corgo, data=table1)
corgo2 <- ggplot(table1, aes(year, corgo)) + geom_line()

# display plots together
grid.arrange(corgo1, corgo2, ncol = 2)
```

Figure 4.3 presents the results. The pattern in table1 and Figure 4.3 is clear.
The correlation between trade and growth is definitely not stable over time. It
ranges from -0.31 in 1965 to 0.219 in 1968.

At this point, one may naturally ask whether each yearly correlation coefficient is statistically different from zero or not. To answer this question,
we may use the plyr package as well as the broom package to organize and

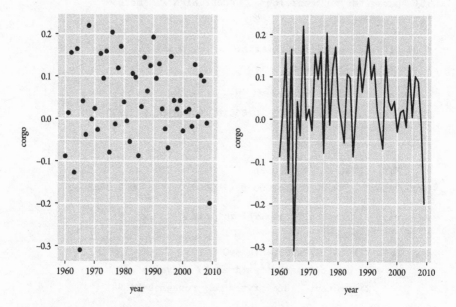

Figure 4.3 Correlation between Trade and Growth over Time.

save the output from the cor.test() function as a dataset table2. The only change in R code is in the use of do() and tidy() functions from the broom package. We then list all variable names in table2. As shown by the output of names(table2), many useful variables are produced, particularly the *p*-value and the confidence interval estimates. We present the summary statistics of two quantities of interest: estimated correlation coefficient and *p* value, as well as the cases when the sample correlation is statistically significant at the 5% level.

```
# load package
library(broom)

# produce tests of annual correlation coefficient
# export output as a data frame to table2
table2 <- pwt7g %>%
            group_by(year) %>%
            do(tidy(cor.test(.$growth,.$openk,
                             use="complete.obs"))) %>%
            as.data.frame()

# display variables in table2
names(table2)

[1] "year"          "estimate"      "statistic"    "p.value"
[5] "parameter"     "conf.low"      "conf.high"    "method"
[9] "alternative"

# display descriptive statistics for estimate and p value
summary(table2$estimate)

    Min.   1st Qu.   Median     Mean   3rd Qu.     Max.
-0.30980  -0.01650  0.03405  0.04019  0.12370  0.21930

summary(table2$p.value)

     Min.    1st Qu.    Median      Mean    3rd Qu.      Max.
0.0008419  0.0909400  0.3357000  0.4159000  0.7443000  0.9883000

# display statistically significant cases
library(stargazer)
stargazer(table2[table2$p.value<=0.05,
                 c("year", "estimate", "p.value")],
          type="text", summary=FALSE, rownames=FALSE)
```

```
========================
year   estimate p.value
------------------------
1,965  -0.310   0.001
1,968   0.219   0.020
1,974   0.159   0.046
1,976   0.204   0.010
1,979   0.171   0.032
1,990   0.193   0.013
1,996   0.147   0.044
2,009  -0.199   0.006
------------------------
```

Figure 4.4 displays the p value for each sample correlation, with year on the horizontal axis and p.value on the vertical axis, and the $\alpha = 0.05$ line is drawn in the figure. As shown in table1, the stargazer() output, and Figure 4.4, only in about eight years, the sample correlation between trade and growth is statistically significant at the 5% level. In many years, the relationship is negative, but in many other years, it is positive. Once again, the relationship between trade and growth does not appear to be strong.

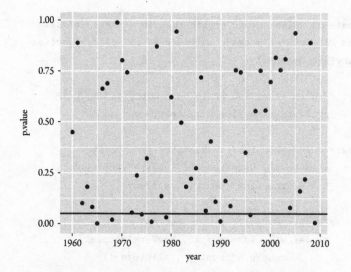

Figure 4.4 P Value of Correlation between Trade and Growth over Time.

Chapter 4 Program Code

Data Preparation Program

```
# install following packages only once, then comment out code
# install.packages(c("DataCombine","ggplot2","dplyr","broom",
#              "gridExtra","stargazer"), dependencies=TRUE)

# before running program, remove all objects in workspace
rm(list=ls(all=TRUE))

# change working directory to project folder
setwd("C:/Project")

# import comma-delimited data file, create data object pwt7
pwt7 <- read.csv("pwt70_w_country_names.csv", header=TRUE,
                strip.white=TRUE, stringsAsFactors = FALSE,
                na.strings=c("NA",""))
# load package
library(ggplot2)

# visualize p value for annual sample correlation
ggplot(table2, aes(year, p.value)) +
    geom_point() +
    geom_hline(yintercept=0.05)
```

```
# create annual economic growth rate in a panel dataset
# load DataCombine package in order to use slide function
library(DataCombine)

# sort data in ascending order by country and by year
pwt7 <- pwt7[order(pwt7$country, pwt7$year),]

# create a one-year leading variable for rgdpl
pwt7 <- slide(pwt7, Var="rgdpl", NewVar="rgdplead",
           GroupVar="country", slideBy=1)

# create a one-year lagged variable for rgdpl
pwt7 <- slide(pwt7, Var="rgdpl", NewVar="rgdplag",
           GroupVar="country", slideBy=-1)

# create annual growth rate based on rgdpl
pwt7$growth <- (pwt7$rgdpl-pwt7$rgdplag)*100/pwt7$rgdplag
```

```
# create a new dataset of pwt7 with six variables
pwt7g <- pwt7[, c("isocode", "country", "year", "rgdpl",
                  "openk", "growth")]

# remove second set of China observations with isocode CH2
pwt7 <- pwt7[pwt7$isocode!="CH2",]

# drop pre-1960 observations
pwt7g<- pwt7g[pwt7g$year>=1960,]

# check variables in and class of pwt7g
names(pwt7g)
class(pwt7g)

# save R dataset
save(pwt7g, file="pwt7g.RData")
```

Data Analysis Program

```
# before running program, remove all objects in workspace
rm(list=ls(all=TRUE))

# change working directory to project folder
setwd("C:/Project")

# load R data
load("pwt7g.RData")

# compute descriptive statstics for growth and openk
summary(pwt7g$growth)
summary(pwt7g$openk)

# load ggplot2 package
library(ggplot2)

# scatter plot of openk and growth
ggplot(pwt7g, aes(x=openk, y=growth))+
  geom_point() +
  geom_vline(xintercept = 73.59) +
  geom_hline(yintercept = 2.304)
```

```r
# sample covariance, only non-missing observations
cov(pwt7g$growth, pwt7g$openk, use="complete.obs")

# sample correlation coefficient, non-missing observations
cor(pwt7g$openk, pwt7g$growth, use="complete.obs")

# making inferences over population correlation between
# openness and growth
cor.test(pwt7g$openk, pwt7g$growth, use="complete.obs",
         "two.sided", "pearson")

# annual sample correlations
# load package
library(dplyr)

# compute correlation coefficient for each year
# export output as a data frame to table1
table1 <- pwt7g %>%
  group_by(year) %>%
  summarize(corgo=cor(growth,openk, use="complete.obs"))%>%
  as.data.frame()

# display sample correlation by year
table1

# compare with example of single-year calculation
cor(pwt7g$openk[pwt7g$year==2008],
    pwt7g$growth[pwt7g$year==2008],
    use="complete.obs")

# load packages
library(ggplot2)
library(gridExtra)

# produce annual sample correlation plot objects
corgo1 <- qplot(year, corgo, data=table1)
corgo2 <- ggplot(table1, aes(year, corgo)) + geom_line()

# display plots together
grid.arrange(corgo1, corgo2, ncol = 2)
```

```
# load package
library(broom)

# produce tests of annual correlation coefficient
# export output as a data frame to table2
table2 <- pwt7g %>%
        group_by(year) %>%
        do(tidy(cor.test(.$growth, .$openk,
                         use="complete.obs"))) %>%
        as.data.frame()

# display variables in table2
names(table2)

# display descriptive statistics for estimate and p value
summary(table2$estimate)
summary(table2$p.value)

# display statistically significant cases
# load package
library(stargazer)
stargazer(table2[table2$p.value<=0.05,
                c("year", "estimate", "p.value")],
          type="text", summary=FALSE, rownames=FALSE)

# load package
library(ggplot2)

# visualize p value for annual sample correlation
ggplot(table2, aes(year, p.value)) +
    geom_point() +
    geom_hline(yintercept=0.05)
```

Summary

This chapter begins with the substantive question of whether trade openness and economic growth are correlated, which motivates both data preparation and statistical analysis. The chapter first illustrates how to get data ready and then demonstrates how to visualize the relationship between two variables using scatter plot. The chapter shows how to use covariance and correlation coefficient to test whether trade openness and economic growth are correlated in the population and to estimate the strength of their correlation. Like in the previous chapter, null hypothesis testing and confidence interval construction are used for statistical inference. The chapter then demonstrates how to derive and test the sample correlation for each year during the sample period. The overall substantive conclusion of the chapter is that the bivariate correlation between economic openness and growth appears to be low and unstable over time. The problem with the correlation coefficient is that it does not control for other confounding factors of economic growth and that it does not identify the marginal effect of trade on growth. To address both issues, we will turn to regression analysis in the next chapter. Before heading into Chapter 5, we will as usual address some miscellaneous questions related to the materials in Chapter 4.

Miscellaneous Q&As for Ambitious Readers
How do we Compute Sample Covariance Step-by-Step?

```
# deviation of growth from mean
d1 <- pwt7g$growth - mean(pwt7g$growth, na.rm=TRUE)


# deviation of openness from mean
d2 <- pwt7g$openk - mean(pwt7g$openk, na.rm=TRUE)


# sample size minus one
s1 <- sum(!is.na(pwt7g$growth)&!is.na(pwt7g$openk))-1
s1

[1] 7943

# sample covariance
sum(d1*d2, na.rm=TRUE)/s1

[1] 17.41489

# doing everything in one step
(sum((pwt7g$growth - mean(pwt7g$growth, na.rm=TRUE))*
      (pwt7g$openk - mean(pwt7g$openk,na.rm=TRUE)), na.rm=TRUE))/
      (sum(!is.na(pwt7g$growth)&!is.na(pwt7g$openk))-1)

[1] 17.41489

# confirm step-by-step calculation
cov(pwt7g$growth, pwt7g$openk, use="complete.obs")

[1] 17.41489
```

How do we Compute Pearson Correlation Coefficient Step by Step?

```
# compute Pearson correlation coefficient step by step
c1 <- cov(pwt7g$openk, pwt7g$growth, use="complete.obs")
v1 <- var(pwt7g$openk, na.rm=TRUE)
v2 <- var(pwt7g$growth, na.rm=TRUE)
correlation <- c1/sqrt(v1*v2)

# display computed results
cbind(c1, v1, v2, correlation)

          c1       v1       v2 correlation
[1,] 17.41489 2421.516 58.30534  0.04634714

# confirm results above
cor(pwt7g$openk, pwt7g$growth, use="complete.obs")

[1] 0.04632766
```

Anscombe's Quartet and the Failures of the Correlation Coefficient

As we noted earlier, the correlation coefficient does not pick up any non-linear relationship in the data, and it is heavily influenced by outliers. This can be best illustrated using Anscombe's quartet, referring to the four datasets with 11 observations each, constructed by Francis Anscombe in 1973. Anscombe illustrated that across the four artificial datasets, the two variables produce an identical correlation coefficient. But when displayed in a scatter plot, the relationship between the two variables appears to differ dramatically among the four datasets. The patterns in the Anscombe quartet, as shown below, demonstrate the weaknesses of the correlation coefficient and the importance of data visualization. As shown in Figure 4.5, Plot f1 shows a normal scatter plot, f2 shows a non-linear relationship, f3 and f4 show the strong impact of outliers.

```
# display Anscombe quartet
anscombe

  x1 x2 x3 x4    y1   y2    y3    y4
1 10 10 10  8  8.04 9.14  7.46  6.58
2  8  8  8  8  6.95 8.14  6.77  5.76
3 13 13 13  8  7.58 8.74 12.74  7.71
4  9  9  9  8  8.81 8.77  7.11  8.84
5 11 11 11  8  8.33 9.26  7.81  8.47
6 14 14 14  8  9.96 8.10  8.84  7.04
```

```
7    6  6  6  8  7.24 6.13  6.08  5.25
8    4  4  4 19  4.26 3.10  5.39 12.50
9   12 12 12  8 10.84 9.13  8.15  5.56
10   7  7  7  8  4.82 7.26  6.42  7.91
11   5  5  5  8  5.68 4.74  5.73  6.89
```

```
# display identical correlation coefficient
cor(anscombe$x1, anscombe$y1)
```

```
[1] 0.8164205
```

```
cor(anscombe$x2, anscombe$y2)
```

```
[1] 0.8162365
```

```
cor(anscombe$x3, anscombe$y3)
```

```
[1] 0.8162867
```

```
cor(anscombe$x4, anscombe$y4)
```

```
[1] 0.8165214
```

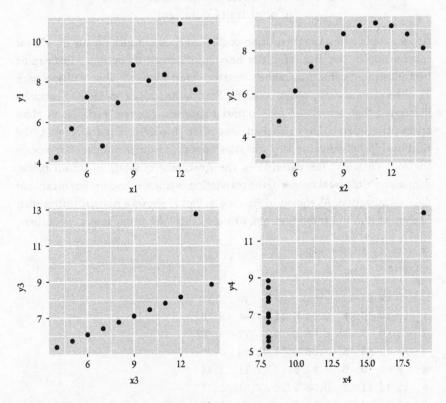

Figure 4.5 Anscombe Quartet Scatter Plot.

```
# load two packages used to data visualization
library(ggplot2)
library(gridExtra)

# generate four scatter plots with regression lines
f1 <- ggplot(anscombe)+aes(x1,y1)+geom_point()
f2 <- ggplot(anscombe)+aes(x2,y2)+geom_point()
f3 <- ggplot(anscombe)+aes(x3,y3)+geom_point()
f4 <- ggplot(anscombe)+aes(x4,y4)+geom_point()

# display four scatter plots together
grid.arrange(f1,f2,f3,f4, ncol = 2)
```

Other Correlation Test Statistics

In addition to the Pearson correlation coefficient, there are also other correlation test statistics, such as Spearman's rank-order correlation and Kendall's Tau Correlation. The Spearman's correlation is a nonparametric measure of the correlation between two variables. The variables need to be either ordinal or continuous variables, and their relationship should be monotonic, which is less restrictive than linearity. A monotonic relationship means two variables are positively or negatively correlated, but their correlation need not be constant. The R code and output for the spearman correlation are as follows:

```
# making inferences over population correlation between
# openness and growth
cor.test(pwt7g$openk, pwt7g$growth, use = "complete.obs",
    "two.sided", "spearman")


Spearman's rank correlation rho

data:  pwt7g$openk and pwt7g$growth
S = 7.8427e+10, p-value = 4.407e-08
alternative hypothesis: true rho is not equal to 0
sample estimates:
       rho
0.06136524
```

The Kendall's Tau rank correlation also is a nonparametric measure of the correlation between two continuous or ordinal variables. It is an alternative to Pearson's correlation or Spearman's correlation when assumptions for the other two test statistics are violated. Like Spearman's correlation, it also assumes a monotonic relationship between two variables. However, it works better with small sample size and with tied ranks in data. The R code and output are as follows:

```
# making inferences over population correlation between
# openness and growth
cor.test(pwt7g$openk, pwt7g$growth, use = "complete.obs",
    "two.sided", "kendall")


Kendall's rank correlation tau

data:  pwt7g$openk and pwt7g$growth
z = 5.3566, p-value = 8.478e-08
alternative hypothesis: true tau is not equal to 0
sample estimates:
    tau
0.0400754
```

The correlation estimates from these two nonparametric tests are not much different from the Pearson correlation coefficient estimate. So the bivariate correlation between trade and growth does not appear to be sensitive to the test statistics used.

Exercises

1. How are government partisanship and the reduction of income inequality related? Specify a hypothesis that answers this question based on the Soskice and Iversen (2006) article. Use hypothesis testing and confidence interval to answer the question and test the hypothesis, based on their dataset. Please be sure to discuss the procedures and test statistics clearly and interpret the substantive meaning of the findings for the question.

2. How are the duration of a military conflict and its geographical spread related? Specify a hypothesis to answer the question based on the Braithwaite (2006) article. Use hypothesis testing and confidence interval to answer the question and test the hypothesis. Discuss the procedures and test statistics clearly and interpret the findings.

3. Use the correlation test and the data from Benabou et al. (2015) in Chapter 7 to evaluate if respondents' church attendance are related to their attitudes toward the importance of child independence.

4. Use data from Benabou et al. (2015) in Chapter 7 to evaluate if respondents' attitudes toward the importance of child independence, child imagination, and child determination are correlated.

5

Regression Analysis

Chapter Objectives

In this chapter, we will use R to conduct regression analysis of the relationship between variables, in which the outcome variable is continuous and the other variables can be continuous or discrete. A continuous variable can take an infinite number of possible values within an interval such as economic growth or height; in contrast, a discrete variable only takes a countable number of values, such as the income group variable created in Chapter 2.

For illustration, we will address the following substantive question: Does trade promote economic growth? While the correlation coefficient between trade and growth provided useful information about their relationship in the previous chapter, it does not tell us the size of the effect of trade on growth. More importantly, it does not take into consideration that some other variables might affect both trade and growth, confounding their bivariate correlation. A regression model is a useful way to address both issues.

We will first provide a brief but important introduction to regression modeling in terms of conceptualization, identification, and estimation technique. We will discuss how to specify a statistical model from a theoretical argument, prepare data, estimate a regression model in both theory and practice, and interpret the estimated coefficients. Next, we will use the estimated regression model to conduct statistical inferences including hypothesis testing and confidence interval construction to answer the question of interest. In addition, we will discuss how to understand the notion of sum of squares regarding the outcome variable and interpret overall model fit. Finally, we will demonstrate how to report our regression model results.

Our objectives in this chapter are as follows:

1. Learn to separate data preparation and analysis into different program files.
2. Learn about the logic of regression models and identify both population and sample models.
3. Learn to estimate sample regression models using ordinary least squares (OLS) and interpret regression coefficient estimates.

4. Learn to make statistical inferences from sample coefficient estimates to population parameters.
5. Learn about three types of sum of squares and overall model fit.
6. Learn to present regression results.

Conceptual Preparation: How to Understand Regression Analysis

Does trade promote economic growth? According to many economists, trade openness promotes growth in the long run because international commerce increases market competition, re-allocates domestic resources to more efficient use, encourages technologies to spread, and expands the market size. Statistical evidence of the relationship between trade openness and growth, however, has been rather mixed and open to various methodological criticisms. In this section, we will provide a simple example from the trade-growth studies to illustrate how we use R and cross-sectional regression analysis to evaluate the effect of trade on economic growth.

Our example draws on a highly influential paper that has a Google Scholar citation count of over 5,000:

Frankel, Jeffrey A., and David Romer. 1999. "Does trade cause growth?" *American Economic Review* 89(3): 379–99.

Using this example, we aim to illustrate the following issues in regression analysis:

1. How do we identify a statistical model from a theoretical argument?
2. How do we understand the logic of regression analysis?
3. How do we prepare data for the variables in the statistical model?
4. How do we estimate the statistical model?
5. How do we interpret the model estimates?
6. How do we make statistical inferences based on the model estimates?
7. How do we explain overall model fit?

To study the effect of trade on growth, Frankel and Romer (1999) start with the following theoretical premise:

$$lnY_i = \alpha + \beta T_i + \gamma W_i + \varepsilon_i$$

where Y_i is income per person, T_i indicates international trade, W_i denotes within-country trade, and ε_i represents other influences on income.

The left-hand side dependent variable, Y_i, is what we are trying to explain using the right-hand side independent variables. The subscript i indicates country. The right-hand side variables include international trade, denoted by T_i, and domestic trade, denoted by W_i. β and γ represent the partial effects of international and domestic trade on growth, that is, the effect of one variable on growth while holding the other variable in the model constant; α is the level of the dependent variable when all independent variables are equal to zero (i.e., for a country without any international or domestic trade, which is neither a reasonable nor common scenario); ε_i represents the random error or other influences uncorrelated with trade.

According to Frankel and Romer, a country's average per capita income is a function of its international trade with other countries, its commerce within the country, and other factors. Both international trade and within-country commerce cause average per capita income in a country to grow. That is, $\beta > 0$, and $\gamma > 0$. Frankel and Romer further posit that a country's within-country trade can be measured by its population and land area, denoted as N_i and A_i, respectively. Based on the discussion, we can rewrite the equation above as a population regression model as follows:

$$lnY_i = \beta_0 + \beta_1 T_i + \beta_2 N_i + \beta_3 A_i + \varepsilon_i$$

Two differences are worth noting. First, the within-country trade W_i is now represented by N_i and A_i. Second, the population parameters are denoted by a vector of β, including β_0, β_1, β_2, and β_3. According to Frankel and Romer, we should expect that $\beta_1 > 0$ and that $(\beta_2 + \beta_3) > 0$.

To test whether $\beta_1 > 0$ holds in the population, Frankel and Romer use sample data to estimate the sample variant of the population regression model. The sample regression model is specified as follows in Frankel and Romer:

$$lnY_i = a + bT_i + c_1 lnN_i + c_2 lnA_i + u_i$$

To estimate this model, Frankel and Romer use two estimation samples: one with 150 countries, and the other with 98 countries, both for the year 1985.

What is the relationship between the population and sample regression models? Specifically, b, c_1, and c_2 represent the sample model coefficient estimates of the corresponding parameters β_1, β_2, and β_3 in the population regression. In the sample regression model, u_i represents the random noise and sampling error in the sample regression model, called the residual. The residual is assumed to be normally distributed, of zero mean and constant variance, and uncorrelated with any right-hand side variable. Note that the residual u_i in the sample regression is an estimate of the random component ε_i in the population regression, but they also differ. The residual consists of both random noise and sampling error, whereas the latter only random noise.

The technique for obtaining b, c_1, and c_2 is called Ordinary Least Squares (OLS). According to the technique, the OLS estimates b, c_1, and c_2 are the values that minimize the residual sum of squares (hence, "least squares"). In other words, the set of estimates that gives us the smallest $\sum u_i^2$ will be the OLS estimates of the population parameters.

To answer the research question, the b value estimated from the sample data will be used to make inferences about β_1. Once again, hypothesis testing and confidence interval will be employed. The former involves a test with respect to the sampling distribution centered on the hypothetical population parameter in the null hypothesis (i.e., $\beta_1 = 0$); the latter represents a range of estimates of the true population parameter at a predefined level of confidence, based on the sampling distribution centered on the true population parameter. The logic resembles what we saw in Figure 3.1 in Chapter 3.

The validity of the answer depends on how good an estimator b is for β_1. The mathematical foundation for the property of the OLS estimator is provided by the Gauss-Markov theorem. According to the theorem, if a set of assumptions is satisfied, then the OLS estimator b is the best linear unbiased estimator (BLUE) of the population regression parameter β_1 among all unbiased estimators. Thus, an important task in regression analysis is to diagnose whether these assumptions are met and the impact of assumption violations on statistical inference, which is the focus of the next chapter.

In sum, regression analysis involves identifying the population and sample models, estimating the coefficients in the sample regression model, making inferences from sample coefficient estimates to population parameters, and checking whether model assumptions are satisfied.

Now, we return to the Frankel and Romer analysis. Their innovation is to propose a new way to deal with the problem that international trade's impact on growth may be due to the possibility that trade itself is a function of other factors. As a result, the estimated effect of trade does not really represent the effect of trade itself. Their solution to the problem is to find a so-called instrument for trade that correlates with trade but is uncorrelated with income. As a result, the estimated effect of the instrumental variable represents only the effect of trade, uncontaminated by other confounding factors. Specifically, they use distance to predict the share of international trade in a country's national economy to obtain an unbiased estimate of β_1 through instrumental variable regression.

In their paper, Frankel and Romer estimate both OLS and instrumental regression models for two samples: one with 150 countries and the other with 98. The original results in Table 3 from Frankel and Romer (1999) are reproduced in Figure 5.1.

Figure 5.1 reports the results from four models, among which we focus on the first one. In Model 1, based on OLS for 150 countries, the coefficient estimate of

	(1)	(2)	(3)	(4)
Estimation	OLS	IV	OLS	IV
Constant	7.40	4.96	6.95	1.62
	(0.66)	(2.20)	(1.12)	(3.85)
Trade share	0.85	1.97	0.82	2.96
	(0.25)	(0.99)	(0.32)	(1.49)
Ln population	0.12	0.19	0.21	0.35
	(0.06)	(0.09)	(0.10)	(0.15)
Ln area	−0.01	0.09	−0.05	0.20
	(0.06)	(0.10)	(0.08)	(0.19)
Sample size	150	150	98	98
R^2	0.09	0.09	0.11	0.09
SE of regression	1.00	1.06	1.04	1.27
First-stage F on excluded instrument		13.13		8.45

Notes: The dependent variable is log income per person in 1985. The 150-country sample includes all countries for which the data are available; the 98-country sample includes only the countries considered by Mankiw et al. (1992). Standard errors are in parentheses.

Figure 5.1 Original Statistical Results from Frankel and Romer (1999).

trade share is 0.85. The t statistic, which equals the coefficient estimate divided by the standard error (i.e., 0.85/0.25), is 3.5, which is associated with a very small p value. Hence, the coefficient estimate 0.85 is statistically different from zero and positive, meaning that international trade has a positive effect on growth. Substantively, a 1% increase in the share of international trade in the national economy is associated with a 0.85% increase in income per person. The instrumental regression estimate for trade share is 1.97, which is also statistically significant and positive. Its size more than doubles the coefficient from Model 1.

In this chapter, we will focus on the process of reproducing and understanding the results in Model 1 of Table 3 in Frankel and Romer. In the process, we will show how to put a dataset together, estimate a statistical model, interpret the results, and conduct statistical inference.

Before moving on, we need to highlight an important issue related to the interpretation of coefficient estimates. Each coefficient estimate represents the marginal effect of an independent variable on the dependent variable. Ordinarily, it indicates the corresponding change in the dependent variable due to a one-unit change in that independent variable. However, when a variable, dependent or independent, is log transformed, a common practice to correct for skew distributions of variables in applied research, then the interpretation of the coefficient estimate varies.

Table 5.1 presents four types of models that do or do not use log transformed variables. The same coefficient 0.5 of the variable x is interpreted differently depending on whether only x is logged, only y is logged, or both, or neither.

Table 5.1 **Coefficient Interpretation in Log or Unlogged Models**

Type	Model	Interpretation of Coefficient of x	Formula
level-level	$y = b_0 + 0.5x + u$	A 1 unit increase in x is associated with a 0.5 unit increase in y.	
log-log	$ln(y) = b_0 + 0.5ln(x) + u$	A 1% increase in x is associated with a 0.5% increase in y.	$[100 * (1.01^{b_1} - 1)]$ $\approx b_1$
log-level	$ln(y) = b_0 + 0.5(x) + u$	A 1 unit increase in x is associated with a 65% increase in y.	$[100 * (exp^{b_1} - 1)]$
level-log	$y = b_0 + 0.5ln(x) + u$	A 1% increase in x is associated with a 0.005 unit increase in y.	$[b_1 * log(1.01)] \approx$ $(b_1/100)$

Table 5.1 helps us to understand the interpretation of the model of Frankel and Romer, which has log income per person as the dependent variable and trade as a percent of GDP as an independent variable. So the coefficient implies the percent change in per capita income as trade share increases by one unit (i.e., one percent).

Data Preparation

In the note of Appendix Table A1, Frankel and Romer list their variable definitions and data sources. We reproduce the information below to help with our reconstructing their dataset.

* Actual trade share: Ratio of imports plus exports to GDP, 1985 (Penn World Table, Mark 5.6, Series OPEN).
* Area: Rand McNally (1993).
* Population: Economically active population, 1985 (Penn World Table, Mark 5.6, constructed as RGDPCH*POP/RGDPW, where RGDPCH is real GDP per capita, RGDPW is real GDP per worker, and POP is total population).
* Income per worker: Real GDP per worker, 1985; 1985 international prices (dollars) (Penn World Table, Mark 5.6, Series RGDPCH).

Before we reconstruct the dataset, several important issues are worth noting. First, following Frankel and Romer, we will use the Penn World Table 5.6 dataset, which is part of the pwt package in R. This means that we must first install the pwt package before we can load it using the library() function. Details regarding the pwt package can be accessed at https://cran.r-project.org/web/packages/pwt/pwt.pdf, which contains the codebooks for various versions of the Penn World Table data. To facilitate reference, we list the codebook for Penn World Table 5.6 below.

- Description: Purchasing power parity (PPP) and national income accounts in international prices for 152 countries over 1950–1992 (1985 as base year).
- Usage: data("pwt5.6")
- Format: A data frame with 6,536 observations of 34 variables.

country: factor with country name.

wbcode: factor with World Bank country code.

continent: factor indicating continent.

benchmark factor: Has the country ever participated in an international benchmark study?

year: year.

pop: population in 1000s.

rgdpch: real GDP per capita (chain-weighted index, in constant US dollars).

rgdpl: real GDP per capita (Laspeyres index, US dollars in 1985 prices).

c: real consumption share of GDP (% in 1985 prices).

i: real investment share of GDP (% in 1985 prices).

g: real government share of GDP (% in 1985 prices).

rgdptt: real GDP per capita in constant dollars adjusted for changes in terms of trade (1985 international prices for domestic absorption and current prices for exports and imports).

y: per capita GDP relative to US (US=100, % in current prices).

cgdp: real gross domestic product (GDP) per capita (US dollars in current prices).

cc: real consumption share of per capita GDP (% in current prices).

ci: real investment share of per capita GDP (% in current prices).

cg: real government share of per capita GDP (% in current prices).

p: price level of GDP (PPP GDP/ US dollar exchange rate).

pc: price level of consumption (% [PPP of c]/xrat).

pi: price level of investment (% [PPP of i]/xrat).

pg: price level of government (% [PPP of g]/xrat).

xrat exchange rate (US dollars).

rgdpeqa: real GDP per equivalent adult (US dollars in 1985 prices).

rgdpwok: real GDP per worker (US dollars in 1985 prices).

kapw: non-residential capital stock per worker (US dollars in 1985 prices).

kdur: producer durables (% of kapw) (in 1985 prices).

knres: non-residential construction (% of kapw in 1985 prices).

kother: other construction (% of kapw in 1985 prices).

kres: residential construction (% of kapw in 1985 prices).

ktranp: transportation equipment (% of kapw in 1985 prices).

open: openness (exports+imports)/nominal GDP.

rgnp: real gross national product (% of per capita GDP).

ipri: gross domestic private investment (% of gross domestic investment in current prices).

`stliv`: standard of living index (consumption plus government consumption minus military expenditure, % of GDP).

- Details: The Penn World Table provides purchasing power parity and national income accounts converted to international prices for 152 countries for some or all of the years 1950–1992. This version contains data from PWT version 5.6. As far as possible the original data from PWT has been preserved. For example, percentages have been maintained rather than converted to fractions.
- Source: Alan Heston and Robert Summers, PennWorld Table Version 5.6. http://pwt.econ.upenn.edu/.

The second issue worth clarifying is that the economically active population variable needs to be computed using other variables in the dataset. This follows the formula *RGDPCH ∗ POP/RGDPWOK* (written as *RGDPCH ∗ POP/RGDPW* in Note to Table A1 in Frankel and Romer).

Finally, the area variable is from a different source, which needs to be collected and merged with the Penn World Table data. We will extract the land area variable from the World Bank statistics, which contains several hundred variables and can be used for future exercises.

In data preparation, we will first get the needed variables from the `pwt56` dataset, then extract the land area variable from the World Bank statistics, and next merge it with the Penn World Table data to produce a final dataset for use in analysis.

The relevant R code and output are as follows:

```
# Data Preparation Program
# install following packages only once, then comment out code
# install.packages(c("devtools", "data.table", "stargazer",
#                 "ggplot2", "gridExtra", "car", "pwt", "broom",
#                 "GGally"), dependencies=TRUE)

# Extract data from PWT5.6
# before running program, remove all objects in workspace
rm(list=ls(all=TRUE))

# change working directory to project folder
setwd("C:/Project")

# load pwt56 data
library(pwt)
data(pwt5.6)
```

```
# check variable names
names(pwt5.6)

 [1] "country"   "wbcode"   "continent" "benchmark"
 [5] "year"      "pop"      "rgdpch"    "rgdpl"
 [9] "c"         "i"        "g"         "rgdptt"
[13] "y"         "cgdp"     "cc"        "ci"
[17] "cg"        "p"        "pc"        "pi"
[21] "pg"        "xrat"     "rgdpeqa"   "rgdpwok"
[25] "kapw"      "kdur"     "knres"     "kother"
[29] "kres"      "ktranp"   "open"      "rgnp"
[33] "ipri"      "stliv"

# create new variable: economically active population
pwt5.6$labor <- pwt5.6$rgdpch*pwt5.6$pop/pwt5.6$rgdpwok

# compare total population and new population variables
summary(pwt5.6$pop)

   Min. 1st Qu.  Median    Mean 3rd Qu.     Max.    NA's
     39    2172    6342   28570   18710  1162000    1464

summary(pwt5.6$labor)

   Min. 1st Qu.   Median     Mean  3rd Qu.      Max.
   20.9   811.2   2586.0  11920.0   7287.0  685700.0
   NA's
   1726

# create new dataset: subset of pwt5.6, select variables, 1985
pwt.85 <- pwt5.6[pwt5.6$year==1985, c("wbcode", "country",
   "year", "rgdpwok", "rgdpch", "open", "labor", "continent")]
```

The pwt.85 dataset contains seven variables. Now, we turn to extract the land area variable from the World Bank statistics. We first install two packages, dev-tools and wbstats, with the latter one installed from the package developer's page so that the most up-to-date version can be downloaded. Then, we install a third package, data.table, to help with processing data. After package installation, we load two packages, wbstats and data.table. Next, we use the wbsearch() function to list the variables related to total area, and we use the data.table() function to extract a land area variable based on an indicator identified from the output of the wbsearch() function. We then inspect one observation from the new data object called area, and rename some variable names to be consistent with those in pwt.85 (e.g., rename date as year) or for the sake of convenience (e.g., rename AG.LND.TOTL.K2 as landarea).

```
# Extract land area variable from World Bank statistics
# install new package for extracting most up to date data
#install.packages("devtools")
devtools::install_github("GIST-ORNL/wbstats")

# load packages
library(wbstats)
library(data.table)

# search for a list of area related variables
# choose one needed
wbsearch(pattern = "total area")

              indicatorID
7516          LND.TOTL.K2
7769          EN.POP.DNST
11560       AG.LND.TOTL.K2
11561       AG.LND.TOTL.HA
12222       AG.SRF.TOTL.K2
12223       AG.SRF.TOTL.HA
15153 IN.AGR.GR.IRRIG.AREA

                                                  indicator
7516                             Total Area (in Km²)
7769   Population density (people per sq. km of land area)
11560                             Land area (sq. km)
11561                             Land area (hectares)
12222                             Surface area (sq. km)
12223                             Surface area (ha)
15153 Gross Irrigated Area under all crops ('000 hectares)

# extract land area variable based on indicator, sq km
area <- data.table(
      wb(country="all", indicator = c("AG.LND.TOTL.K2"))
      )

# view the last observation extracted
tail(area, n=1)

    value date    indicatorID          indicator iso2c
1: 386850 1961 AG.LND.TOTL.K2 Land area (sq. km)    ZW
```

```
    country
1: Zimbabwe

# rename variables
names(area)[names(area)=="value"] <- "landarea"
names(area)[names(area)=="date"] <- "year"

# list variable names
names(area)

[1] "landarea"    "year"         "indicatorID" "indicator"
[5] "iso2c"       "country"
```

It turns out that the two datasets area and pwt.85 have different matching
id variables, with iso2c in the former and wbcode (i.e., iso3c) in the latter.
Although both datasets have the country variable, different datasets often spell
the name of the same country differently and thus, country is not a good
matching id variable.

To solve this problem, we extract some country mapping data from the
wbstats package, referred to as countries. Next, we use the merge() function
to merge the two datasets area and countries, matched on the iso2c variable.
We assign the merged dataset the same name, area, to overwrite the old dataset
and then apply the data.frame() function to make sure area is a data frame.
For our analysis, we only need six variables—iso3c, landarea, year, region,
lat (latitude), long (longitude)—for 1985 only from the area dataset, which
we select as a subset and overwrite the old area dataset. We then rename the
iso3c variable as wbcode in the area dataset in order to match and merge with
the pwt.85 dataset.

```
# download country mappings from wbstat package
countries <- data.table(wbcountries())

# list variable names in countries
names(countries)

 [1] "iso3c"     "iso2c"    "country"   "capital"
 [5] "long"      "lat"      "regionID"  "region"
 [9] "adminID"   "admin"    "incomeID"  "income"
[13] "lendingID" "lending"

# merge area and countries according to iso2c
area <- merge(area, countries, by=c("iso2c"), sort=TRUE)
area <- data.frame(area)
```

```
# keep needed variables and observations from area dataset
area <- area[area$year==1985, c("iso3c","landarea","year",
                                "region","lat","long")]

# rename iso3c to wbcode to merge with pwt.85
names(area)[names(area)=="iso3c"] <- "wbcode"

# list variable names in dataset
names(area)

[1] "wbcode"    "landarea" "year"      "region"    "lat"
[6] "long"
```

We then merge pwt.85 and area, matched on the wbcode and year variables. The option all.x=TRUE means that all observations from the first listed dataset are kept, i.e., observations from area that do not match are dropped. Next, we inspect the merged dataset by examining its object class, variable names, and last observation. The next step is to create log transformed variables as required by the model. The last step is to save the file as an R dataset for use in the analysis program later.

```
# merge area1 and pwt.85 to create the analysis dataset
# keep only observations that match with pwt.85 data
final.85 <- merge(pwt.85, area, by=c("wbcode", "year"),
                  all.x=TRUE, sort=TRUE)

# display object class, variable names, and last observation
class(final.85)

[1] "data.frame"

names(final.85)

 [1] "wbcode"    "year"      "country"   "rgdpwok"
 [5] "rgdpch"    "open"      "labor"     "continent"
 [9] "landarea"  "region"    "lat"       "long"

tail(final.85, n=1)

    wbcode year        country rgdpwok rgdpch  open    labor
152    WSM 1985 Western Samoa    5388   1726 92.17 50.29362
    continent landarea              region      lat
152   Oceania     2830 East Asia & Pacific -13.8314
        long
```

```
152 -171.752

# create new variables for analysis
final.85$logy <- log(final.85$rgdpch)
final.85$loglab <- log(final.85$labor)
final.85$logland <- log(final.85$landarea)

# save R dataset
save(final.85, file="final.85.RData")
```

Having reconstructed the dataset, we will now start a data analysis program file with the following R code:

```
# Data Analysis Program
# before running program, remove all objects in workspace
rm(list=ls(all=TRUE))

# change working directory to project folder
setwd("C:/Project")

# load R data
load("final.85.RData")
```

Visualize and Inspect Data

Once the dataset is ready, the first thing we should do is to examine the descriptive statistics of the variables and graph the key scatter plot so that we may spot unusual data patterns, including possible coding errors. Like in Chapter 1, we can apply the stargazer package and report the descriptive statistics in Table 5.2.

```
# load stargazer into R
library(stargazer)

# produce formatted descriptive statistics in pwt56.final
stargazer(final.85, type="text",  median = TRUE)
```

As shown in Table 5.2, real income per person, rgdpch, has an average of 4,423 international dollars but a median of 2,564 international dollars, which suggests a rather skewed distribution; in contrast, the log real income per person, logy, has an average of 7.891 and a median of 7.849. Hence, the log transformation has made the distribution of the variable more symmetric.

Table 5.2 **Descriptive Statistics of Final Dataset**

Statistic	N	Mean	St. Dev.	Min	Median	Max
year	152	1,985.000	0.000	1,985	1,985	1,985
rgdpwok	151	10,696.670	9,635.187	705	7,091	38,190
rgdpch	152	4,423.257	4,423.595	299	2,564	19,648
open	152	73.874	45.928	13.160	63.715	318.070
labor	150	13,314.110	56,733.470	29.314	2,547.374	612,363.100
landarea	141	716,704.000	1,653,680.000	260	196,850	9,388,250
logy	152	7.891	1.042	5.700	7.849	9.886
loglab	150	7.663	1.931	3.378	7.843	13.325
logland	141	11.679	2.421	5.561	12.190	16.055

The following R code compares the histograms of rgdpch and logy. Note how we use the geom_vline() option to draw a line denoting the mean of each variable. Figure 5.2 shows the two histograms.

```
# load packages
library(ggplot2)
library(gridExtra)

# histogram of rgdpch as data object
hist1 <- ggplot(final.85, aes(rgdpch)) +
        geom_histogram() +
        geom_vline(xintercept=4423, color="red")

# histogram of logy as data object
hist2 <- ggplot(final.85, aes(logy)) +
        geom_histogram() +
        geom_vline(xintercept=7.891, color="red")

# display plots together
grid.arrange(hist1, hist2, ncol=2)
```

Following the example in Chapter 4, we can construct a scatter plot between open and logy, with their mean values drawn from their respective axes. Figure 5.3 helps us to visualize the relationship between the two variables. The R code is identical to that in Chapter 4, with one exception. We add the geom_text() with aes(label=country) embedded to indicate that we label each data point with its value of the country variable.

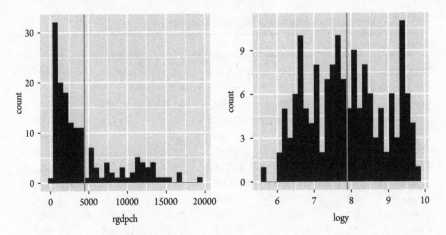

Figure 5.2 Comparing Unlogged and Logged Income per Person.

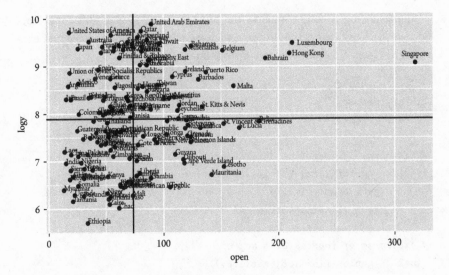

Figure 5.3 Trade Openness and Log of Income per Person.

```
# scatter plot of open and log of real income per capita
ggplot(final.85, aes(x=open, y=logy))+
  geom_point() +
  geom_vline(xintercept = 73.874) +
  geom_hline(yintercept = 7.891) +
  geom_text(aes(label=country),hjust=0,vjust=0)
```

Figure 5.3 indicates a positive relationship between the two variables in 1985, with most observations falling in the upper right and lower left quadrants.

Countries like Singapore and Luxembourg are high in both dimensions, whereas Ethiopia and Myanmar are low on both variables. Still, there are many other countries in the lower right quadrant, like Lesotho and Mauritania that are open to trade but very low in per capita income. Interestingly, we find in the upper left quadrant such advanced economies as the United States and Japan that have very high per capita income and yet very low trade openness.

How to Estimate and Interpret OLS Model Coefficients

What technique should we use to estimate the sample regression model? As noted earlier, we use OLS, which is to find a set of coefficient estimates that minimizes the residual sum of squares. The specific OLS estimator (or equation) for the vector of coefficients in the sample model, denoted as B containing a, b, c_1, and c_2, can be expressed as follows:

$$B = (\mathbf{X'X})^{-1}\mathbf{X'Y} = \left(\sum \mathbf{x}_i \mathbf{x}'_i\right)^{-1}\left(\sum \mathbf{x}_i y_i\right)$$

The essence of the formula is that it allows us to find the set of B (i.e., a, b, c_1, and c_2) that minimizes the residual sum of squares.

The R code for obtaining the OLS coefficient estimates and related output is straightforward. We begin with the lm() function, which represents a linear model. The argument inside the function includes the dependent variable, followed by a tilde and the independent variables connected by plus sign, and the data= option for specifying the dataset. Once the model is estimated, the output from the lm() function is assigned to some object, which we refer to as model1. To demonstrate the content of the model output, we simply apply the summary() function to model1.

```
# estimate OLS model and create output object
model1 <- lm(logy ~ open + loglab + logland, data=final.85)


# show model output
summary(model1)


Call:
lm(formula = logy ~ open + loglab + logland, data = final.85)

Residuals:
     Min       1Q   Median       3Q      Max
-2.07067 -0.82670 -0.08307  0.64393  2.10651
```

```
Coefficients:
            Estimate Std. Error t value Pr(>|t|)
(Intercept)  6.588159   0.720802   9.140  8.3e-16 ***
open         0.008280   0.002583   3.206  0.00168 **
loglab       0.154185   0.066221   2.328  0.02138 *
logland     -0.044109   0.056274  -0.784  0.43451
---
Signif. codes:
0 '***' 0.001 '**' 0.01 '*' 0.05 '.' 0.1 ' ' 1

Residual standard error: 0.9875 on 135 degrees of freedom
  (13 observations deleted due to missingness)
Multiple R-squared:  0.1007,Adjusted R-squared:  0.08069
F-statistic: 5.038 on 3 and 135 DF,  p-value: 0.002434
```

The output shows the model estimated, summary information for the residuals, OLS coefficient estimates (Estimate), their standard errors (Std. Error), t statistics (t value), p values ($Pr(> abs(t))$), statistical significance indicated by the asterisks, the residual standard error, the degree of freedom (i.e., sample size minus the number of coefficient estimates), multiple R-squared, adjusted R-squared, and F-test statistic information.

We focus on interpreting the coefficient of open, which is shown to be 0.00828 in the column Estimate. Based on Table 5.1, since the dependent variable is logged and open is not, the coefficient should be transformed as $[100 * (exp^{b_1} - 1)] = [100 * (exp^{0.00828} - 1)] \approx 0.831\%$. This means that holding everything else constant, a one-unit increase in trade openness, which is equivalent to a 1% increase in the share of international trade in GDP, is associated with a 0.831% increase in real income per person.

This effect is certainly consistent with, though slightly smaller than, the 0.85% estimate in Frankel and Romer's Model 1 in Figure 5.1. This small discrepancy might be accounted for by one difference in data. Our model is based on 139 observations (i.e., the degree of freedom plus number of coefficient estimates and intercept), whereas the Frankel and Romer model is based on 150 observations. We have 11 fewer observations, probably due to missing values of the land area variable. Overall, however, our estimate is almost exactly the same as theirs.

Our estimates of the intercept (6.588), loglab (0.154), and logland (−0.044) are also consistent with those in Model 1 of Table 3 in Frankel and Romer, which are 7.40, 0.12, and −0.01, respectively. According to Table 5.1, the coefficient of loglab means that holding everything else constant, a 1% increase in the active labor force is associated with a 0.154 percent increase in real income per person, and the coefficient of logland means that a 1% increase in land area is associated with a 0.044 percent decrease in real income per person. According to Frankel and Romer, because both the active labor force and land area capture the size of domestic commerce, their effects should be interpreted and tested together, an issue we will address in the Miscellaneous section of the chapter.

Having obtained the coefficient estimate b of open, what shall we do next in statistical inference? In other words, if we accept it as a valid estimate of the population parameter β_1, what inferences can we make about the effect of trade openness on growth in the population? The answer is that we must also find out the standard error around the coefficient estimate, which captures the uncertainty we have, so that we can carry out null hypothesis testing and confidence interval construction like in previous chapters.

How to Estimate Standard Error of Coefficient

We already know β_1 is constant, about which we make inferences based on b. Like discussed in previous chapters, since a sample statistic like b changes from one sample to another, it behaves like a random variable and follows some probability distribution (called sampling distribution). The standard error of the sample statistic like b captures the uncertainty in that sampling distribution. Once we establish the standard error of b, we may carry out statistical inferences like before.

We first need to estimate the variance of b, denoted as $Var(b)$, whose square root is the standard error of b. We will obtain $Var(b)$ from the variance and covariance matrix of the OLS estimator B. It is a matrix because the sample model includes a, b, c_1, and c_2, and it can be formally defined as follows:

$$Var(B) = E[(B - \beta)(B - \beta)'] = (X'X)^{-1}X'E[\varepsilon\varepsilon']X(X'X)^{-1} = \sigma^2(X'X)^{-1}$$

In the expression, σ^2 is the true variance of the error term ε in the population regression model. Since σ^2 is unknown, we have to estimate it using its sample variant, i.e., s^2 (the variance of the residual u_i in the sample regression model). Hence, the estimated variance-covariance matrix of B is $s^2(X'X)^{-1}$.

The notational form of the variance-covariance matrix of the OLS estimator B looks as follows:

$$Var(B) = E[(B - \beta)(B - \beta)'] = \begin{bmatrix} var(a) & cov(a,b) & cov(a,c_1) & cov(a,c_2) \\ cov(b,a) & var(b) & cov(b,c_1) & cov(b,c_2) \\ cov(c_1,a) & cov(c_1,b) & var(c_1) & cov(c_1,c_2) \\ cov(c_2,a) & cov(c_2,b) & cov(c_2,c_1) & var(c_2) \end{bmatrix}$$

Along the diagonal of this variance-covariance matrix lies the variance of each coefficient in the vector B, denoted by $var(a)$, $var(b)$, $var(c_1)$, and $var(c_2)$.

In R, we request the estimated variance-covariance matrix of B using the vcov() function.

```
# show variance-covariance matrix of B in model1
vcov(model1)
```

	(Intercept)	open	loglab
(Intercept)	0.519556111	-1.497506e-03	-1.311325e-02
open	-0.001497506	6.670097e-06	4.603039e-05
loglab	-0.013113254	4.603039e-05	4.385185e-03
logland	-0.025911639	5.626562e-05	-2.011784e-03

	logland
(Intercept)	-2.591164e-02
open	5.626562e-05
loglab	-2.011784e-03
logland	3.166816e-03

The variance of b from model1, which is in the second row and second column, is $6.670097e - 06$. Its square root, i.e., the standard error of b, is 0.002583, which is identical to the value for open in the Std. Error column in the model1 output shown earlier. Interested readers may verify the results of other variables by hand.

How to Make an Inference about the Population Parameter of Interest

We may think about the relationship between the sample estimate b and the population parameter β_1 within the context of OLS estimation and the Gauss-Markov theorem as follows:

$$b \sim N(\beta_1, Var(b))$$

According to the expression, the sample regression coefficient b is assumed to be normally distributed with mean β_1 and variance $Var(b)$.

It is essential for us to understand the nature of this expression because the statistical inferences we are making later on hinge on the following thought experiment. If we draw a first sample from the population and apply the OLS estimator equation listed in the previous section, we will obtain one b value as the first estimate of β_1; if we repeat the process with a second sample, we will obtain a second b value as the second estimate of β_1; and if we estimate our model in repeated samples, we will obtain as many b estimates as the number of samples we draw from the population. As a result, b behaves like a random variable, i.e., its value varies from one sample to another. These estimates of b from repeated samples form a probability distribution, called the sampling distribution of the sample regression coefficient estimator b. As noted, b is assumed to be normally distributed with mean β_1 and variance $Var(b)$.

Based on this background information, we will use null hypothesis testing and confidence interval construction to make two types of statistical inferences from the sample coefficient b to the population parameter β_1. Below we will discuss them in turn using the results from model1.

Hypothesis Testing

One method of statistical inferences is to test a hypothesis regarding a hypothetical population parameter value of β_1.

Null hypothesis $H_0 : \beta_1 = 0$. Trade openness has no effect on economic growth in the population.
Alternative hypothesis $H_a : \beta_1 \neq 0$. Trade openness has an effect on economic growth in the population.

To test the null hypothesis directly, we have to construct a test statistic, denoted as t.

$$t = \frac{b - \beta_1}{se(b)}$$

This t-test statistic is similar in spirit to the t-test statistic on a hypothetical population mean introduced in Chapter 3. They are both essentially the difference between the sample estimate and the hypothetical population parameter, weighted by the standard error of the sample estimate. In both scenarios, the test statistic follows a t-distribution and hence, is referred to as the t-statistic.

Take the results from model1 as an example. The estimated b value in model1 is 0.00828, and the $se(b)$ value is 0.002583. The hypothesized β_1 value is 0. Hence, the test statistic can be rewritten as:

$$t = \frac{b - \beta_1}{se(b)} = \frac{0.00828 - 0}{0.002583} = 3.205575$$

The t value, as shown in the t value column in the model1 output, is 3.206.

As in previous null hypothesis testing, we must find the p value associated with the computed test statistic value 3.206, and then compare it against our acceptable Type I error rate α, in order to make our decision. If the p value is smaller than α, the null hypothesis will be rejected, and we will conclude that trade openness has an effect on growth; if the p value is larger than α, the null hypothesis will not be rejected, and we will conclude that trade openness has no effect on growth. As shown in the $Pr(> abs(t))$ column of the model1 output, the

p value for the t statistic for open is 0.00168, which is far below the conventional α level 0.05. Hence, we conclude that trade openness has a statistically significant and positive effect on growth.

Confidence Interval

A second method of making inference about the population parameter β_1 is to estimate a confidence interval using the sample estimate b and a margin of error. In the context of regression models, we may apply the following formula:

$$b \pm t_{(1-\alpha/2),n-k} \times se(b)$$

where α is the acceptable Type I error rate and $(1-\alpha)100\%$ is the confidence level chosen by the analyst.

In the context of open in model1, the 95% confidence interval for β_1 can be represented as:

$$b \pm t_{(1-\alpha/2),n-k} \times se(b) = 0.00828 \pm t_{95\%,139} \times 0.002583$$

To request the confidence interval estimates in R, we apply the *confint*() function to model1. The output below shows the lower bound value at 2.5% and the upper bound value at 97.5%, which constitutes the 95% confidence interval.

```
# confidence interval estimates from model1
confint(model1)

                 2.5 %      97.5 %
(Intercept)  5.162633541 8.01368425
open         0.003172303 0.01338769
loglab       0.023221048 0.28514950
logland     -0.155403059 0.06718410
```

We may interpret the confidence interval estimates as follows. We are 95% confident that the effect of trade on growth in the population ranges between 0.003172296 and 0.01338768. Substantively speaking, we are 95% confident that a 1% increase in trade openness is associated with an increase in real income per person somewhere between 0.32% and 1.34%.

How to Interpret Overall Model Fit

It is worth noting that the lm() function provides other useful information, particularly overall model fit, about the statistical model we have estimated. In this section, we explain those statistics in model1 output and their conceptual logic.

Conceptually, a dependent variable Y, whose behaviors we seek to explain, can be decomposed into a systematic component predicted by our substantive theory, $\hat{Y}$, and a random component, ε, which can not be explained by our theory. We can represent the idea for the population as follows:

$$Y_i = \hat{Y}_i + \varepsilon_i$$

Its sample equivalent would be:

$$y_i = \hat{y}_i + e_i$$

The expression above can be further redefined in detail as follows:

1. Total variations in y, i.e., Total Sum of Squares (TSS).

$$\sum_{i=1}^{n} (y_i - \bar{y})^2$$

It means the sum of squared deviations of actual y from mean of y (i.e., $\bar{y}$) across observations.

2. Explained variations in y, i.e., Explained Sum of Squares (ESS).

$$\sum_{i=1}^{n} (\hat{y}_i - \bar{y})^2$$

It means the sum of squared deviations of predicted $\hat{y}$ from mean $\bar{y}$ across observations.

3. Unexplained variations in y, i.e., Residual Sum of Squares (RSS).

$$\sum_{i=1}^{n} (y_i - \hat{y})^2$$

It means the sum of squared deviations of actual y from predicted $\hat{y}$ across observations, or the sum of squared residuals u_i.

4. Total Sum of Squares = Explained Sum of Squares + Residual Sum of Squares.

$$\sum_{i=1}^{n} (y_i - \bar{y})^2 = \sum_{i=1}^{n} (\hat{y}_i - \bar{y})^2 + \sum_{i=1}^{n} (y_i - \hat{y})^2$$

That is, TSS = ESS + RSS.

5. The principle of OLS is to find the set of coefficient estimates that minimizes RSS. How good a model is can be measured by the share of ESS in TSS, which is called model R-squared.

In R, we may use the anova() function to request these results.

```
# show ESS and RSS from model output
anova(model1)

Analysis of Variance Table

Response: logy
            Df  Sum Sq  Mean Sq  F value   Pr(>F)
open         1   9.143   9.1433   9.3755 0.002654 **
loglab       1   4.996   4.9959   5.1228 0.025209 *
logland      1   0.599   0.5992   0.6144 0.434514
Residuals  135 131.656   0.9752
---
Signif. codes:
0 '***' 0.001 '**' 0.01 '*' 0.05 '.' 0.1 ' ' 1
```

The sum-of-squares output is shown in the second column Sum Sq. The RSS is 131.656, and the ESS is the sum of squares across open, loglab, and logland, which is 14.738 (the sum of 9.143, 4.996, and 0.599). Hence, the TSS is the sum of RSS and ESS, which equals 146.394 (not shown in the anova output).

The model fit statistic, R-squared, is defined as follows:

$$R^2 = \frac{ESS}{TSS} = \frac{\sum_{i=1}^{n} \left(\hat{y}_i - \bar{y} \right)^2}{\sum_{i=1}^{n} \left(y_i - \bar{y} \right)^2}$$

As a result, R^2 is ESS as a share of TSS. In other words, it measures the amount of variations in the dependent variable explained by the systematic component of the model. Based on the values of ESS and TSS above, we can compute the R-squared, which is 0.10. This is identical to the value in the model1 output. The result means that the model explains roughly 10% of the total variations in the dependent variable. Given how simple the model is, this result is hardly surprising. The model1 output also reports the adjusted R-squared (0.08), which downward adjusts the R-squared value as the number of independent variables increases in a model.

Another model fit test statistic is F-statistic. It tests the null hypothesis that all coefficients are simultaneously equal to zero. In other words, none of the independent variables explains the dependent variable. This is not a very interesting hypothesis since we have no interest in estimating a model that does not explain the dependent variable at all. The alternative hypothesis is that at least one of the independent variables explains the dependent variable. The F-statistic value for the model1 output is 5.038, with a p value of 0.0024. If we set α at 5%, the null hypothesis that none of the independent variables explains the variations in the dependent variable will be rejected.

How to Present Statistical Results

Regression results are often reported in tables and graphs. To present regression results in a formatted table, we may utilize the stargazer package.

```
# report regression results
library(stargazer)
stargazer(model1, type="text", no.space=TRUE,
          omit.stat=c("ser"), model.names=FALSE,
          dep.var.labels.include=FALSE, dep.var.caption="")
```

In the stargazer() function, we first specify the model output object model1 to be reported and then the type of table reported, followed by a series of options to customize table format. Option no.space=TRUE removes empty lines; omit.stat=c("ser") omits residual standard error; dep.var.labels.include= FALSE and dep.var.caption="" suppress dependent variable caption and label; model.names=FALSE suppresses model name. Other useful options not employed here include ci=TRUE and ci.level=0.95, which request that 95% confidence intervals be reported.

To plot the regression coefficients and their confidence intervals, we use the ggcoef() function from the GGally package, which also requires loading the broom package. In the ggcoef() function, we simply list the model output object. Note that the model estimated earlier has a very large intercept, making other coefficients difficult to see in the plot. Hence, we exclude the intercept from the

Table 5.3 **Effect of Trade Openness on Real Income per Person**

open	0.008***
	(0.003)
loglab	0.154**
	(0.066)
logland	−0.044
	(0.056)
Constant	6.588***
	(0.721)
Observations	139
R2	0.101
Adjusted R2	0.081
Note:	*p<0.1; **p<0.05; ***p<0.01

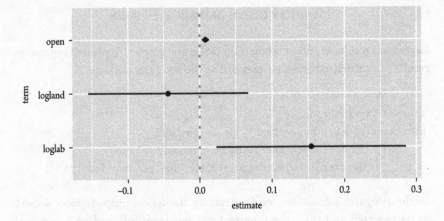

Figure 5.4 Coefficients Plot for Model 1.

plot in the ggcoef() function. Table 5.1 reports the model results and Figure 5.4 presents the model results graphically.

```
# load required packages
library(broom)
library(GGally)

# plot coefficients
ggcoef(model1, exclude_intercept = TRUE)
```

Chapter 5 Program Code

Data Preparation Program

```
# install following packages only once, then comment out code
# install.packages(c("devtools", "data.table", "stargazer",
#            "ggplot2", "gridExtra", "car", "pwt", "broom",
#            "GGally"), dependencies=TRUE)


# Extract data from PWT5.6
# before running program, remove all objects in workspace
rm(list=ls(all=TRUE))


# change working directory to project folder
setwd("C:/Project")


# load pwt56 data
```

```
library(pwt)
data(pwt5.6)

# check variable names
names(pwt5.6)

# create new variable-economically active population
pwt5.6$labor <- pwt5.6$rgdpch*pwt5.6$pop/pwt5.6$rgdpwok

# compare total population and new population variables
summary(pwt5.6$pop)
summary(pwt5.6$labor)

# create new dataset: subset of pwt5.6, select variables, 1985
pwt.85 <- pwt5.6[pwt5.6$year==1985, c("wbcode", "country",
    "year", "rgdpwok", "rgdpch", "open", "labor", "continent")]

# Extract land area variable from World Bank statistics
# install new package for extracting most up to date data
#install.packages("devtools")
devtools::install_github("GIST-ORNL/wbstats")

# load packages
library(wbstats)
library(data.table)

# search for a list of area related variables
# choose one needed
wbsearch(pattern = "total area")

# extract land area variable based on indicator, sq km
area <- data.table(
        wb(country="all", indicator = c("AG.LND.TOTL.K2"))
        )

# view the last observation extracted
tail(area, n=1)

# rename variables
names(area)[names(area)=="value"] <- "landarea"
names(area)[names(area)=="date"] <- "year"
```

```r
# list variable names
names(area)

# download country mappings from wbstat package
countries <- data.table(wbcountries())

# list variable names in countries
names(countries)

# merge area and countries according to iso2c
area <- merge(area, countries, by=c("iso2c"), sort=TRUE)
area <- data.frame(area)

# keep needed variables and observations from area dataset
area <- area[area$year==1985, c("iso3c","landarea","year",
                                "region","lat","long")]

# rename iso3c to wbcode to merge with pwt.85
names(area)[names(area)=="iso3c"] <- "wbcode"

# list variable names in dataset
names(area)

# merge area1 and pwt.85 to create the analysis dataset
# keep only observations that match with pwt.85 data
final.85 <- merge(pwt.85, area, by=c("wbcode", "year"),
                  all.x=TRUE, sort=TRUE)

# display object class, variable names, and last observation
class(final.85)
names(final.85)
tail(final.85, n=1)

# create new variables for analysis
final.85$logy <- log(final.85$rgdpch)
final.85$loglab <- log(final.85$labor)
final.85$logland <- log(final.85$landarea)

# save R dataset
save(final.85, file="final.85.RData")
```

Data Analysis Program

```r
# before running program, remove all objects in workspace
rm(list=ls(all=TRUE))

# change working directory to project folder
setwd("C:/Project")

# load R data
load("final.85.RData")

# load stargazer into R
library(stargazer)

# produce formatted descriptive statistics in pwt56.final
stargazer(final.85, type="text",  median = TRUE)

# load packages
library(ggplot2)
library(gridExtra)

# histogram of rgdpch as data object
hist1 <- ggplot(final.85, aes(rgdpch)) +
        geom_histogram() +
        geom_vline(xintercept=4423, color="red")

# histogram of logy as data object
hist2 <- ggplot(final.85, aes(logy)) +
        geom_histogram() +
        geom_vline(xintercept=7.891, color="red")

# display plots together
grid.arrange(hist1, hist2, ncol=2)

# scatter plot of open and log of real income per capita
ggplot(final.85, aes(x=open, y=logy))+
  geom_point() +
  geom_vline(xintercept = 73.874) +
  geom_hline(yintercept = 7.891) +
  geom_text(aes(label=country),hjust=0,vjust=0)

# estimate OLS model and create output object
```

```
model1 <- lm(logy ~ open + loglab + logland, data=final.85)

# show model output
summary(model1)

# show variance-covariance matrix of B in model1
vcov(model1)

# show confidence interval estimates from model1
confint(model1)

# show ESS and RSS from model output
anova(model1)

# report regression results
library(stargazer)
stargazer(model1, type="text", no.space=TRUE,
          omit.stat=c("ser"), model.names=FALSE,
          dep.var.labels.include=FALSE, dep.var.caption="")

# load required packages
library(broom)
library(GGally)

# plot coefficients
ggcoef(model1, exclude_intercept = TRUE)
```

Summary

In this chapter, we have learned how to use R and regression analysis to answer the question: Does trade promote economic growth? We have learned about the logic of regression analysis, the relationship between population and sample regression models, the estimation of sample regression model using OLS, the interpretation of estimation results, the statistical inference in regression analysis, and the types of sum of squares and overall model fit. As indicated in various parts of the chapter, the validity of regression analysis depends on the assumptions of the Gauss-Markov theorem being met. Notably, the model is linear in parameters and correctly specified; the independent variables are not perfectly correlated; the long-run average of the error term is zero; the error variance is constant across observations; the error term and the independent variables are uncorrelated; the observations of the error term are not serially correlated. In the next chapter, therefore, we will learn how to diagnose and correct for various assumption violations in R.

Miscellaneous Q&As for Ambitious Readers
What Information can we get from lm() Model Output?

```
# estimate OLS model and create output object
model1 <- lm(logy ~ open + loglab + logland, data=final.85)

# understand the nature of model output
names(model1)
class(model1)
mode(model1)

#request various estimation output
# anova table and results
anova(model1)

# model coefficients
coefficients(model1)

# confidence interval of coefficient estimates, 95% and 99%
confint(model1)
confint(model1, level=0.99)

# covariance matrix for model coefficient estimates
vcov(model1)

# Other useful functions
# list predicted values of the fitted model
fitted(model1)

# list residuals of the fitted model
residuals(model1)

# use fitted model to get predicted y
predict(model1)
```

How do we use Matrix Algebra to Solve for OLS Coefficient Estimates Step by Step?

We can use the lm() function to obtain the OLS coefficient estimates as follows:

```
# estimate OLS model and show output
model1 <- lm(logy ~ open + loglab + logland, data = final.85)


coefficients(model1)

 (Intercept)          open       loglab       logland
 6.588158896   0.008279996   0.154185276  -0.044109479
```

Here for those readers familiar with matrix algebra, we show how we can solve for the same coefficient estimates in a step-by-step manner. We first select only observations that do not have missing values on the variables in the model, using the complete.cases() function. Then we create a matrix x including the three independent variables plus a column of ones for the intercept term, and we assign the dependent variable to a vector y.

```
# preparing data
final.85 <- final.85[complete.cases(final.85),]

x <- cbind(1, as.matrix(final.85[, c("open", "loglab",
                                     "logland")]))

y <- final.85[, "logy"]
```

Finally, we solve for the OLS coefficient estimates as defined by the following formula earlier in the chapter,

$$B = (\mathbf{X'X})^{-1}\mathbf{X'Y} = \left(\sum \mathbf{x}_i \mathbf{x'}_i\right)^{-1}\left(\sum \mathbf{x}_i y_i\right)$$

The corresponding R code is as follows:

```
# matrix calculation of OLS estimates
solve(t(x) %*% x) %*% t(x) %*% y

                  [,1]
           6.588158896
open       0.008279996
loglab     0.154185276
logland   -0.044109479
```

The %*% operator represents matrix multiplication; the t() function finds the transpose of the matrix *x*; the solve() function computes the inverse of any matrix.

How do we Compute TSS, ESS, and RSS by Formula?

```
# compute TSS, ESS, and RSS TSS-total sum of squares in y
sum((final.85$logy - mean(final.85$logy))^2)

[1] 146.3949

# ESS-explained sum of squares in y
sum((predict(model1) - mean(final.85$logy))^2)

[1] 14.73841

# RSS-residual sum of squares in y
sum((final.85$logy - predict(model1))^2)

[1] 131.6565
```

How do we Understand Holding Everything Else Constant Through Partial Regression?

The coefficient of an independent variable on the dependent variable is interpreted as the effect of the independent variable, while holding other variables in the model constant. We can understand the meaning of holding other variables constant via an example of partial regression.

Take the model used earlier as an example. We first regress logy on the other two independent variables loglab and logland, obtain the residual, and call it yres, which represents the component of logy unexplained by population and land area. Then, we regress open on the other two independent variables loglab and logland, obtain the residual, and call it openres, which represents the component of open unexplained by population and land area. Note how the option na.action = na.exclude is included in the lm() function so that missing values are excluded rather than omitted. Without this option, an error message will be produced in including the residual and fitted value variables into the original dataset.

Next, when we regress yres on openres, we find that the coefficient of openres is the same as open in the original model (as well as other results).

```
# obtain logy unexplained by population and land
model2 <- lm(logy ~ loglab + logland, data=final.85,
```

```
                na.action = na.exclude)
final.85$yres <- residuals(model2)

# obtain open unexplained by population and land
model3 <- lm(open ~ loglab + logland, data=final.85,
             na.action = na.exclude)
final.85$openres <- residuals(model3)

# effect of open on logy (population and land held constant)
model4<-lm(yres ~ openres, data=final.85)
summary(model4)


Call:
lm(formula = yres ~ openres, data = final.85)

Residuals:
    Min      1Q   Median      3Q     Max
-2.07067 -0.82670 -0.08307  0.64393  2.10651

Coefficients:
             Estimate  Std. Error  t value  Pr(>|t|)
(Intercept) 1.511e-16  8.315e-02   0.00     1.00000
openres     8.280e-03  2.564e-03   3.23     0.00155 **
---
Signif. codes:
0 '***' 0.001 '**' 0.01 '*' 0.05 '.' 0.1 ' ' 1

Residual standard error: 0.9803 on 137 degrees of freedom
Multiple R-squared:  0.07075, Adjusted R-squared:  0.06397
F-statistic: 10.43 on 1 and 137 DF,  p-value: 0.001552
```

We can use ggplot to construct a partial regression plot between yres and openres. The R code is as follows. Note how the option stat_smooth() is added for graphing the partial regression line. Figure 5.5 shows the plot.

```
# partial regression plot
ggplot(final.85, aes(x=openres, y=yres)) +
  geom_point() +
  geom_text(aes(label=country),hjust=0,vjust=0) +
  stat_smooth(method="lm")
```

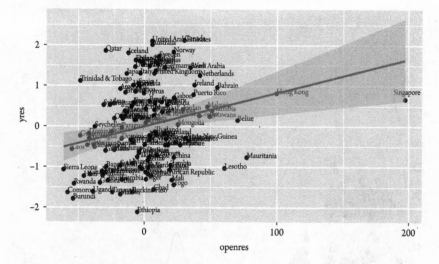

Figure 5.5 Partial Regression Plot.

Alternatively, we could use the avPlot() function in the car package to graphically demonstrate the partial regression plot for each independent variable in the model. The plot is straightforward. The R code is as follows.

```
# produce model estimation output
model1 <- lm(logy ~ open + loglab + logland, data = final.85)

# load packages
library(car)

# partial regression plot
avPlots(model1)
```

How do we Create a Pairwise Scatter Plot Among Multiple Variables?

The R base has the pairs() function that can produce rather primitive pairwise scatterplots. The ggscatmat() function in the GGally package can produce much more—a figure that includes pairwise scatter plots, density plots, and correlation coefficients. It helps us explore the relationships among the variables, in terms of correlation strength and direction, any non-linear pattern, variable distribution, outliers, and possible coding errors. The R code and Figure 5.6 are as follows. As a caveat, the ggscatmat() function only works for numeric data; with categorical data, the ggpairs() function can be used.

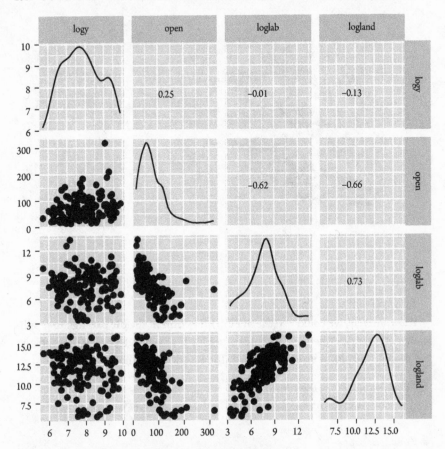

Figure 5.6 Explore Pairwise Relationships among Variables.

```
# explore pairwise relationships among variables
library(GGally)
ggscatmat(final.85v2, columns = c("logy", "open", "loglab",
    "logland"))
```

Exercises

1. Re-estimate the trade-growth model in Frankel and Romer for 1995 and 2005, respectively. Discuss how the effect of trade openness changes over time.
2. Re-estimate the trade-growth model in Frankel and Romer, adding a variable for the share of FDI net inflows over GDP drawn from the World Bank statistics. Discuss the findings and their similarities and differences from the original model results.
3. Design some hypotheses regarding the effects of partisanship and electoral system on wage inequality. Graph the relationship using an appropriate figure,

using the data in Soskice and Iversen (2006). Estimate a regression model. Based on the example in this chapter, interpret the findings. Discuss the substantive meaning of the findings for the question asked.

4. Design some hypotheses regarding the effects of natural resource endowment in a country and its mountainous terrain on the spread of military conflict. Graph the relationship using an appropriate figure, using the data in Braithwaite (2006). Estimate a regression model and interpret the findings. Discuss the substantive meaning of the findings for the question asked.

6

Regression Diagnostics and Sensitivity Analysis

Chapter Objectives

In Chapter 5, we showed how to use regression analysis and R to answer a substantive question: Does trade promote economic growth? We demonstrated how to specify a statistical model from a theoretical argument, prepare data, estimate and interpret the statistical model, and use the estimated results to make inferences and answer the question of interest. As noted at the end of Chapter 5, the validity of our findings depends on whether the assumptions for the statistical model are satisfied or not and how sensitive the results are to assumption violations. In this chapter, we will demonstrate how to conduct diagnostic tests and sensitivity analysis in R. Our objectives in this chapter are as follows:

1. Learn about the assumptions of OLS modeling and their impact.
2. Learn to diagnose assumption violations in OLS modeling.
3. Learn to conduct sensitivity analysis to assumption violations.

Why Are OLS Assumptions and Diagnostics Important?

Since this book emphasizes using R for data analysis, we will not delve into the mathematical details of the properties of OLS estimates. Numerous textbooks provide sufficient discussions for interested readers. However, even in applied work, we need to be aware of the properties of our estimates in order to have confidence in the validity of our findings.

In terms of the OLS estimator of the parameter in the population regression, the Gauss-Markov theorem provides the theoretical foundation for us to evaluate its property. According to the Gauss-Markov theorem, the OLS estimator b is the best linear unbiased estimator (BLUE) of the population parameter β among all unbiased estimators if the following conditions are satisfied:

1. The model is linear in parameter and correctly specified.
2. The independent variables are not perfectly correlated.
3. The long-run average of the error term is zero.
4. The error term and the independent variables are uncorrelated.
5. The error variance is constant across observations.
6. The observations of the error term are not correlated.

If the OLS estimator is BLUE, that is the ideal scenario. It is incumbent upon us as analysts to verify, using a variety of diagnostics, whether these conditions are satisfied or not. When a condition is violated, we need to be aware of its impact on our inference from a sample estimate to the population parameter, and when possible, make corrections to restore the BLUE property of the OLS estimate, and verify if the original findings are sensitive to this correction or not.

In order to conduct hypothesis testing and construct a confidence interval, one additional condition needs to be satisfied: the error term is normally distributed. Without this distributional assumption, we will not be able to conduct the types of statistical tests introduced earlier.

Finally, in applied research, it often happens that certain outliers have undue influences over model estimates or predictions. Hence, it is important to ask why those outliers occur and how sensitive the results are to those outliers.

We will illustrate why it is important to check regression assumptions and what some violations might look like. We will start with Anscombe's quartet example discussed in the Miscellaneous Q&A Section in Chapter 4. In that example, four datasets with eleven observations each produce identical correlation coefficients even though their scatter plots present four distinct bivariate relationships. In fact, if we estimate four regression models, we will obtain four identical sets of regression results in spite of four distinct relationships.

The R code, regression output, and contrasting figure are as follows.

```
# display regression results from Anscombe quartet
a1 <- lm(y1~x1, data=anscombe)
a2 <- lm(y2~x2, data=anscombe)
a3 <- lm(y3~x3, data=anscombe)
a4 <- lm(y4~x4, data=anscombe)


# report Anscombe quartet regression results
library(stargazer)
```

```
stargazer(a1, a2, a3, a4, type="text", no.space=TRUE,
 model.names=FALSE, notes="standard errors in parentheses")

# load two packages used to data visualization
library(ggplot2)
library(gridExtra)

# generate four scatter plots with regression lines
F1 <- ggplot(anscombe)+aes(x1,y1)+geom_point()
            +geom_abline(intercept=3,slope=0.5)
F2 <- ggplot(anscombe)+aes(x2,y2)+geom_point()
            +geom_abline(intercept=3,slope=0.5)
F3 <- ggplot(anscombe)+aes(x3,y3)+geom_point()
            +geom_abline(intercept=3,slope=0.5)
F4 <- ggplot(anscombe)+aes(x4,y4)+geom_point()
            +geom_abline(intercept=3,slope=0.5)

# display four scatter plots together
grid.arrange(F1,F2,F3,F4, ncol = 2)
```

As shown in Table 6.1, in all four models, the slope estimate is 0.5 and the intercept is 3. Obviously, the OLS model is only good at capturing the relationship between $x1$ and $y1$, fails to represent the curvilinear relationship between $x2$ and $y2$, is moderately influenced by one outlier in terms of the effect of $x3$ on $y3$, and is disproportionately driven by one outlier in the relationship between $x4$ and $y4$. Figure 6.1 demonstrates the need for data visualization, which helps to expose any non-linear pattern and the impact of outliers.

The most commonly employed regression diagnostic graph is the residuals-versus-fitted-values plot. It is a scatter plot with residuals on the vertical axis and the fitted or predicted values of the dependent variable on the horizontal axis. It can help us to detect non-linearity, non-constant error variance, and outliers. For illustration, Figure 6.2 displays the residuals-versus-fitted-values plot for the Anscombe quartet models.

To interpret a residuals-versus-fitted-values plot, we need to first establish its link with the original scatter plot in Figure 6.1. In the original $x1$ and $y1$ scatter plot in Figure 6.1, three data points fall on the regression line, with corresponding predicted values of $y1$ being 7, 8, and 10, respectively. Now, turning to the residuals-versus-fitted-values plot for that pair, we find that the data points with fitted values being 7, 8, and 10 on the horizontal axis actually fall on the $residual = 0$ line in Figure 6.2. This is because a data point that falls on the estimated regression line in Figure 6.1 should have a residual value of zero and

Table 6.1 **Regression Results Using Anscombe's Quartet**

	Dependent Variable:			
	$y1$ (1)	$y2$ (2)	$y3$ (3)	$y4$ (4)
$x1$	0.500*** (0.118)			
$x2$		0.500*** (0.118)		
$x3$			0.500*** (0.118)	
$x4$				0.500*** (0.118)
Constant	3.000** (1.125)	3.001** (1.125)	3.002** (1.124)	3.002** (1.124)
Observations	11	11	11	11
R2	0.667	0.666	0.666	0.667
Adjusted R2	0.629	0.629	0.629	0.630
Residual Std. Error (df = 9)	1.237	1.237	1.236	1.236
F Statistic (df = 1; 9)	17.990***	17.966***	17.972***	18.003***

Note: $*p<0.1$; $**p<0.05$; $***p<0.01$.
Standard errors in parentheses.

thus, falls on the *residual* = 0 line in Figure 6.2. The *residual* = 0 line in Figure 6.2 represents the estimated regression line in Figure 6.1. We may find one-to-one connections for other data points between the two scatter plots as well.

For regression assumption violations, we should look for three patterns in a residuals-versus-fitted-values plot: (1) If the linearity and correct model specification assumption holds, the residuals should be distributed randomly around the *residual* = 0 line; any systematic pattern will be a violation of the assumption. (2) If the variance of the error term is constant across observations, the residuals should be distributed within a relatively constant band around the *residual* = 0 line; any fanning-out or funneling-in pattern will be an indication of non-constant error variance. (3) No observation should deviate too far from other observations both in terms of residuals and fitted values.

Turning to Figure 6.2, the residuals-versus-fitted-values plot for $x1$ and $y1$ behaves well with respect to linearity and model specification, constant error variance, and the absence of outliers. The plot for $x2$ and $y2$ clearly indicates a non-linear or curvilinear relationship, with the residuals distributed in a

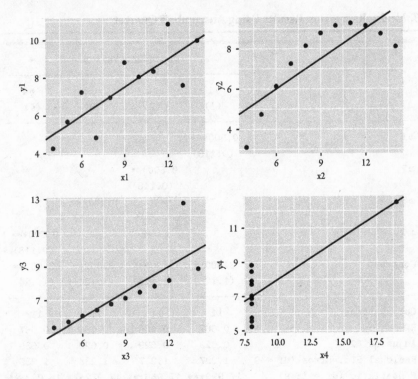

Figure 6.1 Anscombe Quartet Regressions.

systematic pattern. The plot for x3 and y3 shows the impact of one outlier with a really large positive residual, and the residuals appear to fan out along the x-axis, making the residual variance non-constant. The plot for x4 and y4 shows how one outlier heavily influences the regression line, even though other observations suggest the lack of any linear or non-linear relationship between x4 and y4.

Since the Anscombe dataset is extremely small, Figure 6.3 presents six diagnostic graphs based on a simulated regression model that satisfies most of the regression assumptions. Specifically, they are generated from the following regression model: $y = 100 + 3x + u$, where u is the random error with mean equal to zero and variance equal to 3, x is a normal random variable, and sample size n is set to 100. Figure 6.3 includes a scatter plot between x and y, one between residuals and fitted values of y, one between residuals and fitted values of y plus a loess curve fitted to identify specification errors, one between residuals and observation numbers as an example of checking independence among observations, a Normal Q-Q plot to check normality of the residual, and a plot between Cook's D statistics and observation numbers. Thus Figure 6.3 provides a benchmark when we turn to diagnose the trade and growth model estimated in Chapter 5. Further details about these plots will be provided in relevant sections later in the chapter.

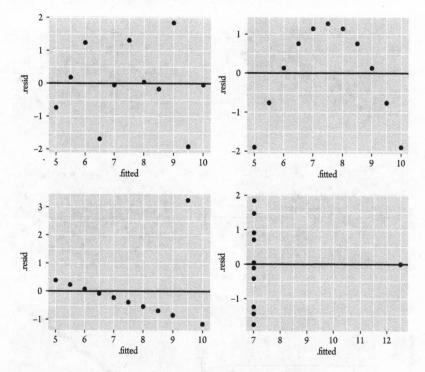

Figure 6.2 Anscombe Quartet Residuals versus Fitted Values Plots.

Data Preparation

For data preparation, we must first clean the workspace, set the working directory to our project folder, load the final.85.RData dataset, reproduce the table of descriptive statistics, re-run the OLS model from Chapter 5, and display the regression output.

```
# Data Analysis Program
#install following packages only once, then comment out code
#install.packages(c("stargazer","ggplot2","gridExtra","broom",
#"car","lmtest","sandwich","interplot","ape"),dependencies=TRUE)

# remove all objects from workspace
rm(list=ls(all=TRUE))

# change working directory to project folder
setwd("C:/Project")

# load R data
load("final.85.RData")
```

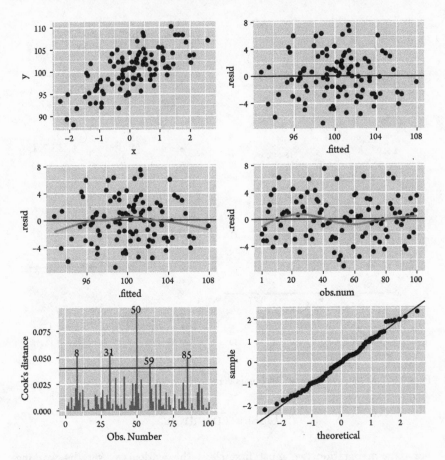

Figure 6.3 Diagnostic Plots for a Well-Behaved Regression.

```
# load packages
library(ggplot2)
library(gridExtra)
library(stargazer)
```

```
# produce formatted descriptive statistics in pwt7.final
stargazer(final.85, type="text", median = TRUE)
```

Statistic	N	Mean	St. Dev.	Min	Median	Max
year	152	1,985.000	0.000	1,985	1,985	1,985
rgdpwok	151	10,696.670	9,635.187	705	7,091	38,190
rgdpch	152	4,423.257	4,423.595	299	2,564	19,648
open	152	73.874	45.928	13.160	63.715	318.070
labor	150	13,314.110	56,733.470	29.314	2,547.374	612,363.100

```
landarea   141  716,704.000  1,653,680.000   260    196,850   9,388,250
logy       152     7.891         1.042       5.700    7.849      9.886
loglab     150     7.663         1.931       3.378    7.843     13.325
logland    141    11.679         2.421       5.561   12.190     16.055
------------------------------------------------------------------------
```

```
# estimate OLS model and create output object
model1 <- lm(logy ~ open + loglab + logland, data=final.85)


# show model output
summary(model1)



Call:
lm(formula = logy ~ open + loglab + logland, data = final.85)

Residuals:
    Min      1Q    Median     3Q      Max
-2.07067  -0.82670  -0.08307  0.64393  2.10651

Coefficients:
              Estimate Std. Error t value Pr(>|t|)
(Intercept)   6.588159   0.720802   9.140  8.3e-16 ***
open          0.008280   0.002583   3.206  0.00168 **
loglab        0.154185   0.066221   2.328  0.02138 *
logland      -0.044109   0.056274  -0.784  0.43451
---
Signif. codes:
0 '***' 0.001 '**' 0.01 '*' 0.05 '.' 0.1 ' ' 1

Residual standard error: 0.9875 on 135 degrees of freedom
  (13 observations deleted due to missingness)
Multiple R-squared:  0.1007,Adjusted R-squared:  0.08069
F-statistic: 5.038 on 3 and 135 DF,  p-value: 0.002434
```

In the following sections, we will provide regression diagnostics for the estimated model and carry out several sensitivity analyses. Before we do so, we will first introduce a new R package and some of its functions that can greatly facilitate diagnostic tests. The new broom package can convert the statistical results above into a tidy data frame via the tidy() function, and add output statistics such as fitted values and residuals as variables to the original data via the augment_columns() function. Notably, the augment_columns() function first specifies the model output object and then the original data, producing a new data object with both the original variables and the new statistics. The R code and output demonstrates this process and displays the variable names and descriptive statistics of the new dataset.

```
# load package
library(broom)

# tidy regression output
tidy(model1)

          term       estimate    std.error   statistic
1 (Intercept)  6.588158896 0.720802408  9.1400345
2        open  0.008279996 0.002582653  3.2060040
3      loglab  0.154185276 0.066220731  2.3283536
4     logland -0.044109479 0.056274468 -0.7838276
           p.value
1 8.297834e-16
2 1.680345e-03
3 2.137907e-02
4 4.345144e-01

# add additional statistics to original data
final.85v2 <- augment_columns(model1, final.85)

# show variables in new data
names(final.85v2)

 [1] "wbcode"     "year"       "country"    "rgdpwok"
 [5] "rgdpch"     "open"       "labor"      "continent"
 [9] "landarea"   "region"     "lat"        "long"
[13] "logy"       "loglab"     "logland"    ".fitted"
[17] ".se.fit"    ".resid"     ".hat"       ".sigma"
[21] ".cooksd"    ".std.resid"

# produce descriptive statistics for new data
stargazer(final.85v2, type = "text", median = TRUE)
```

Statistic	N	Mean	St. Dev.	Min	Median	Max
year	139	1,985.000	0.000	1,985	1,985	1,985
rgdpwok	139	10,411.680	9,483.972	705	6,878	38,190
rgdpch	139	4,250.374	4,346.766	299	2,411	19,648
open	139	73.557	44.818	13.800	64.240	318.070

labor	139	12,757.850	57,876.240	29.314	2,368.962	612,363.100
landarea	139	661,122.600	1,500,333.000	320	196,850	9,388,250
logy	139	7.851	1.030	5.700	7.788	9.886
loglab	139	7.582	1.915	3.378	7.770	13.325
logland	139	11.692	2.353	5.768	12.190	16.055
.fitted	139	7.851	0.327	7.310	7.817	10.027
.se.fit	139	0.156	0.061	0.084	0.144	0.572
.resid	139	-0.000	0.977	-2.071	-0.083	2.107
.hat	139	0.029	0.033	0.007	0.021	0.336
.sigma	139	0.988	0.004	0.974	0.989	0.991
.cooksd	139	0.007	0.017	0.00000	0.003	0.182
.std.resid	139	-0.002	1.003	-2.115	-0.085	2.160

In the R code above, we name the new data frame as final.85v2. By comparing the two descriptive statistics tables for final.85 and final.85v2, we will notice that the latter only includes the observations used in model estimation. The diagnostics below will be carried out with respect to the new dataset. The new diagnostic statistics added as new variables include: .fitted, .se.fit, .resid, .hat, .sigma, .cooksd, and .std.resid, many of which will be discussed and used in the diagnostic tests in later sections.

Linearity and Model Specification

One condition of the Gauss-Markov theorem is that the estimated model is linear in parameters and correctly specified. Correct model specification refers to both the functional form and that no relevant variable is omitted. We will begin with some diagnostic graph.

Figure 6.4 is a residuals-versus-fitted-values scatter plot, plus a loess curve. The R code follows the ggplot code from earlier chapters, with the addition of the geom_smooth() function. The function requests a loess curve and its confidence interval to be fitted to uncover any systematic relationship between residuals and fitted values. The loess (locally weighted smoothing) curve is

```
# load packages
library(ggplot2)
library(gridExtra)

# residuals against fitted values: check linearity
ggplot(final.85v2, aes(x=.fitted, y=.resid)) +
        geom_hline(yintercept=0) +
        geom_point() +
        geom_smooth(method='loess', se=TRUE)
```

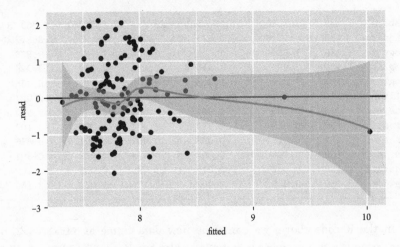

Figure 6.4 Residuals versus Fitted Values: Linearity.

a smooth line through a scatter plot of data points to identify the relationship between two variables without imposing the linearity assumption. Hence, when the loess curve overlaps with or is very close to the *residual* = 0 line, there is little evidence of non-linearity or systematic correlation between residuals and fitted values.

Recall that residuals should be independent of fitted values or independent variables, and the model should be linear in parameters and correctly specified. Any correlation between residuals and fitted values will violate these assumptions. If residuals exhibit any non-linear pattern, such as a curvilinear relationship, the model is incorrectly specified. On the other hand, if the dependent variable is linearly related to the independent variables as correctly specified by the model, the plot should show no systematic relationship between fitted values and residuals.

Figure 6.4 does not show any strong non-linear or correlation pattern between residuals and fitted values. Most data points appear randomly distributed around the *residual* = 0 line, and the confidence interval of the loess curve largely overlaps with the *residual* = 0 line. It is worth noting, though, that the loess curve does appear moderately influenced by one data point whose fitted value is around 10.

We further examine the linearity and model specification assumption via the residuals-versus-independent-variables plots below. The R code and Figure 6.5 are as follows:

```
# load packages
library(ggplot2)
library(gridExtra)
```

```
# residuals against trade
ropen <- ggplot(final.85v2, aes(x=open, y=.resid)) +
        geom_hline(yintercept=0) +
        geom_point() +
        geom_smooth(method='loess', se=TRUE)

# residuals against land
rland <- ggplot(final.85v2, aes(x=logland, y=.resid)) +
        geom_hline(yintercept=0) +
        geom_point() +
        geom_smooth(method='loess', se=TRUE)

# residuals against labor
rlab <- ggplot(final.85v2, aes(x=loglab, y=.resid)) +
        geom_hline(yintercept=0) +
        geom_point() +
        geom_smooth(method='loess', se=TRUE)

# display plots together
grid.arrange(ropen, rland, rlab, ncol=3)
```

The loess curve confidence interval in each plot in Figure 6.5 largely overlaps with the *residual* = 0 line. But the residuals-versus-open plot seems to indicate a relatively clear curvilinear relationship, an issue worth further exploring.

While Figure 6.4 and Figure 6.5 are illuminating, they can not replace formal diagnostic tests. We can use Ramsey's regression specification error test (RESET) to examine whether the functional form is misspecified. In this

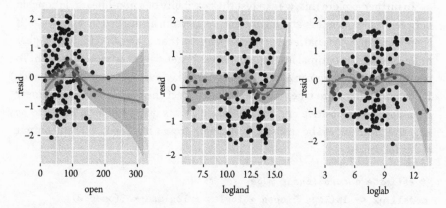

Figure 6.5 Residuals versus Independent Variables: Linearity.

test, we re-estimate the original model plus the quadratic or cubic terms of the fitted or predicted y (i.e., $\hat{y}_i^2$ or $\hat{y}_i^3$). We use an F-statistic to test the null hypothesis that the original and expanded models explain the same amount of variations of the dependent variable. If the null hypothesis is rejected, then some of the independent variables affect the dependent variable in a non-linear fashion.

The R code and output for a quadratic functional form test is as follows. Note how the quadratic term is being specified; an alternative is to create a new variable for the squared term first and then include the new variable in the model.

```
# regression specification error test expanded model
model1.q1 <- lm(logy ~ open + loglab + logland + I(.fitted^2),
    data = final.85v2)

# F test of model difference
anova(model1, model1.q1)

Analysis of Variance Table

Model 1: logy ~ open + loglab + logland
Model 2: logy ~ open + loglab + logland + I(.fitted^2)
  Res.Df    RSS Df Sum of Sq      F Pr(>F)
1     135 131.66
2     134 130.10  1    1.5581 1.6048 0.2074
```

The F-statistic is 1.6048, with a p value 0.2074. If we apply the 5% significance level, we will fail to reject the null hypothesis that these two models are identical. The result is consistent with the loess curve pattern in Figure 6.4.

To further explore this, we can test the possibility of a non-linear relationship between trade openness and log income per person, as implied by Figure 6.4. If there were some optimal level of trade openness, then a level that is either higher or lower than the optimal level would be less beneficial for economic growth. To test this possibility, we can add a quadratic term, i.e., $open^2$, to the original model. If the possibility were true, then we should expect the coefficient for the linear term open to be positive and the coefficient for its quadratic term $open^2$ to be negative. Both should be statistically different from zero. The R code and output are as follows:

```
# estimate a curvilinear model for trade
model1.q2 <- lm(logy ~ open + loglab + logland + I(open^2),
                data=final.85v2)
```

```
# F test of model difference
anova(model1, model1.q2)

Analysis of Variance Table

Model 1: logy ~ open + loglab + logland
Model 2: logy ~ open + loglab + logland + I(open^2)
  Res.Df    RSS Df Sum of Sq      F  Pr(>F)
1    135 131.66
2    134 127.29  1    4.3701 4.6006 0.03376 *
---
Signif. codes:
0 '***' 0.001 '**' 0.01 '*' 0.05 '.' 0.1 ' ' 1

summary(model1.q2)


Call:
lm(formula = logy ~ open + loglab + logland + I(open^2),
   data = final.85v2)

Residuals:
     Min       1Q   Median       3Q      Max
-2.02458 -0.74207 -0.08419  0.62834  2.12034

Coefficients:
             Estimate Std. Error t value Pr(>|t|)
(Intercept) 5.720e+00  8.186e-01   6.988 1.19e-10 ***
open        1.998e-02  6.019e-03   3.319  0.00116 **
loglab      2.268e-01  7.359e-02   3.081  0.00250 **
logland    -6.102e-02  5.610e-02  -1.088  0.27867
I(open^2)  -4.651e-05  2.168e-05  -2.145  0.03376 *
---
Signif. codes:
0 '***' 0.001 '**' 0.01 '*' 0.05 '.' 0.1 ' ' 1

Residual standard error: 0.9746 on 134 degrees of freedom
Multiple R-squared:  0.1305,Adjusted R-squared:  0.1046
F-statistic: 5.029 on 4 and 134 DF,  p-value: 0.0008297
```

The F-statistic is 4.6, with a p value 0.034. If we apply the 5% significance level, we will reject the null hypothesis that these two models are identical. This result appears to contradict the earlier RESET test based on the squared fitted values.

More specifically, the coefficient of open is positive and statistically significant, whereas the coefficient of I(open^2), i.e., $open^2$, is negative and statistically significant. The results suggest that the effect of trade openness on growth first rises and then declines. Based on the model estimates, we can actually identify the turning point of trade openness using the following formula: $|\frac{coef_{open}}{2*coef_{open^2}}| = |\frac{1.998e-02}{2*-4.651e-05}| \approx 215$. According to this finding, trade and growth are positively associated in those countries whose trade openness is below 215%, and yet for those above the turning point, the relationship is negative.

Figure 6.6 provides a sctter plot of trade openness and log of income per person for the estimation sample. It shows that Hong Kong and Singapore are the only two data points above the turning point in the sample. Hence, the curvilinear relationship may well be driven by these two observations, an issue to be further examined below.

Finally, we can also use an F test to investigate if some new variable actually belongs to the model in question in the sense that it is correlated with trade and with the dependent variable. In this scenario, excluding the new variable causes what is commonly known as an omitted variable bias because its omission causes the coefficient of trade to be biased. One may first visually inspect the residuals-versus-new-variable scatter plot and then apply the anova() function and the F test to address this issue. Interested readers may use the procedures above to explore this possibility.

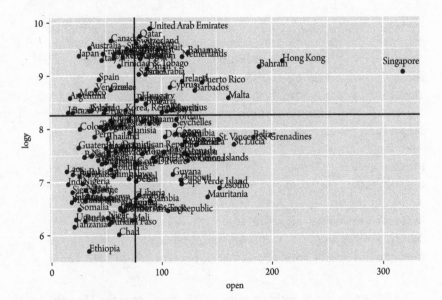

Figure 6.6 Trade Openness and Log of Income per Person.

Perfect and High Multicollinearity

A second condition of the Gauss-Markov theorem is that the independent variables can not be perfectly correlated. For illustration, we will provide an example. Suppose we create a new variable, open4, which simply equals four times the open variable, thus making the two variables perfectly correlated. For illustration, we will re-estimate the original model twice—first with open entered before open4, and then in reverse order—using the lm() function. The R code and output are as follows:

```
# create a variable perfectly correlating with open
final.85v2$open4 <- 4 * final.85v2$open

# check correlation between two variables
cor(final.85v2$open, final.85v2$open4, use = "complete.obs")

[1] 1

# estimate model 1 adding open4 in two different orderings OLS model
lm(logy ~ open + open4 + loglab + logland, data = final.85v2)


Call:
lm(formula = logy ~ open + open4 + loglab + logland,
   data = final.85v2)

Coefficients:
(Intercept)          open         open4         loglab
    6.58816       0.00828            NA        0.15419
    logland
   -0.04411

lm(logy ~ open4 + open + loglab + logland, data = final.85v2)


Call:
lm(formula = logy ~ open4 + open + loglab + logland,
   data = final.85v2)

Coefficients:
(Intercept)         open4          open         loglab
    6.58816       0.00207            NA        0.15419
    logland
   -0.04411
```

The output indicates that because open and open4 are perfectly correlated, they can not be estimated simultaneously, and whichever enters second will be dropped from estimation.

Perfect multicollinearity is rare. Often, independent variables may be highly correlated. In the presence of high multicollinearity, the OLS estimator remains unbiased; its sampling distribution still centers on the true parameter value if the model specification is correct. The OLS estimator remains BLUE, and the standard error and t-test remain valid. However, when two independent variables are highly correlated, least squares estimates become sensitive to small changes in data and model specification. They tend to change erratically when the model specification or sample changes. In addition, standard errors are larger than in the absence of multicollinearity, and t-statistics are smaller, making it harder to reject the null hypothesis.

The variance inflation factor (VIF) is most commonly used to diagnose high multicollinearity. The term literally means the factor that inflates the standard error of a regression coefficient estimator. Take the VIF for the variable open for example. It is formally defined as follows:

$$VIF = \frac{1}{1 - R_{open}^2}$$

where R_{open}^2 is the R-squared value from a new regression with open as the dependent variable on all other independent variables in the original model.

To understand how VIF is a good indicator of high collinearity, we may look at an alternative way to estimate the variance of b.

$$\widehat{var}(b) = \frac{s^2}{(n-1)\widehat{var}(open)} \cdot \frac{1}{1 - R_{open}^2}$$

where R_{open}^2 is as defined above, s^2 is the sample mean squared error (an estimate of the true variance of the error term in the population regression model), and $\widehat{var}(open)$ is the sample variance of open. Note that $\frac{1}{1-R_{open}^2}$ is the variance inflation factor (VIF). Hence, when VIF increases, $var(b)$ rises and the t-statistic decreases.

If VIF is equal to one, then R_{open}^2 is equal to zero, meaning open is completely independent of other independent variables in the original model. In this case, there is no multicollinearity at all. However, if VIF equals 10, then R_{open}^2 equals 0.9, meaning that 90% of the variations in open can be explained by other independent variables in the original model. In this case, we should be concerned about the influence of multicollinearity and use caution in interpreting the findings since only 10% of the variations in open are used to estimate its *ceteris paribus* effect. Many consider a VIF value of 10 as a sign of serious multicollinearity.

The vif() function from the car package can provide the diagnostic test.

```
# compute vif statistics
library(car)
vif(model1)

    open   loglab  logland
1.895843 2.274622 2.481816
```

In this case, none of the three independent variables from the original model appears to suffer from serious multicollinearity.

Constant Error Variance

The Gauss-Markov theorem assumes that the error variance should remain constant across observations. When this assumption is violated, we have non-constant error variance, also referred to as heteroskedastic error variance. In the presence of non-constant error variance, OLS parameter estimates remain unbiased and consistent, but the standard errors of regression coefficients are estimated incorrectly and hence, the t-tests using the standard error estimates become invalid.

The first diagnostic tool is the residuals-versus-fitted-values plot, as shown in Figure 6.4, as well as the residuals-versus-independent-variables plots in Figure 6.5. In Figure 6.4, it looks like there is a pattern of residuals slightly funneling in as the fitted values increases, as shown by the confidence band of the loess curve. This pattern is more obvious in the residuals-versus-open plot in Figure 6.5. As shown in Figure 6.6, a couple of countries with very high trade openness might have contributed to this pattern.

Using R, we can conduct two formal diagnostic tests: Breush/Pagan and Cook/Weisberg score tests. For both tests, the null hypothesis is constant error variance, and the alternative hypothesis is that the error variance is not constant. Hence, if the null hypothesis is rejected, then the error variance is not constant. The decision rule remains the same as before: Compare the p value for a test statistic against the acceptable Type I error rate α to draw conclusions.

```
# test heteroskedasticity,
# estimate OLS model and create output object
model1 <- lm(logy ~ open + loglab + logland, data = final.85v2)

# Cook/Weisberg score test of constant error variance
```

```
library(car)
ncvTest(model1)

Non-constant Variance Score Test
Variance formula: ~ fitted.values
Chisquare = 0.5594459    Df = 1      p = 0.4544836

# Breush/Pagan test of constant error variance
library(lmtest)
bptest(model1)


studentized Breusch-Pagan test

data:  model1
BP = 4.2832, df = 3, p-value = 0.2325
```

The p values for the test statistics are 0.45 and 0.23, respectively. The null hypothesis of constant error variance fails to be rejected when the acceptable Type I error rate is 0.05.

Even though the assumption of constant error variance is not violated for our model, it is still useful from a pedagogical perspective to discuss some common solutions used to correct for non-constant error variance. One method is to log-transform a skewed variable that is likely to be the source of non-constant error variance. It is worth noting that both pop and landarea are highly skewed variables and their log-transformation could have helped.

A second method is to use weighted least squares (WLS), assuming that the variance of the residuals is proportional to one of the independent variables. WLS estimates the coefficients by minimizing a weighted residual sum of squares (with one over the identified independent variable as the weight). The R code and output for WLS are as follows:

```
# weighted least squares
model1.wls <- lm(logy ~ open+loglab+logland,
                 weights=1/open, data=final.85v2)
summary(model1.wls)


Call:
lm(formula = logy ~ open + loglab + logland, data = final.85v2,
    weights = 1/open)
```

```
Weighted Residuals:
    Min       1Q    Median       3Q       Max
-0.33791  -0.09702  -0.00591  0.09324   0.33650


Coefficients:
            Estimate Std. Error t value Pr(>|t|)
(Intercept) 5.456484   0.776028   7.031 9.25e-11 ***
open        0.013540   0.003224   4.200 4.82e-05 ***
loglab      0.115856   0.069859   1.658   0.0996 .
logland     0.044447   0.062822   0.708   0.4805
---
Signif. codes:
0 '***' 0.001 '**' 0.01 '*' 0.05 '.' 0.1 ' ' 1


Residual standard error: 0.136 on 135 degrees of freedom
Multiple R-squared:  0.117,Adjusted R-squared:  0.09733
F-statistic:  5.96 on 3 and 135 DF,  p-value: 0.0007581
```

The WLS results are broadly consistent with those from the OLS model. The effect of open remain positive and statistically significant, though the size of the effect has increased to 1.35%. The effect of loglab remains positive and significant, and the effect of logland turns positive though is still statistically insignificant.

A third method is to estimate new standard errors that correct for the impact of non-constant error variance, which are referred to as the White heteroskedasticity consistent robust standard errors. While this is commonly used in applied work, several caveats are worth noting. The White robust standard errors only have asymptotic justification, that is, valid for large samples. When the sample size is small, the White robust standard error-based t statistics will not have a probability distribution close to the t, and statistical inferences may be incorrect. Also, the OLS estimator is inefficient with White robust standard errors.

Two packages in R, lmtest and sandwich, offer functions for computing the White robust standard errors. Note that there are variants of different sandwich corrections. With the vcovHC() function in the sandwich package, one could request slightly different estimators of White robust standard errors, ranging from HC0 to HC5, as shown in the sandwich manual at https://cran.r-project.org/web/packages/sandwich/sandwich.pdf. For our purposes, it is important to know that the variance-covariance matrix HC3 is the default reported by the vcovHC() function. In practice, many analysts compare the results from R against those produced by a popular software Stata, whose default White robust standard error estimator is equivalent to the variance-covariance matrix HC1 of the vcovHC() function in the sandwich package. Below, we report both types of White robust standard errors to see their differences.

The R code is as follows. We use the coeftest() function from the lmtest package, first specifying the model output object model1 produced earlier and then the type of robust standard errors to be reported by revising the type= option.

```
# load packages
library(lmtest)
library(sandwich)


# report default HC3 robust standard errors
model1.hc3 <- coeftest(model1, vcov=vcovHC)
model1.hc3


t test of coefficients:

            Estimate Std. Error t value  Pr(>|t|)
(Intercept) 6.5881589  0.7338756  8.9772 2.099e-15 ***
open        0.0082800  0.0028039  2.9530  0.003713 **
loglab      0.1541853  0.0674633  2.2855  0.023844 *
logland    -0.0441095  0.0573772 -0.7688  0.443377
---
Signif. codes:
0 '***' 0.001 '**' 0.01 '*' 0.05 '.' 0.1 ' ' 1

# report HC1 robust standard errors as Stata
# variants:"HC3","HC","HC0","HC1","HC2","HC4","HC4m","HC5"
model1.hc1 <- coeftest(model1, vcov=vcovHC(model1, type="HC1"))
model1.hc1


t test of coefficients:

            Estimate Std. Error t value  Pr(>|t|)
(Intercept) 6.5881589  0.6779671  9.7175 < 2.2e-16 ***
open        0.0082800  0.0023576  3.5120 0.0006053 ***
loglab      0.1541853  0.0626915  2.4594 0.0151805 *
logland    -0.0441095  0.0559666 -0.7881 0.4319969
---
Signif. codes:
0 '***' 0.001 '**' 0.01 '*' 0.05 '.' 0.1 ' ' 1
```

Two observations are worth noting about these results. First, all coefficient estimates remain unchanged since White robust standard error corrections only apply to standard error estimates. Second, focusing on the open variable, we can see that the two corrections provide slightly different standard error estimates, but the effect of open remains statistically significant at the conventional level regardless of which standard error estimator is used.

The corresponding variance-covariance matrices can be requested as follows. Interested readers can verify their correspondence with the standard error estimates above by taking the square root of the diagonal elements below.

```
# request the variance-covariance matrix HC3
vcovHC(model1, type = "HC3")

            (Intercept)          open          loglab
(Intercept)  0.538573356 -1.755419e-03 -1.357727e-02
open         -0.001755419  7.862004e-06  5.581238e-05
loglab       -0.013577274  5.581238e-05  4.551300e-03
logland      -0.026354579  6.555593e-05 -2.144378e-03
                 logland
(Intercept) -2.635458e-02
open         6.555593e-05
loglab      -2.144378e-03
logland      3.292145e-03

# request the variance-covariance matrix HC1
vcovHC(model1, type = "HC1")

            (Intercept)          open          loglab
(Intercept)  0.459639431 -1.348921e-03 -8.331623e-03
open         -0.001348921  5.558300e-06  2.544375e-05
loglab       -0.008331623  2.544375e-05  3.930227e-03
logland      -0.025380567  6.393592e-05 -2.012949e-03
                 logland
(Intercept) -2.538057e-02
open         6.393592e-05
loglab      -2.012949e-03
logland      3.132260e-03
```

Independence of Error Term Observations

The Gauss-Markov theorem assumes that the observations of the error term are independent and uncorrelated. However, observations that are collected over time or across regions are likely to be correlated over time or within a region. If the temporal or spatial dependence is not modeled explicitly, the residuals will be correlated over time or spatially, causing standard error estimates to be biased. Since our focus in this book is the cross-sectional design, we will not explore the time dependence, usually referred to as autocorrelation in the residuals. The dataset final.85v2 does have a spatial dimension. Hence, we will explore whether there is any systematic pattern in the residuals that are correlated with regions.

Figure 6.7 plots residuals-versus-fitted-values by continent, a variable for regions. The R code is as before, with the only addition of facet_wrap() to wrap the sequence of figure panels for regions.

```
# distribution of residuals in each region
ggplot(final.85v2, aes(.fitted, .resid)) +
        geom_hline(yintercept=0) +
    geom_point() +
    facet_wrap(~continent)
```

Figure 6.7 demonstrates some clear regional patterns. All residuals for Europe are positive, meaning that the model systematically underpredicts log income per person for European countries in 1985. The same pattern applies to South America, except for one country. In contrast, most residuals for Africa are negative, meaning that the model systematically overpredicts income per person

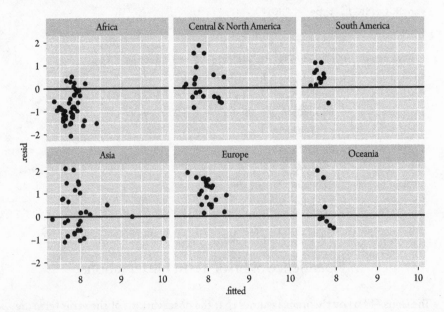

Figure 6.7 Distribution of Residuals by Region.

for many African countries. These patterns suggest that some commonalities for many countries in the same region, indicating a lack of independence among countries, are not captured by the Frankel and Romer statistical model.

One formal test statistic of spatial correlation is Moran's I, which we can use to test whether the values of log income per person for geographically proximate countries are more similar than those values for geographically distance countries. If this were true, then it would be evidence of dependence among observations in the dependent variable. We will demonstrate how to carry out this test in the Miscellaneous Q&A section later in the chapter. At the moment, we will take the graphic pattern as sufficient evidence for the presence of spatial correlation. The key question for the Frankel and Romer analysis is whether the spatial correlation could affect the estimated effect of trade on growth and how to address it. We begin with a scatter plot of logy and open by region to see if the linear relationship holds across different regions. It is likely that countries within a region are closely related to each other such that there are large differences between regions. Examining the relationship between trade and income region is a good place to start. The R code and Figure 6.8 are as follows. Note that a regression line without confidence interval is drawn within each region by adding the stat_smooth() option.

```
# scatter plot of trade and income by region
ggplot(final.85, aes(open, logy)) +
  geom_point() +
  facet_wrap( ~ continent) +
  stat_smooth(method = "lm", se = FALSE)
```

Figure 6.8 shows that indeed, there are large differences between regions. It appears that trade and income are positively related in three regions: Africa, Asia, and Europe; but they are either unrelated in Central & North America or negatively related in South America and Oceania. In this case, the spatial correlation appears to indicate a misspecification error in the original Frankel and Romer model. Figure 6.8 seems to indicate that both the intercept and the coefficient of open of the original model might differ among regions. If so, the Frankel and Romer model should be re-specified to account for the differences among regions. Below, we demonstrate how to re-specify the original Frankel and Romer model to account for regional differences.

Recall the original Frankel and Romer model is as follows:

$$lnY_i = \beta_0 + \beta_1 T_i + \beta_2 N_i + \beta_2 A_i + \varepsilon_i$$

If regional differences only affect the intercept β_0, then we can create six dummy variables replacing the original intercept, as shown in the following equation. The coefficient of a regional dummy such as Africa, that is, β_{af},

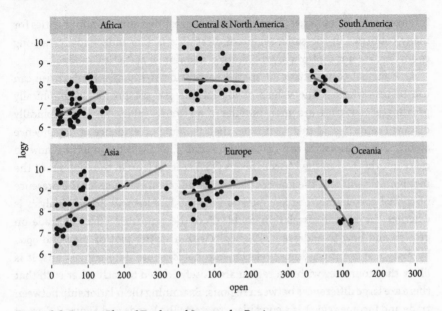

Figure 6.8 Scatter Plot of Trade and Income by Region.

represents the level of log income per person for an average African country when all other variables in the model are equal to zero.

$$lnY_i = \beta_{af}Africa + \beta_{cn}C.N.America + \beta_{sa}S.America + \beta_{as}Asia + \beta_{e}Europe$$
$$+ \beta_{o}Oceania + \beta_1 T_i + \beta_2 N_i + \beta_2 A_i + \varepsilon_i$$

The R code and output are as follows. Three issues are worth noting. First, continent is a factor variable, meaning that internally, R stores integer values 1, 2, 3, 4, 5, and 6 for the six regional names as value labels, respectively. Before we run the model, we will first simplify the long value labels for regional names so that they become easier to read below. We first show the attributes of the continent variable using the attributes() function, then use the level() function to change the value labels, and then confirm the changes by showing the attributes again. Second, when we include the factor variable continent in the model, R creates a dummy variable for each level (i.e., region) in regression. Third, the intercept is excluded by adding 0+ after the ~ sign.

```
# show attributes
attributes(final.85v2$continent)

$levels
[1] "Africa"              "Central & North America"
[3] "South America"       "Asia"
[5] "Europe"              "Oceania"
```

```
$class
[1] "factor"

# change value labels of factor variable continent
levels(final.85v2$continent) <- c(".Africa", ".C.N.America",
    ".S.America", ".Asia", ".Europe", ".Oceania")

# confirm the change
attributes(final.85v2$continent)

$levels
[1] ".Africa"      ".C.N.America" ".S.America"
[4] ".Asia"        ".Europe"      ".Oceania"

$class
[1] "factor"

# model with all regional dummies and no intercept
lm(logy ~ 0 + continent + open + loglab + logland,
    data = final.85v2)


Call:
lm(formula = logy ~ 0 + continent + open + loglab + logland,
    data = final.85v2)

Coefficients:
     continent.Africa  continent.C.N.America
              5.85086                6.97531
  continent.S.America        continent.Asia
              6.98705                7.06399
    continent.Europe      continent.Oceania
              7.94885                6.86145
                 open                 loglab
              0.00641               -0.01615
              logland
              0.06393
```

Alternatively, we may estimate the model above but with the intercept included; one region will be automatically excluded due to perfect multicollinearity as shown earlier. In this case, the excluded region, measured by the intercept, serves as the reference category for other regional dummies such that the coefficient of an included region is the difference between the included and excluded regions. As shown in the output below, R automatically uses Africa as the baseline category.

```
# display model with all regional dummies but one
lm(logy ~ continent+open+loglab+logland, data=final.85v2)

Call:
lm(formula = logy ~ continent + open + loglab + logland,
   data = final.85v2)

Coefficients:
          (Intercept)    continent.C.N.America
              5.85086                  1.12445
  continent.S.America          continent.Asia
              1.13619                  1.21313
     continent.Europe        continent.Oceania
              2.09799                  1.01059
                 open                   loglab
              0.00641                 -0.01615
              logland
              0.06393
```

By comparing the output of the two models, we will see that they are mathematically equivalent. In the intercept-free model, each region has a coefficient; the coefficient of Africa is 5.85086, the one for South America is 6.98705, and so forth. In the model with intercept, each region except for Africa has a coefficient; the intercept is 5.85086, and the one for South America is 1.13619, which equals exactly the difference between 6.98705 (South America) and 5.85086 (Africa) in the intercept-free model.

The full model output is as follows. In addition, we carry out an F test to compare against the original model. The null hypothesis is that the two models are indistinguishable; in other words, there are no regional differences.

```
# display full model ouput
model1.reg <- lm(logy ~ continent + open + loglab + logland,
   data = final.85v2)

# display model output
summary(model1.reg)

Call:
lm(formula = logy ~ continent + open + loglab + logland,
   data = final.85v2)
```

```
Residuals:
    Min      1Q  Median      3Q     Max
-1.5393 -0.5051 -0.1059  0.4129  1.6415
```

```
Coefficients:
```

	Estimate	Std. Error	t value	Pr(>|t|)
(Intercept)	5.850858	0.554950	10.543	< 2e-16
continent.C.N.America	1.124454	0.198251	5.672	8.73e-08
continent.S.America	1.136190	0.230289	4.934	2.42e-06
continent.Asia	1.213131	0.176252	6.883	2.24e-10
continent.Europe	2.097989	0.191067	10.980	< 2e-16
continent.Oceania	1.010595	0.276448	3.656	0.000371
open	0.006410	0.001885	3.400	0.000894
loglab	-0.016153	0.054946	-0.294	0.769245
logland	0.063926	0.043466	1.471	0.143782

```
(Intercept)           ***
continent.C.N.America ***
continent.S.America   ***
continent.Asia        ***
continent.Europe      ***
continent.Oceania     ***
open                  ***
loglab
logland
---
Signif. codes:
0 '***' 0.001 '**' 0.01 '*' 0.05 '.' 0.1 ' ' 1
```

```
Residual standard error: 0.7004 on 130 degrees of freedom
Multiple R-squared:  0.5644,Adjusted R-squared:  0.5376
F-statistic: 21.05 on 8 and 130 DF,  p-value: < 2.2e-16
```

```
# compare against original model
anova(model1, model1.reg)
```

```
Analysis of Variance Table
```

```
Model 1: logy ~ open + loglab + logland
Model 2: logy ~ continent + open + loglab + logland
  Res.Df    RSS Df Sum of Sq      F    Pr(>F)
```

```
1      135 131.66
2      130  63.77  5      67.887 27.679 < 2.2e-16 ***
---
Signif. codes:
0 '***' 0.001 '**' 0.01 '*' 0.05 '.' 0.1 ' ' 1
```

The results demonstrate several useful findings. First, the effect of open remains positive and statistically significant, even after regional differences are controlled for. But the size of effect is smaller than before. A 1% increase in trade openness is now associated with a 0.64% increase in income per person. Second, relative to Africa, each of the other five regions has a statistically significant and higher level of income. Third, after controlling for regional differences, both loglab and logland become statistically insignificant. Fourth, the overall model fit, R-squared, has improved dramatically after accounting for regional differences in income. The model explains about 56% of the variations in log income per person. Finally, the test between the model with regions and the original one has an F-statistic 27.679, rejecting the null hypothesis that the two models are indistinguishable.

If the effect of trade varies between regions, then the coefficient β_1 in the original Frankel and Romer model should be re-specified as follows:

$$lnY_i = \beta_{af}Africa + \beta_{cn}CNAmerica + \beta_{sa}SAmerica + \beta_{as}Asia + \beta_e Europe$$
$$+ \beta_o Oceania + \beta_{1af}Africa * T_i + \beta_{1cn}CNAmerica * T_i$$
$$+ \beta_{1sa}SAmerica * T_i + \beta_{1as}Asia * T_i + \beta_{1e}Europe * T_i$$
$$+ \beta_{1o}Oceania * T_i + \beta_2 N_i + \beta_2 A_i + \varepsilon_i$$

The R code and output are as follows. Note how the interaction model can be easily specified in R (alternatively, an interaction term could be created and included). In addition, we conduct two model comparison tests: one between the original and interaction models, and the other between the region and interaction models.

```
# interaction model
model1.int <- lm(logy ~ open * continent + loglab + logland,
    data = final.85v2)

# compare models
anova(model1, model1.int)

Analysis of Variance Table

Model 1: logy ~ open + loglab + logland
Model 2: logy ~ open * continent + loglab + logland
```

```
   Res.Df     RSS Df Sum of Sq      F    Pr(>F)
1     135 131.656
2     125  53.819 10     77.837 18.078 < 2.2e-16 ***
---
Signif. codes:
0 '***' 0.001 '**' 0.01 '*' 0.05 '.' 0.1 ' ' 1

anova(model1.reg, model1.int)

Analysis of Variance Table

Model 1: logy ~ continent + open + loglab + logland
Model 2: logy ~ open * continent + loglab + logland
   Res.Df     RSS Df Sum of Sq      F    Pr(>F)
1     130  63.770
2     125  53.819  5     9.9503 4.6221 0.0006643 ***
---
Signif. codes:
0 '***' 0.001 '**' 0.01 '*' 0.05 '.' 0.1 ' ' 1

# display output
summary(model1.int)


Call:
lm(formula = logy ~ open * continent + loglab + logland,
     data = final.85v2)

Residuals:
    Min      1Q   Median     3Q      Max
-1.64503 -0.44733 -0.09181  0.38105  1.75245

Coefficients:
```

	Estimate	Std. Error	t value
(Intercept)	6.3266688	0.5556540	11.386
open	0.0073966	0.0030342	2.438
continent.C.N.America	1.5586340	0.3742021	4.165
continent.S.America	2.0492782	0.4524259	4.530
continent.Asia	1.2039049	0.2803122	4.295
continent.Europe	2.7438566	0.4459053	6.153
continent.Oceania	4.0066062	0.8371850	4.786
loglab	-0.0704607	0.0551576	-1.277
logland	0.0527409	0.0421710	1.251

```
open:continent.C.N.America  -0.0061018   0.0041246   -1.479
open:continent.S.America    -0.0181383   0.0079835   -2.272
open:continent.Asia          0.0006836   0.0034438    0.198
open:continent.Europe       -0.0081190   0.0055471   -1.464
open:continent.Oceania      -0.0346147   0.0090520   -3.824
                            Pr(>|t|)
(Intercept)                  < 2e-16 ***
open                         0.016186 *
continent.C.N.America        5.75e-05 ***
continent.S.America          1.36e-05 ***
continent.Asia               3.48e-05 ***
continent.Europe             9.47e-09 ***
continent.Oceania            4.72e-06 ***
loglab                       0.203813
logland                      0.213401
open:continent.C.N.America   0.141552
open:continent.S.America     0.024796 *
open:continent.Asia          0.842987
open:continent.Europe        0.145798
open:continent.Oceania       0.000206 ***
---
Signif. codes:
0 '***' 0.001 '**' 0.01 '*' 0.05 '.' 0.1 ' ' 1


Residual standard error: 0.6562 on 125 degrees of freedom
Multiple R-squared:  0.6324,Adjusted R-squared:  0.5941
F-statistic: 16.54 on 13 and 125 DF,  p-value: < 2.2e-16
```

We start with the model comparison results first. The test between the original and interaction models has an F-statistic of 18.078, and the test between the region and interaction models has an F-statistic 4.622. Both tests are statistically significant, suggesting that the interaction model has more explanatory power than either the original model or the model with region dummies only.

The results for the interaction model require some clarification. Note that since Africa is the excluded baseline category, the intercept 6.327 is African's log income per person when all other variables in the model are equal to zero, and the coefficient of open, 0.0074, is the effect of trade for African countries in the sample. The effect of trade for the other region in the model equals 0.0074 plus its respective coefficient. Hence, the effect of trade is (0.0074-0.0061)=0.0013 in Central & North America, (0.0074-0.018)=-0.0106 in South America, (0.0074+0.00068)=0.00808 in Asia, (0.0074-0.0081)=0.0007 in Europe, (0.0074-0.0346)=-0.0272 in Oceania.

The effect of trade appears to differ among regions. The question is whether the effect is due to chance or actually different from zero in the population. The answer is not obvious from the model results because only the significance test for the effect of trade in Africa is directly reported. Thus, to answer the question, we employ a new R package interplot to examine the effect of trade and its 95% confidence interval in each region.

The R code and Figure 6.9 are as follows. In the interplot() function, we specify the model output model1.int, then the variable whose effect is to be plotted with var1=, and the conditioning or moderating variable with var2=. To mark statistical significance, we insert a dashed line representing coefficient=0, using the geom_hline() option.

```
# load package
library(interplot)

# plot effect of trade conditional on region
interplot(model1.int, var1 = "open", var2 = "continent") +
    geom_hline(yintercept = 0, linetype = "dashed")
```

Each panel in Figure 6.9 has two point estimates and respective confidence intervals. In each panel, the estimate on the left is when a region dummy equals zero, thus representing the effect of trade in Africa, and the estimate on the right

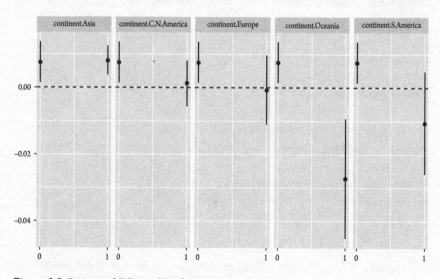

Figure 6.9 Estimated Effect of Trade on Income by Region.

is when the respective region dummy equals one, thus representing the effect of trade in that particular region.

Figure 6.9 demonstrates that the 95% confidence interval for the effect of trade is positive and never crosses the zero-effect dashed line for African and Asian countries only, it crosses the zero-effect line for three regions: Central & North America, Europe, and South America, and it turns negative and does not cross the zero-effect line for Oceania. These results suggest that trade has a positive and significant effect on Africa and Asia, a negative and significant effect on Oceania, and no effect on Central & North America, Europe, and South America.

So far we have treated the dependence among observations as a model misspecification error. This is desirable when we know the source of data dependence and can model it explicitly. However, in applied work, this is not always possible. In those situations, one common solution is to compute robust standard errors clustered over a particular unit-level (e.g., class within school, or school within district). The clustered standard error estimator allows for correlation among observations within a unit-level or cluster (in our case, a region can be thought of as a cluster). But its validity depends on a large sample, particularly the presence of many clusters. In our case, we have only six regions and thus, applying the clustered standard errors is not appropriate. Yet for pedagogical purposes, we will demonstrate how to estimate clustered standard errors in R. We first use the cluster.vcov() function in the multiwayvcov package to obtain the clustered variance-covariance matrix, and then apply the coeftest() function of the lmtest package to compute test statistics and p values based on the clustered matrix. The R code and output are as follows. The output shows rather small differences between the clustered and regular OLS standard errors.

```
# load packages
library(lmtest)
library(multiwayvcov)

# estimate OLS model and create output object
model1 <- lm(logy ~ open + loglab + logland, data = final.85v2)

# show OLS results for comparison
summary(model1)


Call:
lm(formula = logy ~ open + loglab + logland, data = final.85v2)
```

```
Residuals:
    Min      1Q    Median     3Q      Max
-2.07067 -0.82670 -0.08307  0.64393  2.10651
```

```
Coefficients:
            Estimate Std. Error t value Pr(>|t|)
(Intercept)  6.588159   0.720802   9.140  8.3e-16 ***
open         0.008280   0.002583   3.206  0.00168 **
loglab       0.154185   0.066221   2.328  0.02138 *
logland     -0.044109   0.056274  -0.784  0.43451
---
Signif. codes:
0 '***' 0.001 '**' 0.01 '*' 0.05 '.' 0.1 ' ' 1
```

```
Residual standard error: 0.9875 on 135 degrees of freedom
Multiple R-squared:  0.1007,Adjusted R-squared:  0.08069
F-statistic: 5.038 on 3 and 135 DF,  p-value: 0.002434
```

```
# request clustered variance and covariance matrix
vcov_region <- cluster.vcov(model1, final.85v2$continent)
```

```
# display clustered matrix
vcov_region
```

```
              (Intercept)          open         loglab
(Intercept)  0.378688904 -1.077383e-03 -0.0643315181
open        -0.001077383  4.577988e-06  0.0002341682
loglab      -0.064331518  2.341682e-04  0.0146384290
logland      0.022730464 -1.205310e-04 -0.0059365002
                  logland
(Intercept)  0.022730464
open        -0.000120531
loglab      -0.005936500
logland      0.003635146
```

```
# request test statistics and p values
model1.cl <- coeftest(model1, vcov_region)
model1.cl
```

```
t test of coefficients:

            Estimate Std. Error t value  Pr(>|t|)
```

```
(Intercept)   6.5881589   0.6153770 10.7059 < 2.2e-16 ***
open          0.0082800   0.0021396  3.8698 0.0001688 ***
loglab        0.1541853   0.1209894  1.2744 0.2047215
logland      -0.0441095   0.0602922 -0.7316 0.4656835
---
Signif. codes:
0 '***' 0.001 '**' 0.01 '*' 0.05 '.' 0.1 ' ' 1
```

Influential Observations

One important regression diagnostic concerns influential observations. A regression coefficient represents the average effect of an independent variable on a dependent variable, holding other variables constant. Yet some observations may have excessive influences over the coefficient estimates, the predicted values, and the overall fit of a regression model. This introduces much uncertainty as to whether it is the presence or absence of such observations that gives us good or bad estimates of the population parameter. As noted in the Anscombe example, the presence of such observations could be highly problematic, causing misleading conclusions in statistical inference.

Influential observations tend to be associated with both large absolute values of residuals and high leverage. The residual outliers refer to observations with very large absolute residual values, that is, observed values of the dependent variable are far away from its predicted values; observations with high leverage refer to those with extreme values on an independent variable, that is, observed values of an independent variable are far away from its mean. Influential observations influence both the coefficient estimates and the predicted values of a regression model. Hence, it is important to identify such observations and evaluate how sensitive the model results are to their presence.

A large number of statistics are often applied to detect influential observations. We focus on three of these, with particular attention to Cook's D statistics. The first statistic is the studentized residual for each observation, which is based on the standard error of the regression re-estimated without that observation. As the studentized residuals follow a t distribution, observations outside the ± 2 range are residual outliers.

The second statistic is the hat value for each observation, which measures its degree of leverage. It is constructed based on a weighted measure of an observation's distance from the point of means of different independent variables. It is bounded between $1/n$ and 1.

The third statistic is the Cook's Distance (Cook's D). It is worth our particular attention as it is based on both the studentized residual and the hat value for each observation.

$$Cook's\ D_i = \frac{\sum_{j=1}^{n}(\hat{y}_j - \hat{y}_{j(i)})^2}{p \times MSE}$$

where *Cook's* D_i is the Cook's D value for observation i, $\hat{y}_j$ is the prediction for observation j from regression, $\hat{y_{j(i)}}$ is the prediction for observation j from a new regression omitting observation i, p is the number of parameters in the model, and MSE is the model mean squared error.

For each observation, as we apply the augment_columns() function of the broom package to the model output model1 and the original data final.85, these three statistics have been generated as three new variables: .std.resid, .hat, and .cooksd, and they have been saved into the new dataset final.85v2.

The influence plot from the car package illustrates all three statistics simultaneously, with the hat values on the horizontal axis, the studentized residuals on the y-axis, and the Cook's D represented by the relative size of the circle for each observation.

```
# load package
library(car)

# influence plot for influential observations
influencePlot(model1)
```

Figure 6.10 shows that several observations such as 102 have studentized residuals outside the ±2 range, one observation, 104, has an extremely large hat value, and several observations appear to have relatively large Cook's D values. While Figure 6.10 is illustrative and informative, it does not indicate exactly which observations are above a certain threshold of concern, for which we turn to the Cook's D statistic.

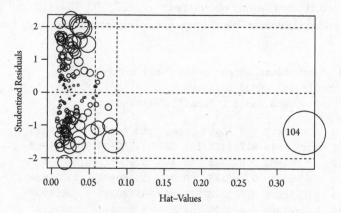

Figure 6.10 Influence Plot of Influential Observations.

A commonly used cutoff for Cook's D is 4/(n-k-1), with n indicating the number of observations and k the number of independent variables. When observations have Cook's D values larger than the threshold, they are considered to be overly influential. For model1, n is 139, k is 3, and the threshold should be about 0.03.

In the R code below, we demonstrate how to construct a plot of Cook's D against observation numbers, with those above the cutoff identified explicitly. We first use the row.names() function to give each observation an id and convert the character vector output into numeric using the as.numeric() function. Then we use ggplot() to identify dataset final.85v2 and variables id and .cooksd for plot, with geom_bar() to specify a bar chart, xlab() and ylab() to specify the axis labels, geom_hline() to specify the cutoff value line, and geom_text() to specify that only observations with .cooksd>0.03 are marked by id values above the bars and otherwise unmarked.

```
# create observation id
final.85v2$id <- as.numeric(row.names(final.85v2))


# load library
library(ggplot2)


# identify obs with Cook's D above cutoff
ggplot(final.85v2, aes(id, .cooksd))+
  geom_bar(stat="identity", position="identity")+
    xlab("Obs. Number")+ylab("Cook's distance")+
    geom_hline(yintercept=0.03)+
    geom_text(aes(label=ifelse((.cooksd>0.03),id,"")),
              vjust=-0.2, hjust=0.5)
```

Figure 6.11 identifies six observations—28, 52, 102, 104, 119, and 132—as having undue influences. We display those observations and related variables below.

```
# list observations whose cook's D above threshold
final.85v2[final.85v2$.cooksd > 0.03, c("id", "country", "logy",
    "open", ".std.resid", ".hat", ".cooksd")]
```

	id	country	logy	open	.std.resid	.hat
28	28	Mauritania	6.714171	141.56	-1.482906	0.08164658
52	52	Canada	9.654321	54.48	1.928715	0.04003432
102	102	Qatar	9.740145	80.94	2.160486	0.02519534
104	104	Singapore	9.061376	318.07	-1.199398	0.33596207
119	119	Iceland	9.409929	81.83	1.966874	0.03725787
132	132	Australia	9.516574	35.28	2.023071	0.03543545

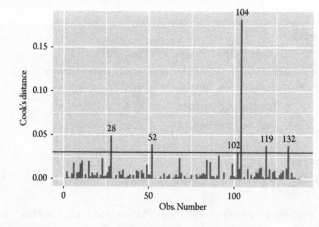

Figure 6.11 Influential Observations Above Cook's D Threshold.

```
         .cooksd
28   0.04887600
52   0.03878400
102  0.03016099
104  0.18195511
119  0.03742840
132  0.03758969
```

Clearly, Singapore has the largest Cook's D, trade openness, and hat value, but not the largest residual absolute value. Other identified observations have some large values to varying degrees. At this point, the question is whether our statistical inference over the effect of trade will change or not if we remove those influential observations.

We estimate two robustness models: one with only Singapore removed, and the other with all six observations removed. Note how we use the indexing method to exclude the observations.

```
# re-estimate model 1 without Singapore
model1.no1 <- lm(logy ~ open + loglab + logland,
                 data=final.85v2[final.85v2$.cooksd<0.18,])
summary(model1.no1)

Call:
lm(formula = logy ~ open + loglab + logland,
   data = final.85v2[final.85v2$.cooksd < 0.18, ])

Residuals:
     Min       1Q   Median       3Q      Max
-2.06329 -0.79338 -0.07195  0.65377  2.14759
```

```
Coefficients:
            Estimate Std. Error t value Pr(>|t|)
(Intercept)  6.262904   0.768866   8.146 2.33e-13 ***
open         0.010242   0.003052   3.356  0.00103 **
loglab       0.183232   0.070395   2.603  0.01028 *
logland     -0.046574   0.056220  -0.828  0.40890
---
Signif. codes:
0 '***' 0.001 '**' 0.01 '*' 0.05 '.' 0.1 ' ' 1

Residual standard error: 0.9859 on 134 degrees of freedom
Multiple R-squared:  0.1012,Adjusted R-squared:  0.08107
F-statistic: 5.029 on 3 and 134 DF,  p-value: 0.002467
```

```
# re-estimate model 1 without Singapore and five others
model1.no2 <- lm(logy ~ open + loglab + logland,
                 data=final.85v2[final.85v2$.cooksd<0.03,])
summary(model1.no2)


Call:
lm(formula = logy ~ open + loglab + logland,
     data = final.85v2[final.85v2$.cooksd < 0.03, ])


Residuals:
    Min      1Q  Median      3Q     Max
-2.01252 -0.74545 -0.02962  0.59824  2.09918

Coefficients:
            Estimate Std. Error t value Pr(>|t|)
(Intercept)  6.027796   0.758572   7.946 8.32e-13 ***
open         0.011691   0.002971   3.935 0.000135 ***
loglab       0.231452   0.068136   3.397 0.000907 ***
logland     -0.070915   0.056397  -1.257 0.210870
---
Signif. codes:
0 '***' 0.001 '**' 0.01 '*' 0.05 '.' 0.1 ' ' 1

Residual standard error: 0.9286 on 129 degrees of freedom
Multiple R-squared:  0.1524,Adjusted R-squared:  0.1326
F-statistic: 7.729 on 3 and 129 DF,  p-value: 8.677e-05
```

In both models, the effect of trade remains statistically significant and positive. The primary difference is that after removing influential observations, the size of the effect increases in both models, more so in the second model. Therefore, the primary impact of those influential observations is to weaken the estimated effect of trade in the original model.

Normality Test

The Gauss-Markov theorem does not require that the error term is normally distributed. However, inferences based on z or t statistics do need the error term to be normally distributed. In addition, when the error term is not normally distributed, it can be skewed or heavy-tailed, affecting the efficiency of estimation.

The quantile comparison plot from the car package is an effective way to check whether the residuals from regression are approximately normally distributed or not. The qqPlot() function plot compares the empirical quantiles of studentized residuals from model1 against the theoretical or expected quantiles of a benchmark t or *normal* distribution, with a confidence envelope. The closer the residuals follow the quartile line, the closer the studentized residuals meet the theoretical distribution. Note that if we want to compare the quantiles of studentized residuals against a theoretical normal distribution, we can simply replace "t" in the R code with norm instead. The option simulate=TRUE means the confidence envelope is based on parametric bootstrap. Figure 6.12 shows that most residuals lie within the confidence envelope and close to the line of quartile-pairs, but some appear to deviate away from the quartile line.

A variety of normality tests have been designed, but many are shown to be overly sensitive in capturing small deviations from normality in large samples

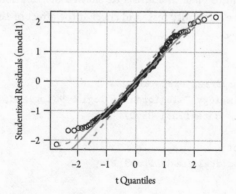

Figure 6.12 Normality Assumption Diagnostic Plot.

but not capturing big deviations in small samples. Here we apply one common normality test, the Shapiro-Wilk normality test. The null hypothesis is that the residuals have a normal distribution. The *p* value of the test statistic

```
# Normality diagnostic plot
library(car)
qqPlot(model1, distribution = "t", simulate = TRUE)
```

is smaller than 0.05, suggesting that the null hypothesis of normality is rejected.

```
# normality test
shapiro.test(final.85v2$.resid)


Shapiro-Wilk normality test

data:  final.85v2$.resid
W = 0.97508, p-value = 0.01202
```

Two responses are often offered to the violation of the normality assumption in applied work. In the first response, many analysts argue that given the central limit theorem, even if the residuals are not normally distributed, the OLS estimator can still be asymptotically normal, that is, if the sample is sufficiently large. When the sample size is considered large enough, the assumption violation can be ignored.

In the second response, some transformation is applied to the variable that might be causing the assumption violation. In this case, we know from the earlier sections that the very skewed open variable (think about the large value of Singapore!) might have caused the problem. Thus we might apply log-transformation to open to address its skewed distribution, re-estimate the model, conduct the normality test, and check if the effect of log(open) changes our earlier findings.

```
# test log-transformed open variable
model1.no3 <- lm(logy ~ log(open) + loglab + logland,
                 data=final.85v2)

# normality test
shapiro.test(residuals(model1.no3))


Shapiro-Wilk normality test
```

```
data:  residuals(model1.no3)
W = 0.98172, p-value = 0.05974

# show model output
summary(model1.no3)

Call:
lm(formula = logy ~ log(open) + loglab + logland, data = final.85v2)

Residuals:
    Min      1Q   Median      3Q     Max
-2.0467 -0.7291 -0.0815  0.6641  2.0720

Coefficients:
             Estimate Std. Error t value Pr(>|t|)
(Intercept)  3.77407    1.22228    3.088  0.00245 **
log(open)    0.76200    0.18722    4.070 7.96e-05 ***
loglab       0.21225    0.06856    3.096  0.00239 **
logland     -0.05758    0.05265   -1.094  0.27609
---
Signif. codes:
0 '***' 0.001 '**' 0.01 '*' 0.05 '.' 0.1 ' ' 1

Residual standard error: 0.9668 on 135 degrees of freedom
Multiple R-squared:  0.138,Adjusted R-squared:  0.1188
F-statistic: 7.203 on 3 and 135 DF,  p-value: 0.0001605
```

The Shapiro-Wilk normality test shows a p value 0.06, larger than the 0.05 level. Log-transforming the trade variable does help to address the issue, to the extent that one accepts the 0.05 Type I error threshold.

The model results show that the effect of trade, now measured by log(open), remains positive and statistically significant. The interpretation of the size of effect requires some clarification. According to Table 5.1, since open, which is the percent share of trade over GDP, is logged, the coefficient 0.76 of log(open) means that when the percent share of trade over GDP increases by 1%, the real income per person increases by 0.76%.

Report Findings

By now, we have accumulated a lot of statistical findings from 10 models related to estimation, diagnostics, and corrective tests. If we were to simply include the original computer output in a paper, it would appear confusing and unprofessional. Readers always expect to see nicely formatted tables of statistical results in professional writings. For illustration, we report the statistical results from 10 models in two separate tables.

We use the stargazer() function to compile the results tables. The R code is specified similarly as in the previous chapter, with a couple more options including column.labels=() for model types.

```
# robustness checks I
stargazer(model1,model1.q2,model1.wls,model1.hc1,model1.hc3,
        model1.no1, model1.no2, type="text", no.space=TRUE,
        covariate.labels = NULL, label="",
        omit.stat=c("f","ser"), model.names=FALSE,
        dep.var.labels.include=FALSE, dep.var.caption="",
        column.labels=c("OLS","Quadratic","WLS","Robust.hc1",
                        "Robust.hc3", "Singapore","outliers")
        )


# robustness checks II
stargazer(model1.cl, model1.reg, model1.int, model1.no3,
        type="text", no.space=TRUE, covariate.labels = NULL,
        label="", omit.stat=c("f","ser"), model.names=FALSE,
        dep.var.labels.include=FALSE, dep.var.caption="",
        column.labels = c("cluster.se", "regions",
                        "interaction", "logopen")
        )
```

Table 6.2 includes the results from seven models: original OLS, curvilinear model, weighted least squares, OLS with White robust standard errors (HC1), OLS with White robust standard errors (HC3), OLS excluding Singapore, and OLS excluding six influential observations. Table 6.3 includes four models: OLS with robust standard errors clustered over region, OLS with regional dummies, OLS with interactions between trade and regions, and OLS with log-transformed trade variable.

Since we have discussed each model earlier, we will not repeat our detailed discussion here and will focus on a broad summary of the findings instead. Overall, the effect of trade on income is quite robust, remaining statistically significant and positive under a variety of diagnostic and robustness tests. However, the positive and significant effect of trade appears to be limited to specific regions, Asia and Africa in particular, and it is not robust when it comes to other regions in the world. Hence, the positive effect of trade is not generalizable across regions.

Table 6.2 **Effect of Trade on Income: Robustness Checks Part I**

	OLS (1)	Quadratic (2)	WLS (3)	Robust.hc1 (4)	Robust.hc3 (5)	Singapore (6)	outliers (7)
open	0.008***	0.020***	0.014***	0.008***	0.008***	0.010***	0.012***
	(0.003)	(0.006)	(0.003)	(0.002)	(0.003)	(0.003)	(0.003)
loglab	0.154**	0.227***	0.116*	0.154**	0.154**	0.183**	0.231***
	(0.066)	(0.074)	(0.070)	(0.063)	(0.067)	(0.070)	(0.068)
logland	-0.044	-0.061	0.044	-0.044	-0.044	-0.047	-0.071
	(0.056)	(0.056)	(0.063)	(0.056)	(0.057)	(0.056)	(0.056)
I(open2)		-0.00005**					
		(0.00002)					
Constant	6.588***	5.720***	5.456***	6.588***	6.588***	6.263***	6.028***
	(0.721)	(0.819)	(0.776)	(0.678)	(0.734)	(0.769)	(0.759)
Observations	139	139	139			138	133
R2	0.101	0.131	0.117			0.101	0.152
Adjusted R2	0.081	0.105	0.097			0.081	0.133

Note: *p<0.1; **p<0.05; ***p<0.01

249

Table 6.3 **Effect of Trade on Income: Robustness Checks Part II**

	cluster.se (1)	logopen (2)	regions (3)	interaction (4)
continent.C.N.America			1.124*** (0.198)	1.559*** (0.374)
continent.S.America			1.136*** (0.230)	2.049*** (0.452)
continent.Asia			1.213*** (0.176)	1.204*** (0.280)
continent.Europe			2.098*** (0.191)	2.744*** (0.446)
continent.Oceania			1.011*** (0.276)	4.007*** (0.837)
open	0.008*** (0.002)		0.006*** (0.002)	0.007** (0.003)
log(open)		0.762*** (0.187)		
loglab	0.154 (0.121)	0.212*** (0.069)	-0.016 (0.055)	-0.070 (0.055)
logland	-0.044 (0.060)	-0.058 (0.053)	0.064 (0.043)	0.053 (0.042)
open:continent.C.N.America				-0.006 (0.004)
open:continent.S.America				-0.018** (0.008)
open:continent.Asia				0.001 (0.003)
open:continent.Europe				-0.008 (0.006)
open:continent.Oceania				-0.035*** (0.009)
Constant	6.588*** (0.615)	3.774*** (1.222)	5.851*** (0.555)	6.327*** (0.556)
Observations		139	139	139
R2		0.138	0.564	0.632
Adjusted R2		0.119	0.538	0.594

Note: *p<0.1; **p<0.05; ***p<0.01

Chapter 6 Program Code

```
#install following packages only once, then comment out code
#install.packages(c("stargazer","ggplot2","gridExtra","broom",
#"car","lmtest","sandwich","interplot","ape"),dependencies=TRUE)

# display regression results from Anscombe quartet
a1 <- lm(y1~x1, data=anscombe)
a2 <- lm(y2~x2, data=anscombe)
a3 <- lm(y3~x3, data=anscombe)
a4 <- lm(y4~x4, data=anscombe)

# report Anscombe quartet regression results
library(stargazer)
stargazer(a1, a2, a3, a4, type="text", no.space=TRUE,
 model.names=FALSE, notes="standard errors in parentheses")

# load two packages used to data visualization
library(ggplot2)
library(gridExtra)

# generate four scatterplots with regression lines
F1 <- ggplot(anscombe)+aes(x1,y1)+geom_point()
            +geom_abline(intercept=3,slope=0.5)
F2 <- ggplot(anscombe)+aes(x2,y2)+geom_point()
            +geom_abline(intercept=3,slope=0.5)
F3 <- ggplot(anscombe)+aes(x3,y3)+geom_point()
            +geom_abline(intercept=3,slope=0.5)
F4 <- ggplot(anscombe)+aes(x4,y4)+geom_point()
            +geom_abline(intercept=3,slope=0.5)

# display four scatter plots together
grid.arrange(F1,F2,F3,F4, ncol = 2)

# remove all objects from workspace
rm(list=ls(all=TRUE))

# change working directory to project folder
setwd("C:/Project")

# load R data
```

```
load("final.85.RData")

# load packages
library(ggplot2)
library(gridExtra)
library(stargazer)

# produce formatted descriptive statistics in pwt7.final
stargazer(final.85, type="text",  median = TRUE)

# estimate OLS model and create output object
model1 <- lm(logy ~ open + loglab + logland, data=final.85)

# show model output
summary(model1)

# load package
library(broom)

# tidy regression output
tidy(model1)

# add additional statistics to original data
final.85v2 <- augment_columns(model1, final.85)

# show variables in new data
names(final.85v2)

# produce descriptive statistics for new data
stargazer(final.85v2, type="text",  median = TRUE)

# load packages
library(ggplot2)
library(gridExtra)

# residuals against fitted values: check linearity
ggplot(final.85v2, aes(x=.fitted, y=.resid)) +
        geom_hline(yintercept=0) +
        geom_point() +
        geom_smooth(method='loess', se=TRUE)
```

```
# residuals against trade
ropen <- ggplot(final.85v2, aes(x=open, y=.resid)) +
        geom_hline(yintercept=0) +
        geom_point() +
        geom_smooth(method='loess', se=TRUE)


# residuals against land
rland <- ggplot(final.85v2, aes(x=logland, y=.resid)) +
        geom_hline(yintercept=0) +
        geom_point() +
        geom_smooth(method='loess', se=TRUE)


# residuals against labor
rlab <- ggplot(final.85v2, aes(x=loglab, y=.resid)) +
        geom_hline(yintercept=0) +
        geom_point() +
        geom_smooth(method='loess', se=TRUE)


# display plots together
grid.arrange(ropen, rland, rlab, ncol=3)


# regression specification error test
# expanded model
model1.q1 <- lm(logy ~ open + loglab + logland + I(.fitted^2),
                data=final.85v2)


# F test of model difference
anova(model1, model1.q1)


# estimate a curvilinear model for trade
model1.q2 <- lm(logy ~ open + loglab + logland + I(open^2),
                data=final.85v2)


# F test of model difference
anova(model1, model1.q2)
summary(model1.q2)


# scatter plot of open and log of real income per capita
ggplot(final.85v2, aes(x=open, y=logy))+
  geom_point() +
  geom_vline(xintercept = 76.129) +
```

```
  geom_hline(yintercept = 8.256) +
  geom_text(aes(label=country),hjust=0,vjust=0)


# create a variable perfectly correlating with open
final.85v2$open4 <- 4*final.85v2$open


# check correlation between two variables
cor(final.85v2$open, final.85v2$open4, use="complete.obs")


# estimate model 1 adding open4 in two different orderings
lm(logy ~ open + open4 + loglab + logland, data=final.85v2)


lm(logy ~ open4 + open + loglab + logland, data=final.85v2)


# compute vif statistics
library(car)
vif(model1)


#  test heteroskedasticity
# estimate OLS model and create output object
model1 <- lm(logy ~ open + loglab + logland, data=final.85v2)


# Cook/Weisberg score test of constant error variance
library(car)
ncvTest(model1)


# Breush/Pagan test of constant error variance
library(lmtest)
bptest(model1)


# weighted least squares
model1.wls <- lm(logy ~ open+loglab+logland,
                 weights=1/open, data=final.85v2)
summary(model1.wls)


# load packages
library(lmtest)
library(sandwich)


# report default HC3 robust standard errors
model1.hc3 <- coeftest(model1, vcov=vcovHC)
```

```
model1.hc3

# report HC1 robust standard errors as Stata
# variants:"HC3","HC","HC0","HC1","HC2","HC4","HC4m","HC5"
model1.hc1 <- coeftest(model1, vcov=vcovHC(model1, type="HC1"))
model1.hc1

# request the variance-covariance matrix HC3
vcovHC(model1, type="HC3")

# request the variance-covariance matrix HC1
vcovHC(model1, type="HC1")

# distribution of residuals in each region
ggplot(final.85v2, aes(.fitted, .resid)) +
            geom_hline(yintercept=0) +
      geom_point() +
      facet_wrap(~continent)

# scatter plot of trade and income by region
ggplot(final.85, aes(open, logy)) +
      geom_point() +
      facet_wrap( ~ continent) +
      stat_smooth(method = "lm", se = FALSE)

# scatter plot open and logy by region
ggplot(final.85, aes(open, logy)) +
      geom_point() +
      facet_wrap( ~ continent) +
      stat_smooth(method = "lm", se = FALSE)

# show attributes
attributes(final.85v2$continent)

# change value labels of factor variable continent
levels(final.85v2$continent) <- c(".Africa", ".C.N.America",
      ".S.America", ".Asia", ".Europe", ".Oceania")

# confirm the change
attributes(final.85v2$continent)
```

```
# model with all regional dummies and no intercept
lm(logy ~ 0 + continent + open + loglab + logland,
   data=final.85v2)


# display model with all regional dummies but one
lm(logy ~ continent + open + loglab + logland, data=final.85v2)


# display full model ouput
model1.reg <- lm(logy ~ continent + open + loglab + logland,
                 data=final.85v2)


# display model output
summary(model1.reg)


# compare against original model
anova(model1, model1.reg)


# interaction model
model1.int <- lm(logy ~ open*continent + loglab + logland,
                 data=final.85v2)


# compare models
anova(model1, model1.int)
anova(model1.reg, model1.int)


# display output
summary(model1.int)


# load package
library(interplot)


# plot effect of trade conditional on region
interplot(model1.int, var1="open", var2="continent") +
    geom_hline(yintercept = 0, linetype = "dashed")


# load packages
library(lmtest)
library(multiwayvcov)


# estimate OLS model and create output object
model1 <- lm(logy ~ open + loglab + logland, data=final.85v2)
```

```
# show OLS results for comparison
summary(model1)


# request clustered variance and covariance matrix
vcov_region <- cluster.vcov(model1, final.85v2$continent)


# display clustered matrix
vcov_region


# request test statistics and p values
model1.cl <- coeftest(model1, vcov_region)
model1.cl


# load package
library(car)


# influence plot for influential observations
influencePlot(model1)


# create observation id
final.85v2$id <- as.numeric(row.names(final.85v2))


# load library
library(ggplot2)


# identify obs with Cook's D above cutoff
ggplot(final.85v2, aes(id, .cooksd)) +
    geom_bar(stat="identity", position="identity") +
    xlab("Obs. Number")+ylab("Cook's distance")+
    geom_hline(yintercept=0.03) +
    geom_text(aes(label=ifelse((.cooksd>0.03),id,"")),
              vjust=-0.2, hjust=0.5)


# list observations whose cook's D above threshold
final.85v2[final.85v2$.cooksd>0.03, c("id","country","logy",
                        "open",".std.resid",".hat",".cooksd")]


# re-estimate model 1 without Singapore
model1.no1 <- lm(logy ~ open + loglab + logland,
                data=final.85v2[final.85v2$.cooksd<0.18,])
summary(model1.no1)
```

```
# re-estimate model 1 without Singapore and five others
model1.no2 <- lm(logy ~ open + loglab + logland,
                 data=final.85v2[final.85v2$.cooksd<0.03,])
summary(model1.no2)


# normality diagnostic plot
library(car)
qqPlot(model1, distribution="t", simulate=TRUE)


# normality test
shapiro.test(final.85v2$.resid)


# test log-transformed open variable
model1.no3 <- lm(logy ~ log(open) + loglab + logland,
                 data=final.85v2)


# normality test
shapiro.test(residuals(model1.no3))


# show model output
summary(model1.no3)


# robustness checks I
stargazer(model1,model1.q2,model1.wls,model1.hc1,model1.hc3,
          model1.no1, model1.no2, type="text", no.space=TRUE,
          covariate.labels = NULL, label="",
          omit.stat=c("f","ser"), model.names=FALSE,
          dep.var.labels.include=FALSE, dep.var.caption="",
          column.labels=c("OLS","Quadratic","WLS","Robust.hc1",
                          "Robust.hc3", "Singapore","outliers")
          )


# robustness checks II
stargazer(model1.cl, model1.reg, model1.int, model1.no3,
          type="text", no.space=TRUE, covariate.labels = NULL,
          label="", omit.stat=c("f","ser"), model.names=FALSE,
          dep.var.labels.include=FALSE, dep.var.caption="",
          column.labels = c("cluster.se", "regions",
                            "interaction", "logopen")
          )
```

Summary

In this chapter, we have learned why OLS assumptions are important, how to diagnose assumption violations in OLS regression, and how to conduct sensitivity analysis and correct for some assumption violations. The issues covered include linearity and model specification, perfect and high multicollinearity, constant error variance, independence of error term observations, influential observations, and normality test. A mastery of materials in this chapter is necessary for systematic data analysis of a continuous outcome variable in a cross-sectional design. With this preparation, we are now ready to move on to replicate more published research that also employs OLS regression. As usual, before heading into the next chapter, we will address some miscellaneous questions related to the materials in this chapter.

Miscellaneous Q&As for Ambitious Readers

How do we Show Multiple Diagnostic Plots Simultaneously?

Often we are interested in showing multiple diagnostic plots together. There are two easy ways to do this. First, the lm() function model output allows us to plot six diagnostic plots: (1) residuals-versus-fitted-values; (2) normal Quantile-Quantile plot; (3) Scale-Location plot of the square root of residuals against fitted values; (4) Cook's D versus observation numbers; (5) residuals-versus-leverages; and (6) Cook's D versus leverage divided by one minus leverage. The following R code produces a plot of six figures together. But the option which= allows us to select which one to report.

```
par(mfrow = c(3, 2))
plot(model1, which = 1:6)
```

Second, we may use the GGally and ggplot2 package to request a figure that combines pairwise correlation, variable distribution, and scatter plots through the ggscatmat() function, as well as a diagnostic figure of all independent variables in a model versus four different diagnostic statistics (residuals, sigma, hat, cooksd).

```
library(GGally)
library(ggplot2)

# pairwise correlation, distribution, and scatter plots
ggscatmat(final.85v2, columns = c("logy", "open", "loglab",
    "logland"))
```

```
# independent variables vs. diagnostic statistics:
# residual, sigma, hat, cooksd
ggnostic(model1)
```

How do we Test Spatial Correlation Using Moran's I?

For a test using Moran's I, the null hypothesis is no spatial correlation. The result below suggests that the null hypothesis should be rejected.

```
# create a data object with latitude and longitude
# coordinates
morany <- final.85v2[, c("country", "wbcode", "logy", "lat",
    "long")]
head(morany, n = 1)

  country wbcode    logy    lat    long
1 Algeria   DZA 8.00236 36.7397 3.05097

# create distance matrix
morany.dist <- as.matrix(dist(cbind(morany$long, morany$lat)))

# find an inverse distance matrix with each off-diagonal
# entry equal to 1/(distance between two points)
morany.dist.inv <- 1/morany.dist

# replace diagonal entries with zero
diag(morany.dist.inv) <- 0

# load package
library(ape)

# compute moran's I, null hypothesis: no spatial correlation
# formula z=(I-e(I))/sqr(var(I))
Moran.I(morany$logy, morany.dist.inv)

$observed
[1] 0.2188475

$expected
[1] -0.007246377
```

```
$sd
[1] 0.01559622

$p.value
[1] 0
```

Panel Data Models

Frankel and Romer answer their research question using a cross-sectional design. One could potentially estimate a model using a panel dataset including many countries over many years. Some example R code for two common panel models using pwt7g data is as follows.

```
# load package
library(plm)

# ols with country fixed effects
fixed1 <- plm(log(rgdpl) ~ openk + log(POP), data=pwt7g,
              index="country", model="within")

# ols with country and year fixed effects
fixed2 <- plm(log(rgdpl) ~ openk + log(POP),
    data=pwt7g, index=c("country", "year"), model="within",
    effect="twoways")

# random effects model
random <- plm(log(rgdpl) ~ openk + log(POP), data=pwt7g,
              index=c("country", "year"), model="random")
```

The fixed effects model treats the heterogeneity between countries as being constant over time and captured by distinct intercepts for countries. The random effects model assumes that the between-country heterogeneity follows some distribution and can be estimated as a random component in the error term that varies from country to country.

The model choice depends on the key assumption of whether the country-specific effects are correlated with independent variables or not. The following R code provides a test of this assumption. The null hypothesis is that they are not. If the null hypothesis fails to be rejected, the random effects model is more efficient and preferred; if the null is rejected, then only the fixed effects model is appropriate.

```
phtest(fixed1, random)
```

Exercises

1. Re-estimate the trade-growth model in Frankel and Romer for 1995 and 2005, respectively, as instructed in Chapter 5 Exercises section. Conduct appropriate diagnostic tests to verify if the results are sensitive or not to assumption violations and related corrections where appropriate. Use graphs where appropriate.

2. Re-estimate the trade-growth model in Frankel and Romer, adding a variable for the share of FDI net inflows over GDP drawn from the World Bank statistics. Test whether this variable belongs to the correct model specification or not. Use graphs where appropriate.

3. As instructed in Chapter 5 Exercises section, estimate a regression model of the effects of partisanship and electoral system on wage inequality using the data in Soskice and Iversen (2006). Conduct appropriate diagnostic tests to verify if the results are sensitive or not to assumption violations and related corrections where appropriate. Use graphs where appropriate.

4. As instructed in Chapter 5 Exercises section, estimate a regression model of the effects of natural resource endowment in a country and its mountainous terrain on the spread of military conflict, using the data in Braithwaite (2006). Conduct appropriate diagnostic tests to verify if the results are sensitive or not to assumption violations and related corrections where appropriate. Use graphs where appropriate.

7

Replication of Findings
in Published Analyses

Chapter Objectives

In this chapter, we will demonstrate how to replicate statistical analyses in the following two published articles from international relations and economics, respectively.

1. Braithwaite, Alex. 2006. "The Geographic Spread of Militarized Disputes." *Journal of Peace Research* 43(5): 507–22.
2. Bénabou, Roland, Davide Ticchi, and Andrea Vindigni. 2015. "Religion and Innovation." *American Economic Review* 105(5): 346–51.

The purpose of these replication exercises is to accumulate firsthand experience in conducting social science empirical research. Just as we develop better comprehension of the cumulated knowledge of the physical world by replicating previous experiments in physics and chemistry, we can better understand how statistical findings regarding human behaviors came about by reproducing previous data analyses in social sciences. As noted in the introduction of this book, scientific progress requires that previous findings be replicable and replicated. Only through these replication experiences can we expect to better understand the justifications and potential pitfalls of the modeling choices in previous studies. Replication is one of the most important steps toward producing new knowledge. The importance of replication exercises to empirical social scientific research cannot be overemphasized.

The two studies are of two different styles. The Braithwaite study involves one research question—What influences the geographic spread of military conflict?—and one dependent variable, several independent variables, and a couple of regression models. In contrast, the Bénabou et al. study involves one research question—Does religiosity influence individual attitudes toward innovation?—but many dependent and independent variables, and numerous regression models. Both styles of empirical analysis are common in applied work. Hence, they help us learn about two styles of empirical research.

With the Braithwaite study, we show the step-by-step process of how to lay out the hypotheses tested, relate the hypotheses to the statistical model used, locate the relevant replication dataset and program files, read the dataset into R, replicate the statistical models, carry out diagnostic tests and robustness checks, and report and discuss the results of replication and diagnostic estimations. The process is clear because we focus on evaluating just one model. With the Bénabou et al. study, we demonstrate how a large number of models involving many dependent and independent variables are estimated, and how copious model results are distilled so that only key estimates that test the authors' theoretical expectation are put together, as in the published article.

Before we start, readers should already have the following packages installed: foreign, stargazer, car, lmtest, and sandwich.

What Explains the Geographic Spread of Militarized Interstate Disputes? Replication and Diagnostics of Braithwaite (2006)

In this section, we will replicate and diagnose some key findings in the Braithwaite study following detailed procedures. The process integrates a lot of the lessons we have learned so far in previous chapters and demonstrates how to take a published analysis, understand its internal logic, and replicate and diagnose its key findings.

In this chapter, we will aim to achieve the following objectives:

1. Identify Braithwaite's research question, motivation, and testable hypotheses.
2. Identify the population regression model underlying the research hypotheses and the empirical measures of the variables.
3. Specify the sample model and discuss the author's logic of statistical inference.
4. Obtain the author's dataset, import it into R, and check the imported data to ensure that it corresponds to the one reported in the paper.
5. Replicate the model estimation using the author's statistical procedures.
6. Conduct diagnostic tests and robustness checks to examine whether the author's findings are sensitive to various assumption violations such as heteroskedastic error variance discussed in Chapter 4.
7. Report and discuss the results from replication and diagnostic estimations.

Research Question and Hypotheses

In an article entitled "The Geographic Spread of Militarized Disputes," published in the *Journal of Peace Research*, Alex Braithwaite (2006) seeks to explain the geographic spread of Militarized Interstate Disputes (MID). The research question is: Why do some international conflicts spread geographically more than others? Braithwaite (2006) argues that the geographic attributes of the conflict location, the characteristics of the belligerents, and the issues at dispute provide answers to the research question. Based on his argument, Braithwaite specifies the following testable hypotheses:

- H1: Territorial disputes are more spread out than non-territorial disputes.
- H2: Disputes in countries with valuable natural resources are more spread out than those in other countries.
- H3: Disputes in areas of passable terrain are more spread out than those in areas of impassable terrain.
- H4: Disputes between geographically large states are more spread out than those between small or between large and small states.
- H5: Disputes between states sharing a vital border are more spread out than those between states not sharing a vital border.

Underlying Population Regression Model

The underlying population regression model, motivated by the preceding theoretical expectations, is not explicitly specified by Braithwaite but can be easily specified as follows:

$$Spread = \beta_0 + \beta_1 Territory + \beta_2 Resources + \beta_3 Mountain + \beta_4 Forest + \beta_5 Ocean$$
$$+ \beta_6 Size\ of\ States + \beta_7 VitalBorder + \beta_8 Control.variable + \epsilon$$

According to Braithwaite, the dependent variable, spread, is a circular area measured in squared kilometers, log transformed. The key independent and control variables are on the right-hand side, with all the βs indicating the marginal effects of respective right-hand side variables. Drawn from the article, the key independent variables, their measurements, and expected effects are as follows in Table 7.1.

Sample Model, Measures, and Statistical Inference

To test whether the hypothesized effects hold in the population, Braithwaite estimates the following sample regression model using sample data.

$$Spread = b_0 + b_1 Territory + b_2 Resources + b_3 Mountain + b_4 Forest + b_5 Ocean$$
$$+ b_6 Size\ of\ States + b_7 VitalBorder + b_8 Control.variable + u_i$$

Recall from the previous chapter that the logic of statistical inference in regression analysis is to draw conclusions about the population parameter—β—

Table 7.1 **Variable Measures and Expected Effects**

Variable	*Measure*	*Hypothesis*
Territory	Coded one if at least one participant to an MID considers territory to be the primary issue of dispute, and zero otherwise.	$H1 : \beta_1 > 0$
Resources	Coded one if the dispute occurs on the territory of a state well endowed in oil, gems, or illicit drugs, and zero otherwise.	$H2 : \beta_2 > 0$
Mountain	Mountainous terrain as a percent of the host state territory.	$H3 : \beta_3 < 0$
Forest	Forest-covered terrain as a percent of the host state territory.	$H3 : \beta_4 < 0$
Ocean	Coded one if the initial incident is located at sea, and zero otherwise.	$H3 : \beta_5 < 0$
Size of states	Joint size of the territories of two states, measured in 1000s of km^2, logged.	$H4 : \beta_6 > 0$
Vital border	Vitalness of a shared border, ranging from 0 to 2, with higher values indicating more vital border.	$H5 : \beta_7 > 0$

using sample statistics—b and $se(b)$—and sample data. Once again, we may use null hypothesis testing and confidence interval construction.

Hypothesis testing focuses on testing the null hypothesis: $\beta = 0$. It means that an independent variable has no effect on the spread of military disputes in the population. Note how hypothesis testing is never directly about the alternative or research hypothesis Braithwaite postulates. The test statistic, denoted as t, is as before: $t = \frac{b - \beta}{se(b)}$. The decision rule remains as before. The null hypothesis is rejected if the p value associated with the computed t statistic is smaller than the acceptable Type I error rate α, such as 0.05.

Confidence interval construction is used to estimate the range of b estimates which we are 95% confident contains the true population parameter β. Like before, the estimator is as follows: $b \pm t_{0.95, n-k} \times se(b)$.

Data Preparation

According to Braithwaite, his sample data include 296 MIDs between 1993 and 2001. To replicate his statistical results in Table II on page 515, copied in Table 7.2, we must first conduct necessary data preparation, such as acquiring his replication data and program files, importing data into R, and inspecting and understanding imported data.

Table 7.2 **OLS Regression of Dispute Dispersion (Original Statistical Results Table from Braithwaite, 2006)**

	Model 1	
Variable	*Coeff.*	*Z-score*
Territory	1.624*	3.83
Resources	0.984*	2.22
Mountain	0.026*	3.55
Forest	−0.012	−1.78
Ocean	−0.601	−1.07
Vital border	−0.809*	−2.03
Size of states	0.136	1.21
Peace years	−0.040*	−3.93
Constant	4.496*	2.69
N		296
R-squared		0.15

Robust standard errors. * $p < 0.05$.

Obtain Replication Files

The replication zip file, which includes a Stata format data file and a Stata program file called do file, is located at https://www.prio.org/JPR/Datasets/ in the section of 2006 vol. 43, no. 5. The file can be directly downloaded from the following link: http://file.prio.no/Journals/JPR/2006/43/5/Replication%20Braithwaite.zip, or Alex Braithwaite - The Geographic Spread of Militarized Disputes.

Set up a project folder, download the zip file into the project folder, and unzip it using the 7*zip* free software, located at http://www.7-zip.org/. Inside the zip file are two separate files, `file48280_braith_final_data.dta` and `file48280_braith_final_analysis.do`, which should be unzipped and stored in the project folder.

Import Data Into R

Before we import the dataset into R, we should first remove all objects from the workspace and set the working directory to the location where we saved the Braithwaite data file. We then load the foreign package, import the dataset with the read.dta() function, and assign the imported data file to a new data object called *mid*.

```
# (1) remove all objects in workspace
rm(list = ls(all = TRUE))


# (2) change working directory to project folder
setwd("C:\\Project\\braithwaite")
```

```
# (3) load the foreign package
library(foreign)

# (4) import stata file into R
mid <- read.dta("file48280_braith_final_data.dta")
```

Inspect and Understand Imported Data

As before, to inspect data we use the stargazer package to produce descriptive
statistics for the data we imported. We then compare the output below against
Table I for descriptive statistics on page 512 in Braithwaite (2006), copied below
in Table 7.3.

```
#(5) produce formatted table of descriptive statistics
# load stargazer into R
library(stargazer)

stargazer(mid, type="text", title = "Summary Statistics")


Summary Statistics
==============================================================================
Statistic          N      Mean        St. Dev.        Min          Max
------------------------------------------------------------------------------
dispnum           296    4,162.939      137.022       3,551        4,343
dyadid            296   429,818.200   241,178.300     2,020       910,940
ccode1            296     429.291       241.020         2           910
ccode2            296     527.686       220.901        20           986
year              296    1,996.764       2.685       1,992         2,001
logcap_ratio      296       1.734         1.390       0.048         7.912
allies            296       0.334         0.473         0             1
joint_democ       296       0.169         0.375         0             1
incidents         296       6.378        24.627         1           372
territory         296       0.399         0.490         0             1
sdd               296      70.533       131.808       5.000       804.575
radius            296     113.736       268.100       3.830      1,952.803
final_hostile     296       1.649         0.581         1             3
jointsize         296  5,523,885.000 8,043,434.000 31,013.700 56,776,786.000
log_radius_area   296       6.930         3.621       3.830        16.299
log_sdd_area      296       6.730         3.281       4.364        14.525
pop_dense         296       5.735        11.909       0.000        96.041
water             296       0.179         0.384         0             1
logdurat          296       3.006         2.195       0.000         8.068
cwpceyrs          296       7.024        15.928         0           159
host_mt           296      29.438        27.057       0.000        95.705
host_for          296      29.247        29.263       0.000        90.858
host_resource     296       0.368         0.483         0             1
bord_vital        296       0.676         0.534       0.000         2.000
------------------------------------------------------------------------------
```

In comparison, we can see that the number of observations is 296 in our
output as in Braithwaite's original table. One problem in understanding publicly

Table 7.3 **Original Descriptive Statistics Table in Braithwaite (2006)**

Variable	N	Mean	Standard deviation	Min.	Max.
Spread (logged)	296	6.93	3.62	3.83	16.30
Territory	296	0.40	0.49	0.00	1.00
Resources	296	0.37	0.48	0.00	1.00
Mountain	296	29.44	27.06	0.00	95.71
Forest	296	29.25	29.26	0.00	90.86
Ocean	296	0.18	0.38	0.00	1.00
Vital border	296	0.68	0.53	0.00	2.00
Size of states (logged)	296	14.39	1.67	10.34	17.86
Peace years	296	7.02	15.93	0.00	159.00
Number of incidents	296	6.38	24.63	1.00	372.00
Duration (logged)	296	3.01	2.20	0.00	8.07
Hostility level	296	1.65	0.58	1.00	3.00

available datasets is that variables often do not have labels or they lack a companion codebook. This is also the case here. The variables in the replication data do not have labels and the variable names are not always self-evident in terms of which variables they refer to in relation to those in Table 7.3. Now, even if the variables have labels, it is not always clear whether they need any additional transformation (such as log, etc.) in order to replicate the author's analysis. Hence, we should always look at the author's program file or codebook.

The Stata program file `file48280_braith_final_analysis.do` can be easily opened in any text editor, including the R editor. To do so, we open R, click `File` button on the upper left corner, click `Open script`, go to the folder `C:\Project` where we saved the Stata program file, click the downward arrow for file type selection and click `All files(*.*)`, click `file48280_braith_final_analysis.do`, and finally click the `Open` button to the lower right. The Stata program file will show up in R editor as follows:

```
version 7.0
log using "C:\My Documents\Alex\JPR\braith_jpr_RR.log",replace
#delimit;
set more off;
**********************************************************;
* Braith (Nov 1st, 2005) For JPR: the geog spread of mids *;
**********************************************************;

cd "C:\My Documents\Alex\JPR\";
set mem 100m;
set matsize 100;
```

```
use final_data.dta;

summ;
corr logcap_ratio allies joint_democ territory logsize host_mt
  host_for water cwpceyrs bord_vital host_resource incidents
  logdurat final_hostile;

*******************;
*Specific day one models*;
reg log_radius_area territory logsize host_mt host_for water
cwpceyrs bord_vital host_resource if final_hostile>0, robust;
vif;
hettest;
tobit log_radius_area territory logsize host_mt host_for water
cwpceyrs bord_vital host_resource if final_hostile>0, ll(0);

*models with dyadic controls*;
reg log_radius_area logcap_ratio allies joint_democ territory
logsize host_mt host_for water cwpceyrs bord_vital host_resource
if final_hostile>0, robust;
vif;
hettest;
tobit log_radius_area logcap_ratio allies joint_democ territory
logsize host_mt host_for water cwpceyrs bord_vital host_resource
if final_hostile>0, ll(0);

*models without dyadic and with post-hoc*;
reg log_radius_area incidents logdurat final_hostile territory
logsize host_mt host_for water cwpceyrs bord_vital host_resource
if final_hostile>0, robust;
vif;
hettest;
tobit log_radius_area incidents logdurat final_hostile territory
logsize host_mt host_for water cwpceyrs bord_vital host_resource
if final_hostile>0, ll(0);

save "C:\My Documents\Alex\JPR\final_data.dta", replace ;
exit, clear;
```

To understand the Stata program, we need a brief introduction on the commands used:

- log is a function for creating a log file of Stata output.
- #delimit; tells Stata to use a semicolon to separate different command lines.

- * is the comment line symbol like # in R.
- cd is a function for changing working directory, like setwd in R.
- use is a function for importing Stata data file, like load in R.
- summ is a function for requesting summary statistics for dataset.
- corr is a function for requesting correlation matrix for variables listed.
- reg is a function for requesting OLS regression, like lm in R.
- vif is a function for requesting variance inflation factor (VIF) statistics.
- hettest is a function for requesting a heteroskedastic error variance test.
- tobit is a function for requesting a Tobit regression model.

Replicate Table II in Braithwaite

The Stata command line below the comment line, *Specific day one models*;, is most likely the model that is being reported in Table II in Braithwaite (2006). In this Stata line of code, reg or regress is the function for requesting the OLS regression model. It is first followed by the dependent variable log_radius_area, and then by a list of the independent variables separated by blank space. The if final_hostile>0 condition means that only observations that satisfy the condition will be included in the estimation; that is, the final_hostile variable is greater than zero. The line of code also includes a model option after the comma; the robust option requests White robust standard errors.

```
reg log_radius_area territory logsize host_mt host_for water
cwpceyrs bord_vital host_resource if final_hostile>0, robust;
```

The equivalent R code for this Stata line of code is as follows:

```
lm(log_radius_area ~ territory + logsize + host_mt + host_for
   + water + cwpceyrs + bord_vital + host_resource,
   data=mid[mid$final_hostile>0,])
```

In this line of R code, lm() is the function for requesting the OLS linear regression model, with everything else placed in the argument of the function. The argument of the function includes the dependent variable log_radius_area, followed by tilde to separate the dependent variable from the independent variables, the independent variables connected by the plus signs, and the dataset option data=mid, plus the sample selection [mid$final_hostile>0,] based on the indexing method introduced in Chapter 2. Please note that in this line of R code, we are not yet requesting White robust standard errors like in Stata, an issue which we will discuss in detail later.

Running this line of R code, we will obtain the following output:

```
#(6) replicate Table2
lm(log_radius_area ~ territory + logsize + host_mt + host_for
    + water + cwpceyrs + bord_vital + host_resource,
    data=mid[mid$final_hostile>0,])

Error in eval(expr, envir, enclos): object 'logsize' not found
```

The error message indicates that the `logsize` variable is not found. Thus we have to go back to the descriptive statistics output above, which shows that indeed, the variable name is not in the output. To find out which variable `logsize` represents, we return to the list of hypotheses, Table 7.1, and Table 7.3. Most likely, `logsize` refers to H4, Size of states, and Size of states (logged). Within the descriptive statistics output, the most likely variable is `jointsize`, which needs to be logged. Now we will re-estimate the model above, but with `logsize` replaced by `jointsize` logged using the log() function.

```
# replicate Table2
lm(log_radius_area ~ territory + log(jointsize) + host_mt
    + host_for + water + cwpceyrs + bord_vital + host_resource,
    data=mid[mid$final_hostile>0,])


Call:
lm(formula = log_radius_area ~ territory + log(jointsize) + host_mt
    + host_for + water + cwpceyrs + bord_vital + host_resource,
    data = mid[mid$final_hostile > 0, ])

Coefficients:
    (Intercept)        territory    log(jointsize)
        4.49700          1.62443           0.13565
        host_mt          host_for             water
        0.02587         -0.01204          -0.60051
       cwpceyrs        bord_vital     host_resource
       -0.04050         -0.80915           0.98415

# replicate Table 2 and create an output object
table2 <- lm(log_radius_area ~ territory + log(jointsize)
        + host_mt + host_for + water + cwpceyrs + bord_vital
        + host_resource, data=mid[mid$final_hostile>0,])
```

The estimated coefficients match those in the *Coeff.* column of Table II in Braithwaite (2006), though in a different order. The note to Table II indicates that robust standard errors are employed, which we estimate below.

```
# load packages
library(car)
library(lmtest)
library(sandwich)

# White robust standard errors
table2.r<-coeftest(table2,vcov=vcovHC(table2,type="HC1"))
table2.r


t test of coefficients:

               Estimate Std. Error t value  Pr(>|t|)
(Intercept)    4.4969956  1.6694475  2.6937 0.0074823 **
territory      1.6244297  0.4240554  3.8307 0.0001570 ***
log(jointsize) 0.1356500  0.1122895  1.2080 0.2280269
host_mt        0.0258709  0.0072926  3.5475 0.0004540 ***
host_for      -0.0120354  0.0067672 -1.7785 0.0763825 .
water         -0.6005071  0.5610364 -1.0704 0.2853596
cwpceyrs      -0.0404980  0.0103090 -3.9284 0.0001072 ***
bord_vital    -0.8091476  0.3978571 -2.0338 0.0428950 *
host_resource  0.9841489  0.4425418  2.2239 0.0269364 *
---
Signif. codes:
0 '***' 0.001 '**' 0.01 '*' 0.05 '.' 0.1 ' ' 1
```

Comparing the output against Table II in Braithwaite (2006), we find that the coefficients are identical and that the t statistics in our output are the same as those in the column Z-score in Table II. It is worth noting though that the type="HC1" option in the coeftest() function produces identical standard errors as those implied in Table II, but "HC1" could be replaced by "HC", "HC0", "HC2", "HC3", "HC4", "HC4m", or "HC5" to produce other variants of White robust standard errors. At this moment, we have successfully replicated the results in Table II in Braithwaite (2006).

Diagnostic Tests and Robustness Checks

As noted in the previous chapter, whether the estimation and inference results are valid depends on whether the Gauss-Markov conditions are satisfied or not.

Hence, it is important that we double-check whether the results in Table II in Braithwaite are based on violated assumptions and whether they are sensitive to robustness checks.

Following the example in the previous chapter, we first use the augment_columns() function in the broom package to add various diagnostic statistics as new variables to the original data mid and then create a new diagnostic dataset mid.v2.

```
#(7) add additional diagnostics statistics to original data
library(broom)
mid.v2 <- augment_columns(table2, mid)
```

Model Specification

We first show a plot of residuals against fitted values to visually inspect two assumptions: (1) The residuals should be independent of the fitted values, and (2) the model is linear. Figure 7.1 presents the diagnostic graph.

```
#(8) diagnostic test for model specification
# load package
library(ggplot2)

# residuals against fitted values
ggplot(mid.v2, aes(x=.fitted, y=.resid)) +
        geom_hline(yintercept=0) +
        geom_point() +
        geom_smooth(method='loess', se=TRUE)
```

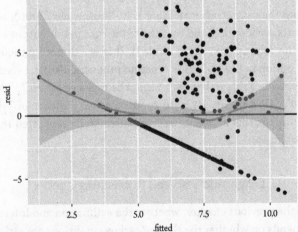

Figure 7.1 Regression Diagnostic Plot: Residuals versus Fitted Values.

Figure 7.1 shows that the loess curve roughly follows the residual=0 line, which is reassuring. But there appears to be some outlying observations (very small fitted values to the left) pulling the loess curve. Also, there appears to be some data truncation as shown in the figure.

To be sure, we conduct Ramsey's regression specification error test (RESET) to test possible non-linearity in the residuals. Recall that for this test, we re-estimate the original model, but also include the quadratic or cubic terms of the predicted y (i.e., $\hat{y}_i$). We use an F-statistic to test the null hypothesis that the two models explain the same amount of variations in the dependent variable. If the null hypothesis is rejected, it indicates that some of the independent variables affect the dependent variable in a non-linear fashion.

```
# OLS estimates for model 2
table2.q <- lm(log_radius_area ~territory + log(jointsize)
      + host_mt + host_for + water + cwpceyrs + bord_vital
      + host_resource + I(.fitted^2), data=mid.v2)

# F test of model difference
anova(table2, table2.q)

Analysis of Variance Table

Model 1: log_radius_area ~ territory + log(jointsize) + host_mt +
    host_for + water + cwpceyrs + bord_vital + host_resource
Model 2: log_radius_area ~ territory + log(jointsize) + host_mt +
    host_for + water + cwpceyrs + bord_vital + host_resource
    + I(.fitted^2)
  Res.Df    RSS Df Sum of Sq      F  Pr(>F)
1    287 3307.2
2    286 3269.6  1      37.6 3.2891 0.07079 .
---
Signif. codes:
0 '***' 0.001 '**' 0.01 '*' 0.05 '.' 0.1 ' ' 1
```

The F test statistic is 3.2891, with a *p* value of 0.07079. If we apply the 5% significance level, we will fail to reject the null hypothesis that these two models are identical. It means that the quadratic model does not do a better job in explaining the dependent variable. But if we apply the 10% significance level, then we will reject the null hypothesis and conclude that there might be some non-linear effect missing in Braithwaite's original model. Overall, the evidence for a quadratic model is not that strong.

Perfect and High Multicollinearity

For the Gauss-Markov theorem to hold, the independent variables cannot be perfectly correlated. Since no variable was dropped in estimation, there is no perfect multicollinearity among the variables.

To diagnose high multicollinearity, we will compute the variance inflation factor (VIF). In this model, none of the variables has a very high VIF value that should cause concern.

```
# (9) diagnose multicollinearity (vif statistics)
library(car)
vif(table2)

    territory log(jointsize)       host_mt       host_for
     1.045411      1.120814      1.132820       1.129070
        water      cwpceyrs    bord_vital  host_resource
     1.176216      1.087304      1.210224       1.112860
```

Constant Error Variance

The Gauss-Markov theorem assumes that the error variance should remain constant across observations. When this assumption is violated, we have non-constant error variance that leads to incorrect standard error estimates. Braithwaite employed White robust standard errors to correct for this assumption violation. Still, it is worth double-checking whether the constant error variance assumption is violated or not because, as noted earlier, White robust standard errors do come with some cost in efficiency.

Like before, we start with the diagnostic graph in Figure 7.1. While there does not appear to be any strong fanning-out or funneling-in pattern in the residuals, the residuals do exhibit some truncation and, notably, most residuals appear to lie above the residuals=0 line. Thus, some formal diagnostic test is useful and necessary.

Again, we conduct two diagnostic tests: Breush/Pagan and Cook/Weisberg score tests. For both tests, the null hypothesis is constant error variance, and the alternative hypothesis is that the error variance is not constant.

```
#(10) test heteroskedasticity
# Cook/Weisberg score test of constant error variance
library(car)
ncvTest(table2)

Non-constant Variance Score Test
Variance formula: ~ fitted.values
```

```
Chisquare = 15.46114     Df = 1      p = 8.421901e-05

# Breush/Pagan test of constant error variance
library(lmtest)
bptest(table2)

studentized Breusch-Pagan test

data:  table2
BP = 22.316, df = 8, p-value = 0.004363
```

The p values in both tests are very small, indicating the constant error variance assumption is violated. Thus, the White robust standard error correction by Braithwaite is justified.

Influential Observations

One main diagnostic test concerns whether the results in Table II in Braithwaite are sensitive to influential observations. As in the previous chapter, we employ the Cook's D statistic to diagnose whether a coefficient estimate varies dramatically with the presence or absence of influential observations or not.

We first present the Cook's distance plot to see if there is any obvious potential outlier. As before, we set the cutoff value for Cook's D at $4/(n-k-1)$; in the formula, "n" indicates the number of observations and equals 296 in this case, "k" is the number of independent variables and equals 8. The computed cutoff is 0.014, which helps identify more accurately the list of influential observations. Figure 7.2 identifies eleven influential observations above the cutoff.

```
#(11) diagnose influential observations
# create observation id
mid.v2$id <- as.numeric(row.names(mid.v2))

# identify obs with Cook's D above cutoff
ggplot(mid.v2, aes(id, .cooksd)) +
    geom_bar(stat="identity", position="identity") +
    xlab("Obs. Number")+ylab("Cook's distance")+
    geom_hline(yintercept=0.014) +
    geom_text(aes(label=ifelse((.cooksd>0.014),id,"")),
              vjust=-0.2, hjust=0.5)
```

We display the dispute number, country codes, the dependent variable log_radius_area, and four diagnostic statistics for these 11 observations below.

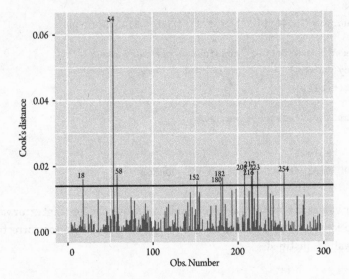

Figure 7.2 Diagnostic Plot for Influential Observations: Cook's D.

```
# list observations whose Cook's D above threshold
mid.v2[mid.v2$.cooksd>0.014, c("dispnum","ccode1","ccode2",
    "year","log_radius_area",".std.resid",".hat",".cooksd")]


    dispnum ccode1 ccode2 year log_radius_area .std.resid
18     4281    710    713 2001       13.424998   2.197770
54     4261      2    101 2000        4.363605   1.099621
58     4283      2    700 2001       16.179976   2.090194
152    4173    365    640 1996        4.363605  -1.791872
180    4271      2    645 1996       13.142159   1.760959
182    4339    490    517 1998       14.061648   2.155569
208    4137    339    345 1998       15.374997   2.825682
216    4186      2    345 2000       14.823683   2.459403
217    4030    710    816 1994       14.055879   2.149420
223    4087    731    732 1994       16.298773   2.793464
254    4016      2     41 1993       15.047297   2.541450
          .hat    .cooksd
18  0.02918300 0.01613298
54  0.32143978 0.06364361
58  0.03454403 0.01736885
152 0.04137509 0.01539791
180 0.04093315 0.01470558
182 0.03077606 0.01639344
208 0.02026260 0.01834803
```

```
216 0.02435228 0.01677503
217 0.03619814 0.01927963
223 0.02073654 0.01836033
254 0.02418082 0.01778370
```

To examine whether the results in Table II in Braithwaite (2006) are sensitive to the exclusion of these observations, we re-estimate the model without those observations. The results appear to be robust as before.

```
# re-estimate model without influential obs
table2.no <- lm(log_radius_area ~ territory + log(jointsize)
          + host_mt + host_for + water + cwpceyrs + bord_vital
          + host_resource, data=mid.v2[mid.v2$.cooksd<0.014,])

# estimation results without outliers
summary(table2.no)


Call:
lm(formula = log_radius_area ~ territory + log(jointsize) + host_mt
    + host_for + water + cwpceyrs + bord_vital + host_resource,
    data = mid.v2[mid.v2$.cooksd < 0.014, ])

Residuals:
    Min      1Q  Median      3Q     Max
-6.0724 -2.3098 -0.8227  2.0987  8.6450

Coefficients:
                Estimate Std. Error t value Pr(>|t|)
(Intercept)     4.249943   1.812386   2.345 0.019739 *
territory       1.865617   0.383800   4.861 1.96e-06 ***
log(jointsize)  0.123944   0.116441   1.064 0.288061
host_mt         0.027678   0.007279   3.803 0.000176 ***
host_for       -0.014094   0.006693  -2.106 0.036140 *
water          -0.751005   0.525275  -1.430 0.153923
cwpceyrs       -0.043022   0.014429  -2.982 0.003123 **
bord_vital     -0.633175   0.382633  -1.655 0.099105 .
host_resource   1.011818   0.403938   2.505 0.012826 *
---
Signif. codes:
0 '***' 0.001 '**' 0.01 '*' 0.05 '.' 0.1 ' ' 1
```

```
Residual standard error: 3.114 on 276 degrees of freedom
Multiple R-squared:  0.1851,Adjusted R-squared:  0.1615
F-statistic: 7.835 on 8 and 276 DF,  p-value: 1.731e-09
```

Normality Test

We first construct the quantile comparison plot for the residuals from both the original model and the model without influential observations. Visually, as shown in Figure 7.3, the residuals do not appear to fit the benchmark t distribution well.

```
#(12) Normality diagnostics
library(car)
qqPlot(table2,distribution="t",simulate=TRUE,grid=TRUE)
qqPlot(table2.no,distribution="t",simulate=TRUE,
       grid=TRUE)
```

We then carry out the Shapiro-Wilk normality test for both models. The null hypothesis that the residuals have a normal distribution appears to be rejected for both models. Hence, the results of the Braithwaite study are subject to the influence of this assumption violation. Our confidence in the results depends on the belief that the OLS estimator can still be asymptotically normal.

```
# normality test
shapiro.test(residuals(table2))


Shapiro-Wilk normality test

data:  residuals(table2)
W = 0.9191, p-value = 1.461e-11

shapiro.test(residuals(table2.no))


Shapiro-Wilk normality test

data:  residuals(table2.no)
W = 0.93066, p-value = 2.843e-10
```

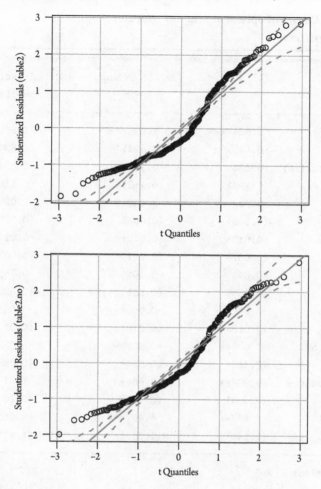

Figure 7.3 Normality Assumption Diagnostic Plot.

Report and Discuss Estimation Results

As before, we report the re-estimated models together in one table using the stargazer() function. Table 7.4 reports three models: OLS, OLS with White robust standard errors, and OLS without outliers. The results in Table 7.4 suggest that the findings in Braithwaite (2006) appear to be rather robust, with the caveat that the normality assumption is violated. To the extent that one accepts that the OLS estimator is asymptotically normal, the statistical tests can be treated as being asymptotically valid.

```
#(13) report results in table
library(stargazer)
stargazer(table2, table2.r, table2.no, type="text",
```

Table 7.4 **Causes of Spread of Military Disputes: Replication and Robustness Tests**

	(1) OLS	(2) OLS-robust SE	(3) OLS-excluding outliers
territory	1.624***	1.624***	1.866***
	(0.412)	(0.424)	(0.384)
log(jointsize)	0.136	0.136	0.124
	(0.125)	(0.112)	(0.116)
host_mt	0.026***	0.026***	0.028***
	(0.008)	(0.007)	(0.007)
host_for	-0.012*	-0.012*	-0.014**
	(0.007)	(0.007)	(0.007)
water	-0.601	-0.601	-0.751
	(0.558)	(0.561)	(0.525)
cwpceyrs	-0.040***	-0.040***	-0.043***
	(0.013)	(0.010)	(0.014)
bord_vital	-0.809**	-0.809**	-0.633*
	(0.408)	(0.398)	(0.383)
host_resource	0.984**	0.984**	1.012**
	(0.432)	(0.443)	(0.404)
Constant	4.497**	4.497***	4.250**
	(1.949)	(1.669)	(1.812)
Observations	296		285
R2	0.145		0.185
Adjusted R2	0.121		0.161
Note:	*p<0.1; **p<0.05; ***p<0.01		

```
no.space=TRUE, omit.stat=c("f","ser"),model.names=FALSE,
dep.var.labels.include=FALSE, dep.var.caption="")
```

Table 7.4 shows that the results are robust to an alternative estimator of the standard errors and the exclusion of outlying observations. According to Table 7.4, the variable territory has a statistically significant positive effect. Conflicts involving territorial issues are much more geographically spread than those on other issues. Since the dependent variable is log transformed and territory is a dummy variable, its size of effect should be recomputed as $100 * (exp^{\hat{\beta}} - 1) = 100 * (exp^{1.624} - 1) \approx 407\%$ following the instruction in Chapter 5. This means that territorial disputes are four times more spread out than non-territorial conflicts. The finding supports Hypothesis 1.

The variable host_resource has a statistically significant positive impact. Conflicts that involve states better endowed in oil, gems, or illicit drugs are more spread out than those that do not. Its effect, based on $100 * (exp^{\hat{\beta}} - 1) = 100 * (exp^{0.984} - 1) \approx 167\%$, means that conflicts in countries endowed with oil, gems, or illicit drugs are 167% more spread out. The finding supports Hypothesis 2.

The variables related to terrain have very different effects, sometimes contradicting Braithwaite's hypotheses. The variable host_mt has a statistically significant positive effect, meaning that conflicts in countries with more mountainous areas are more spread out than those in less mountainous countries. This contradicts Hypothesis 3. In contrast, the variable host_for has a statistically significant negative effect, meaning that conflicts in countries with more forested areas are less spread out than those in countries with less forested areas. This result supports Hypothesis 3. Finally, the variable water, indicating the location of conflict is at sea, has the expected negative sign, but its effect is statistically indistinguishable from zero.

The variable log(jointsize) has no statistically significant effect. Conflicts involving larger states are no more spread out than those involving smaller ones. This finding does not provide empirical support for Hypothesis 4.

The variable border_vital has a statistically significant negative effect. Conflicts involving states sharing a vital border are less spread out than conflicts among states that do not share a vital border. Its effect, based on $100 * (exp^{\hat{\beta}} - 1) = 100 * (exp^{-0.809} - 1) \approx -55\%$, means that as the vital border increases by one unit, the spread of conflicts decreases by about 55%. This finding contradicts Hypothesis 5.

Section Summary

In this section, we demonstrated how to replicate and diagnose the regression model results from a published study. In this process, we also illustrated how to move from theoretical expectations, expressed in hypotheses, to a population regression model, and then how to use the estimates from a sample regression model to make inferences about the parameters in the population regression model. We also showed how to conduct various robustness tests of the original findings, as well as how to report and discuss the estimation results. The process offers a unique experience of empirical research using observational data in social sciences.

Does Religiosity Influence Individual Attitudes toward Innovation? Replication of Bénabou et al. (2015)

In an article entitled "Religion and Innovation," published in the *American Economic Review*, Bénabou, Ticchi, and Vindigni (2015) study the impact of religiosity on innovation. Previous research shows in cross-country regressions that religiosity is negatively correlated with innovation, measured by logged patents per capita. One argument for this negative relationship is that new discoveries, though leading to productivity gains, often challenge existing religious beliefs and doctrines such that a religious sector may be opposed to innovations or must adapt the doctrine to become compatible with the new knowledge. In this paper, Bénabou and his coauthors seek to test whether greater religiosity negatively influences attitudes toward innovation at the individual level.

Bénabou and his coauthors employ data from five waves of the World Value Survey (1980, 1990, 1995, 2000, and 2005, at http://www.worldvaluessurvey. org) to evaluate the effects of five measures of religiosity, both in terms of beliefs and church attendance, on 11 indicators of openness to innovation. Based on a total of 52 regression estimates, they report that greater religiosity is associated with less positive views of innovation.

The empirical analysis in Bénabou et al. (2015) follows a style which is common in empirical work but differs from that of Braithwaite (2006). Recall that Braithwaite (2006) focuses on explaining one dependent variable, reporting only a couple of regression models, one of which we replicated. In contrast, Bénabou et al. (2015) estimate and report a very large number of regressions for a very large number of dependent and independent variables. The rationale is that both religiosity and attitudes toward innovation are concepts difficult to operationalize because both concepts are multidimensional and often hard to observe directly. Using one indicator for either concept is likely to be misleading. As a result, Bénabou et al. (2015) employ a large number of indicators to test their hypothesis.

In this section, we will replicate Table 2 in Bénabou et al. (2015), which reports, based on 15 regression models, 15 coefficient estimates of five key independent variables—religious person, importance of religion, belief in God, importance of God, and church attendance—with respect to three dependent variables—importance of child independence, importance of child imagination, and importance of child determination. The original table is shown in Table 7.5. As shown in the table's notes, a large number of control variables are included in the model though not reported for the sake of space. OLS with robust standard errors is used in estimation.

The purpose of this replication exercise is to expose students to a different style of data analysis that they will often come across in practice, yet this style

Table 7.5 **Most Important Qualities for Children to Have (from Bénabou et al., 2015)**

Dependent variable	Importance of child independence (A029) (1)	Importance of child imagination (A034) (2)	Importance of child determination (A039) (3)
Religious person	−0.045*** (0.005) 93,028 0.141	−0.032*** (0.004) 93,028 0.067	−0.041*** (0.005) 89,348 0.060
Importance of religion	−0.040*** (0.002) 95,902 0.145	−0.024*** (0.002) 95,902 0.068	−0.047*** (0.002) 92,200 0.064
Belief in God	−0.054*** (0.010) 58,294 0.146	−0.038*** (0.009) 58,294 0.067	−0.066*** (0.011) 55,545 0.065
Importance of God	−0.016*** (0.001) 94,827 0.145	−0.008*** (0.001) 94,827 0.068	−0.013*** (0.001) 92,078 0.062
Church attendance	−0.009*** (0.001) 93,242 0.141	−0.006*** (0.001) 93,242 0.069	−0.008*** (0.001) 89,536 0.061

Notes: OLS estimates for alternative measures of religiosity. Robust standard errors in parentheses, followed by *number of observations* and *Adjusted* R^2 both in italics. All regressions include controls (not reported) for sex, age, education, social class, income, town size, religious denomination, country, and year.
***Significant at the 1 percent level.
**Significant at the 5 percent level.
*Significant at the 10 percent level.

of data analysis can often be confusing to students when it comes to implementation. We will unpack the process of "sausage making," demonstrating how the results in Table 2 of Bénabou et al. are produced. Ideally, after this replication exercise, students will no longer be intimidated by this type of empirical work. They will also have the confidence to conduct, on their own, in-depth diagnostic tests and analyses using the data and program codes provided to them.

Locate, Import, and Understand Data

The replication dataset and program codes for Bénabou et al. (2015) are available for download from https://www.aeaweb.org/articles.php?doi=10.1257/aer.p20151032. Once we download the files, we should save them into a newly created folder called "benabou" under our Project folder, unzip the files, and place the unzipped program and data files in the "benabou" folder. Similar to the Braithwaite case, the program and data files are all in stata format. Hence, like before, we need to read the data into R. It is worth noting that we should add the convert.factors=FALSE option inside the read.dta() function to ensure that all numeric variables are read into R as numeric rather than factor variables.

```
# replicate Table 2 in "Religion and Innovation"

#(1) remove all objects in workspace
rm(list=ls(all=TRUE))

#(2) change working directory to project folder
setwd("C:\\Project\\benabou")

#(3) import stata file into R
# load the foreign package
library(foreign)

benabou <- read.dta("aerpp2015btv-dataset.dta",
                    convert.factors=FALSE)
```

We may now try to understand the data by computing summary statistics, as well as importing and showing the variable labels. For a refresher on how to do this in R, readers can refer back to the Miscellaneous Q&A section in Chapter 2.

```
#(4) produce formatted table of descriptive statistics
# load stargazer into R
library(stargazer)

stargazer(benabou, type="text", title = "Summary Statistics")
```

```
Summary Statistics
=================================================
Statistic    N       Mean     St. Dev.  Min    Max
-------------------------------------------------
S002      257,597   3.706     1.133      1      5
S003      257,597   462.970   266.787    8      911
S017      257,597   0.986     0.394      0.001  32.246
A006      236,174   1.912     1.044      1      4
A029      255,656   0.458     0.498      0      1
A034      252,238   0.201     0.401      0      1
A039      247,782   0.357     0.479      0      1
```

A189	70,815	2.696	1.346	1	6
A195	70,748	3.871	1.582	1	6
E046	114,537	5.314	2.904	1	10
E047	17,486	6.063	2.952	1	10
E219	62,930	7.507	2.453	1	10
E220	61,624	5.964	2.959	1	10
E234	65,798	6.756	2.507	1	10
F025	203,036	53.511	14.822	1	90
F028	238,981	4.382	2.581	1	8
F034	231,696	1.327	0.557	1	4
F050	152,038	0.889	0.314	0	1
F063	240,112	7.745	3.019	1	10
F198	66,989	6.243	2.929	1	10
X001	252,941	1.515	0.500	1	2
X003	247,978	40.313	15.914	14	99
X025	230,283	4.408	2.335	1	8
X045	202,706	3.346	0.989	1	5
X047	226,003	4.512	2.392	1	10
X049	159,343	5.050	2.524	1	9
year	257,597	1,998.330	6.200	1,980	2,005
F034rp	231,696	0.717	0.450	0	1
A006m	236,174	-1.912	1.044	-4	-1
F028m	238,981	-4.382	2.581	-8	-1
X001m	252,941	0.515	0.500	0	1
X045m	202,706	-3.346	0.989	-5	-1
X049m	158,787	5.036	2.517	1	8
E220m	61,624	-5.964	2.959	-10	-1
E219m	62,930	-7.507	2.453	-10	-1
A189m	70,815	-2.696	1.346	-6	-1
A195m	70,748	-3.871	1.582	-6	-1

```
#(5) obtain variable labels from original Stata data file
var.labels <- attr(benabou,"var.labels")
bendata.key <- data.frame(var.name=names(benabou),var.labels)
```

We can present the variable labels in bendata.key using the stargazer()
function and show the results in Table 7.6. These variable labels are important
later on as we try to interpret what each variable name means in setting up the
models and constructing the final results table.

Table 7.6 **Variable Labels for Dataset in Bénabou et al. (2015)**

S002	Wave
S003	Country/region
S017	Weight
A006	Important in life: Religion
A029	Importance of child independence (A029)
A034	Importance of child imagination (A034)
A039	Importance of child determination (A039)
A189	Schwartz: It is important to this person to think up new ideas and be creative
A195	Schwartz: It is important to this person adventure and taking risks
E046	New ideas are better than old: agree (E046)
E047	Attitude toward change: welcome possibility (E047)
E219	Science and technology make our way of life change too fast
E220	We depend too much on science and not enough on faith
E234	Science & technology make world better off: agree (E234)
F025	Religious denomination
F028	How often do you attend religious services
F034	Religious person
F050	Belief in God
F063	Importance of God
F198	People shape their own fate: agree (F198)
X001	Sex
X003	Age
X025	Education
X045	Social class (subjective)
X047	Income
X049	Size of town
year	
F034rp	Religious person
A006m	Importance of religion
F028m	Church attendance
X001m	Female
X045m	Social Class

Table 7.6 Continued

X049m	
E220m	Too much dependence on science vs faith: disagree (E220m)
E219m	Science & technology change life too fast: disagree (E219m)
A189m	Importance of new ideas & being creative: agree (A189m)
A195m	Importance of adventure & risk taking: agree (A195m)

```
# show variable labels using stargazer function
stargazer(bendata.key,type="text",summary=F,rownames=F)
```

Replicate Table 2 and Report Findings

Based on the Stata program file, we will demonstrate how the results in row 1 and column 1 of Table 2 of Bénabou et al. (2015) are obtained. The results, concerning the relationship between a religious person (F034rp) and the importance of child independence (A029), include the coefficient -0.045 and the robust standard error 0.005 in parentheses. The R code and output are as follows:

```
#(6) replicate models in table 2
# load car, lmtest, and sandwich packages
library(car)
library(lmtest)
library(sandwich)


# Table 2 Column 1 five models for A029
c1m1 <- lm(A029 ~ F034rp + X001m + X003 + X025 + X045m + X047
        + factor(X049m) + factor(F025) + factor(S003)
        + factor(year), weights=S017, data=benabou)


# White robust standard errors
c1m1.r <- coeftest(c1m1, vcov=vcovHC(c1m1, type="HC1"))


# display estimation results
c1m1.r
t test of coefficients:
                Estimate  Std. Error  t value  Pr(>|t|)
(Intercept)   0.27647883  0.12745442   2.1692  0.0300672 *
F034rp       -0.04463100  0.00460353  -9.6950  < 2.2e-16 ***
X001m         0.00787350  0.00322453   2.4418  0.0146181 *
......[output for 145 variables omitted]
```

Note that the actual model output contains a lot of information. However, for the sake of saving space, the authors only report the results for the F034rp variable in the published article. After rounding, we can see that our results for the F034rp variable match exactly those in Table 2 of Bénabou et al. (2015).

Given this success, we can now proceed to estimate the other 14 models in Table 2 of Bénabou et al. (2015). In the interest of space, we will only show the R code below.

```
# Table 2 Column 1 five models for A029
c1m2 <- lm(A029 ~ A006m + X001m + X003 + X025 + X045m + X047
            + factor(X049m) + factor(F025) + factor(S003)
            + factor(year), weights=S017, data=benabou)
# White robust standard errors
c1m2.r <- coeftest(c1m2, vcov=vcovHC(c1m2, type="HC1"))


c1m3 <- lm(A029 ~ F050 + X001m + X003 + X025 + X045m + X047
            + factor(X049m) + factor(F025) + factor(S003)
            + factor(year), weights=S017, data=benabou)
# White robust standard errors
c1m3.r <- coeftest(c1m3, vcov=vcovHC(c1m3, type="HC1"))


c1m4 <- lm(A029 ~ F063 + X001m + X003 + X025 + X045m + X047
            + factor(X049m) + factor(F025) + factor(S003)
            + factor(year), weights=S017, data=benabou)
# White robust standard errors
c1m4.r <- coeftest(c1m4, vcov=vcovHC(c1m4, type="HC1"))


c1m5 <- lm(A029 ~ F028m + X001m + X003 + X025 + X045m + X047
            + factor(X049m) + factor(F025) + factor(S003)
            + factor(year), weights=S017, data=benabou)
# White robust standard errors
c1m5.r <- coeftest(c1m5, vcov=vcovHC(c1m5, type="HC1"))


# Table 2 Column 2 five models for A034
c2m1 <- lm(A034 ~ F034rp + X001m + X003 + X025 + X045m + X047
            + factor(X049m) + factor(F025) + factor(S003)
            + factor(year), weights=S017, data=benabou)
# White robust standard errors
c2m1.r <- coeftest(c2m1, vcov=vcovHC(c2m1, type="HC1"))


c2m2 <- lm(A034 ~ A006m + X001m + X003 + X025 + X045m + X047
            + factor(X049m) + factor(F025) + factor(S003)
```

```
            + factor(year), weights=S017, data=benabou)
# White robust standard errors
c2m2.r <- coeftest(c2m2, vcov=vcovHC(c2m2, type="HC1"))


c2m3 <- lm(A034 ~ F050 + X001m + X003 + X025 + X045m + X047
            + factor(X049m) + factor(F025) + factor(S003)
            + factor(year), weights=S017, data=benabou)
# White robust standard errors
c2m3.r <- coeftest(c2m3, vcov=vcovHC(c2m3, type="HC1"))


c2m4 <- lm(A034 ~ F063 + X001m + X003 + X025 + X045m + X047
            + factor(X049m) + factor(F025) + factor(S003)
            + factor(year), weights=S017, data=benabou)
# White robust standard errors
c2m4.r <- coeftest(c2m4, vcov=vcovHC(c2m4, type="HC1"))


c2m5 <- lm(A034 ~ F028m + X001m + X003 + X025 + X045m + X047
            + factor(X049m) + factor(F025) + factor(S003)
            + factor(year), weights=S017, data=benabou)
# White robust standard errors
c2m5.r <- coeftest(c2m5, vcov=vcovHC(c2m5, type="HC1"))


# Table 2 Column 3 five models for A039
c3m1 <- lm(A039 ~ F034rp + X001m + X003 + X025 + X045m + X047
            + factor(X049m) + factor(F025) + factor(S003)
            + factor(year), weights=S017, data=benabou)
# White robust standard errors
c3m1.r <- coeftest(c3m1, vcov=vcovHC(c3m1, type="HC1"))


c3m2 <- lm(A039 ~ A006m + X001m + X003 + X025 + X045m + X047
            + factor(X049m) + factor(F025) + factor(S003)
            + factor(year), weights=S017, data=benabou)
# White robust standard errors
c3m2.r <- coeftest(c3m2, vcov=vcovHC(c3m2, type="HC1"))


c3m3 <- lm(A039 ~ F050 + X001m + X003 + X025 + X045m + X047
            + factor(X049m) + factor(F025) + factor(S003)
            + factor(year), weights=S017, data=benabou)
# White robust standard errors
c3m3.r <- coeftest(c3m3, vcov=vcovHC(c3m3, type="HC1"))
```

```
c3m4 <- lm(A039 ~ F063 + X001m + X003 + X025 + X045m + X047
            + factor(X049m) + factor(F025) + factor(S003)
            + factor(year), weights=S017, data=benabou)
# White robust standard errors
c3m4.r <- coeftest(c3m4, vcov=vcovHC(c3m4, type="HC1"))

c3m5 <- lm(A039 ~ F028m + X001m + X003 + X025 + X045m + X047
            + factor(X049m) + factor(F025) + factor(S003)
            + factor(year), weights=S017, data=benabou)
# White robust standard errors
c3m5.r <- coeftest(c3m5, vcov=vcovHC(c3m5, type="HC1"))
```

Once we estimate all the models, we use the stargazer () function to compile the coefficients and standard errors in Table 2 in the Bénabou et al. study. And we report our results in Table 7.7.

```
#(7) Report Replicated Results of Table 2 in Bénabou et al.
library(stargazer)
stargazer(c1m1.r, c1m2.r, c1m3.r, c1m4.r, c1m5.r, type="text",
 no.space=TRUE, keep=c("F034rp","A006m","F050","F063","F028m"),
 dep.var.labels="Importance of child independence (A029)",
 covariate.labels = c("Religious person (F034rp)",
 "Importance of religion (A006m)", "Belief in God (F050)",
 "Importance of God (F063)", "Church attendance (F028m)"),
 out="benabou1")

stargazer(c2m1.r, c2m2.r, c2m3.r, c2m4.r, c2m5.r, type="text",
 no.space=TRUE, keep=c("F034rp","A006m","F050","F063","F028m"),
 dep.var.labels="Importance of child imagination (A034)",
 covariate.labels = c("Religious person (F034rp)",
 "Importance of religion (A006m)", "Belief in God (F050)",
 "Importance of God (F063)", "Church attendance (F028m)"),
 out="benabou2")

stargazer(c3m1.r, c3m2.r, c3m3.r, c3m4.r, c3m5.r, type="text",
 no.space=TRUE, keep=c("F034rp","A006m","F050","F063","F028m"),
 dep.var.labels="Importance of child determination (A039)",
 covariate.labels = c("Religious person (F034rp)",
 "Importance of religion (A006m)", "Belief in God (F050)",
 "Importance of God (F063)", "Church attendance (F028m)"),
 out="benabou3")
```

Looking over the results in Table 7.7, we will see that they are identical to those in Table 2 of Bénabou et al. (2015). Hence, we have successfully replicated this part of their study. More ambitious students may try to replicate the results in Table 1, or apply the diagnostic tests from the previous section to the Bénabou et al. study. The process ought to be relatively easy and straightforward.

The results in Table 7.7 suggest that across all 15 models, all five measures of religiosity are negatively and significantly associated with the three dependent

Table 7.7 **Replicating Table 2 in Bénabout et al. (2015)**

	Dependent variable:				
	Importance of child independence (A029)				
	(1)	(2)	(3)	(4)	(5)
Religious person (F034rp)	−0.045*** (0.005)				
Importance of religion (A006m)		−0.040*** (0.002)			
Belief in God (F050)			−0.054*** (0.010)		
Importance of God (F063)				−0.016*** (0.001)	
Church attendance (F028m)					−0.009*** (0.001)
	Dependent variable:				
	Importance of child imagination (A034)				
	(1)	(2)	(3)	(4)	(5)
Religious person (F034rp)	−0.032*** (0.004)				
Importance of religion (A006m)		−0.024*** (0.002)			
Belief in God (F050)			−0.038*** (0.009)		
Importance of God (F063)				−0.008*** (0.001)	

(continued)

Table 7.7 Continued

	Dependent variable:				
	Importance of child determination (A039)				
	(1)	(2)	(3)	(4)	(5)
Church attendance (F028m)					−0.006*** (0.001)
Religious person (F034rp)	−0.041*** (0.005)				
Importance of religion (A006m)		−0.047*** (0.002)			
Belief in God (F050)			−0.066*** (0.011)		
Importance of God (F063)				−0.013*** (0.001)	
Church attendance (F028m)					−0.008*** (0.001)

Note: *p<0.1; **p<0.05; ***p<0.01

variables: importance of child independence, importance of child imagination, and importance of child determination. Individuals who are more religious, believe in God, and attend church more frequently tend to attach less importance to child independence, imagination, and determination than less religious individuals.

Section summary

In this section, we demonstrated how to replicate a different type of empirical analysis common in applied work. In this case, a lot of dependent variables, a lot of independent variables, and a lot of regression models are involved, but the final published results are condensed, showing only the key estimates of interest. The replication process offers a different type of experience from the one in the previous section, but it is a valuable and realistic one. We encourage readers to carry out, on their own, in-depth diagnostic tests and analyses as conducted in the previous section.

Chapter 7 Program Code

Program for Replicating Braithwaite (2006)

```
#(1) remove all objects in workspace
rm(list=ls(all=TRUE))

#(2) change working directory to project folder
setwd("C:\\Project\\braithwaite")

#(3) load the foreign package
library(foreign)

#(4) import stata file into R
mid <- read.dta("file48280_braith_final_data.dta")

#(5) produce formatted table of descriptive statistics
# load stargazer into R
library(stargazer)

stargazer(mid, type="text", title = "Summary Statistics")

#(6) replicate Table2
lm(log_radius_area ~ territory + logsize + host_mt + host_for
   + water + cwpceyrs + bord_vital + host_resource,
   data=mid[mid$final_hostile>0,])

# replicate Table2
lm(log_radius_area ~ territory + log(jointsize) + host_mt
   + host_for + water + cwpceyrs + bord_vital + host_resource,
   data=mid[mid$final_hostile>0,])

# replicate Table2 and create an output object
table2 <- lm(log_radius_area ~ territory + log(jointsize)
         + host_mt + host_for + water + cwpceyrs + bord_vital
         + host_resource, data=mid[mid$final_hostile>0,])

# load packages
library(car)
library(lmtest)
library(sandwich)
```

```
# White robust standard errors
table2.r<-coeftest(table2,vcov=vcovHC(table2,type="HC1"))
table2.r


#(7) add additional diagnostics statistics to original data
library(broom)
mid.v2 <- augment_columns(table2, mid)


#(8) diagnostic test for model specification
# load package
library(ggplot2)


# residuals against fitted values
ggplot(mid.v2, aes(x=.fitted, y=.resid)) +
        geom_hline(yintercept=0) +
        geom_point() +
        geom_smooth(method='loess', se=TRUE)


# OLS estimates for model 2
table2.q <- lm(log_radius_area ~territory + log(jointsize)
      + host_mt + host_for + water + cwpceyrs + bord_vital
      + host_resource + I(.fitted^2), data=mid.v2)


# F test of model difference
anova(table2, table2.q)


#(9) diagnose multicollinearity (vif statistics)
library(car)
vif(table2)


#(10) test heteroskedasticity
# Cook/Weisberg score test of constant error variance
library(car)
ncvTest(table2)


# Breush/Pagan test of constant error variance
library(lmtest)
bptest(table2)


#(11) diagnose influential observations
# create observation id
```

```
mid.v2$id <- as.numeric(row.names(mid.v2))

# identify obs with Cook's D above cutoff
ggplot(mid.v2, aes(id, .cooksd)) +
    geom_bar(stat="identity", position="identity") +
    xlab("Obs. Number")+ylab("Cook's distance")+
    geom_hline(yintercept=0.014) +
    geom_text(aes(label=ifelse((.cooksd>0.014),id,"")),
              vjust=-0.2, hjust=0.5)

# list observations whose Cook's D above threshold
mid.v2[mid.v2$.cooksd>0.014, c("dispnum","ccode1","ccode2",
    "year","log_radius_area",".std.resid",".hat",".cooksd")]

# re-estimate model without influential obs
table2.no <- lm(log_radius_area ~ territory + log(jointsize)
         + host_mt + host_for + water + cwpceyrs + bord_vital
         + host_resource, data=mid.v2[mid.v2$.cooksd<0.014,])

# estimation results without outliers
summary(table2.no)

#(12) normality diagnostics
library(car)
qqPlot(table2,distribution="t",simulate=TRUE,grid=TRUE)
qqPlot(table2.no,distribution="t",simulate=TRUE,
       grid=TRUE)

# normality test
shapiro.test(residuals(table2))
shapiro.test(residuals(table2.no))

#(13) report results in table
library(stargazer)
stargazer(table2, table2.r, table2.no, type="text",
    no.space=TRUE, omit.stat=c("f","ser"),model.names=FALSE,
    dep.var.labels.include=FALSE, dep.var.caption="")
```

Program for Replicating Bénabou et al. (2015)

```
# replicate Table 2 in "Religion and Innovation"
```

```
#(1) remove all objects in workspace
rm(list=ls(all=TRUE))


#(2) change working directory to project folder
setwd("C:\\Project\\benabou")


#(3) import stata file into R
# load the foreign package
library(foreign)


benabou <- read.dta("aerpp2015btv-dataset.dta",
                    convert.factors=FALSE)


#(4) produce formatted table of descriptive statistics
# load stargazer into R
library(stargazer)


stargazer(benabou, type="text", title = "Summary Statistics")


#(5) obtain variable labels from original Stata data file
# no variable labels in the dataset
var.labels <- attr(benabou,"var.labels")
bendata.key <- data.frame(var.name=names(benabou),var.labels)


# show variable labels using stargazer function
stargazer(bendata.key,type="text",summary=F,rownames=F)


#(6) replicate models in table 2
# load car, lmtest, and sandwich packages
library(car)
library(lmtest)
library(sandwich)


# Table 2 Column 1 five models for A029
c1m2 <- lm(A029 ~ A006m + X001m + X003 + X025 + X045m + X047
           + factor(X049m) + factor(F025) + factor(S003)
           + factor(year), weights=S017, data=benabou)
# White robust standard errors
c1m2.r <- coeftest(c1m2, vcov=vcovHC(c1m2, type="HC1"))


c1m3 <- lm(A029 ~ F050 + X001m + X003 + X025 + X045m + X047
```

```
            + factor(X049m) + factor(F025) + factor(S003)
            + factor(year), weights=S017, data=benabou)
# White robust standard errors
c1m3.r <- coeftest(c1m3, vcov=vcovHC(c1m3, type="HC1"))


c1m4 <- lm(A029 ~ F063 + X001m + X003 + X025 + X045m + X047
            + factor(X049m) + factor(F025) + factor(S003)
            + factor(year), weights=S017, data=benabou)
# White robust standard errors
c1m4.r <- coeftest(c1m4, vcov=vcovHC(c1m4, type="HC1"))


c1m5 <- lm(A029 ~ F028m + X001m + X003 + X025 + X045m + X047
            + factor(X049m) + factor(F025) + factor(S003)
            + factor(year), weights=S017, data=benabou)
# White robust standard errors
c1m5.r <- coeftest(c1m5, vcov=vcovHC(c1m5, type="HC1"))


# Table 2 Column 2 five models for A034
c2m1 <- lm(A034 ~ F034rp + X001m + X003 + X025 + X045m + X047
            + factor(X049m) + factor(F025) + factor(S003)
            + factor(year), weights=S017, data=benabou)
# White robust standard errors
c2m1.r <- coeftest(c2m1, vcov=vcovHC(c2m1, type="HC1"))


c2m2 <- lm(A034 ~ A006m + X001m + X003 + X025 + X045m + X047
            + factor(X049m) + factor(F025) + factor(S003)
            + factor(year), weights=S017, data=benabou)
# White robust standard errors
c2m2.r <- coeftest(c2m2, vcov=vcovHC(c2m2, type="HC1"))


c2m3 <- lm(A034 ~ F050 + X001m + X003 + X025 + X045m + X047
            + factor(X049m) + factor(F025) + factor(S003)
            + factor(year), weights=S017, data=benabou)
# White robust standard errors
c2m3.r <- coeftest(c2m3, vcov=vcovHC(c2m3, type="HC1"))


c2m4 <- lm(A034 ~ F063 + X001m + X003 + X025 + X045m + X047
            + factor(X049m) + factor(F025) + factor(S003)
            + factor(year), weights=S017, data=benabou)
# White robust standard errors
c2m4.r <- coeftest(c2m4, vcov=vcovHC(c2m4, type="HC1"))
```

```
c2m5 <- lm(A034 ~ F028m + X001m + X003 + X025 + X045m + X047
           + factor(X049m) + factor(F025) + factor(S003)
           + factor(year), weights=S017, data=benabou)
# White robust standard errors
c2m5.r <- coeftest(c2m5, vcov=vcovHC(c2m5, type="HC1"))


# Table 2 Column 3 five models for A039
c3m1 <- lm(A039 ~ F034rp + X001m + X003 + X025 + X045m + X047
           + factor(X049m) + factor(F025) + factor(S003)
           + factor(year), weights=S017, data=benabou)
# White robust standard errors
c3m1.r <- coeftest(c3m1, vcov=vcovHC(c3m1, type="HC1"))


c3m2 <- lm(A039 ~ A006m + X001m + X003 + X025 + X045m + X047
           + factor(X049m) + factor(F025) + factor(S003)
           + factor(year), weights=S017, data=benabou)
# White robust standard errors
c3m2.r <- coeftest(c3m2, vcov=vcovHC(c3m2, type="HC1"))


c3m3 <- lm(A039 ~ F050 + X001m + X003 + X025 + X045m + X047
           + factor(X049m) + factor(F025) + factor(S003)
           + factor(year), weights=S017, data=benabou)
# White robust standard errors
c3m3.r <- coeftest(c3m3, vcov=vcovHC(c3m3, type="HC1"))


c3m4 <- lm(A039 ~ F063 + X001m + X003 + X025 + X045m + X047
           + factor(X049m) + factor(F025) + factor(S003)
           + factor(year), weights=S017, data=benabou)
# White robust standard errors
c3m4.r <- coeftest(c3m4, vcov=vcovHC(c3m4, type="HC1"))


c3m5 <- lm(A039 ~ F028m + X001m + X003 + X025 + X045m + X047
           + factor(X049m) + factor(F025) + factor(S003)
           + factor(year), weights=S017, data=benabou)
# White robust standard errors
c3m5.r <- coeftest(c3m5, vcov=vcovHC(c3m5, type="HC1"))


#(7) Report Replicated Results of Table 2 in Bénabou et al.
library(stargazer)
stargazer(c1m1.r, c1m2.r, c1m3.r, c1m4.r, c1m5.r, type="text",
 no.space=TRUE, keep=c("F034rp","A006m","F050","F063","F028m"),
```

```
    dep.var.labels="Importance of child independence (A029)",
    covariate.labels = c("Religious person (F034rp)",
    "Importance of religion (A006m)", "Belief in God (F050)",
    "Importance of God (F063)", "Church attendance (F028m)"),
    out="benabou1")

stargazer(c2m1.r, c2m2.r, c2m3.r, c2m4.r, c2m5.r, type="text",
    no.space=TRUE, keep=c("F034rp","A006m","F050","F063","F028m"),
    dep.var.labels="Importance of child imagination (A034)",
    covariate.labels = c("Religious person (F034rp)",
    "Importance of religion (A006m)", "Belief in God (F050)",
    "Importance of God (F063)", "Church attendance (F028m)"),
    out="benabou2")

stargazer(c3m1.r, c3m2.r, c3m3.r, c3m4.r, c3m5.r, type="text",
    no.space=TRUE, keep=c("F034rp","A006m","F050","F063","F028m"),
    dep.var.labels="Importance of child determination (A039)",
    covariate.labels = c("Religious person (F034rp)",
    "Importance of religion (A006m)", "Belief in God (F050)",
    "Importance of God (F063)", "Church attendance (F028m)"),
    out="benabou3")
```

Summary

If you have reached this point in the textbook, I hope that you will have developed a better appreciation of R, statistical inference, and substantive empirical research in general. Hopefully, our emphasis on a minimalist approach toward R, our focus on a research process- or project-oriented approach toward data analysis, and our demonstration of how to replicate published research have all made the experience of learning R, statistical analysis, and empirical research less overwhelming yet more productive and rewarding than alternative approaches. As enormous amounts of data growingly inundate our lives, the integration of computer programming, data analysis, and substantive empirical research is likely to empower you and make you more competitive in your future careers.

## 8

Appendix: A Brief Introduction to Analyzing Categorical Data and Finding More Data

Objective

This textbook has focused on how to address various substantive questions regarding a continuous dependent variable using basic data management, visualization, and statistical modeling in R. It has demonstrated the practical value and utility of R by reproducing published quantitative analyses. In applied research, however, many dependent variables are not continuous but discrete, such as being binary like life and death, happy or not happy, guilty or not guilty, and so forth. Due to space limitation, it is not possible to cover discrete data analysis in detail in this introductory text. Yet for readers interested in moving further beyond what has been covered, we will provide a brief introduction to two techniques often used with discrete data: testing statistical independence between two discrete variables, and using logistic regression to test the effects of some independent variables on the probability of a dependent variable taking on the value of one rather than zero. We will illustrate the process by focusing on a dichotomous variable measuring self-reported happiness by survey respondents.

Data analysis requires access to data. In the last several years, the amount of data available to the public has increased exponentially, provided by a variety of sources including individual researchers, replication datasets by academic journals, local and national governments, and international organizations. We will provide a short list of such resources available to get readers familiar with the wealth of data that are publicly available.

Getting Data Ready

We will use the World Values Survey (WVS) Wave 6 dataset for analysis, focusing on self-reported happiness and its covariates as an example. Before we introduce related R code for analysis, we must first get data ready.

The WVS data and codebook can be downloaded from http://www.worldvaluessurvey.org/WVSDocumentationWV6.jsp.

We will create a wvs folder under the Project folder and then download the dataset and codebook there. We will first begin with the pdf codebook file: WV6_Official_Questionnaire_v4_June2012.pdf.

Figure 8.1 shows a sample page from the WVS6 codebook. Two pieces of information on this page are most relevant to us. First, the variable V10 is self-reported happiness, the focus of our analysis. Second, the type of missing values with any variable are −1 for Don't Know, −2 for No answer, and −3 for Not applicable. They must be recoded when we clean the data because R does not recognize them as missing values.

The WVS data come in various formats. We simply download the .RData format dataset, named WV6_Data_R_v_2016_01_01.RData. It is worth noting

---

WVS 2010-2012 Wave, revised master, June 2012	2 of 21

(Introduction by interviewer):

Hello. I am from the _____ *(mention name of the interview organization)*. We are carrying out a global study of what people value in life. This study will interview samples representing most of the world's people. Your name has been selected at random as part of a representative sample of the people in _____ *(mention country in which interview is conducted)*. I'd like to ask your views on a number of different subjects. Your input will be treated strictly confidential but it will contribute to a better understanding of what people all over the world believe and want out of life.

(Show Card A)

For each of the following, indicate how important it is in your life. Would you say it is *(read out and code one answer for each)*:

		Very important	Rather important	Not very important	Not at all important
V4.	Family	1	2	3	4
V5.	Friends	1	2	3	4
V6.	Leisure time	1	2	3	4
V7.	Politics	1	2	3	4
V8.	Work	1	2	3	4
V9.	Religion	1	2	3	4

NOTE: Code but do not read out-- here and throughout the interview: -1 Don't know
-2 No answer
-3 Not applicable

V10. Taking all things together, would you say you are *(read out and code one answer)*:

1 Very happy
2 Rather happy
3 Not very happy
4 Not at all happy

Figure 8.1 Sample Page from World Values Survey Codebook.

that the dataset is zipped and thus, must be unzipped and extracted first, as shown in Chapter 2.

In R, we first clean the workspace, set the working directory to the new folder created, and then load the R dataset. Given the size of the dataset, it will take some time to load the file into R. The R code and output are as follows:

```
# Data Preparation Program install following packages only
# once, then comment out code
# install.packages(c('gmodels','MASS'), dependencies=TRUE)

# (1) before running project program, first remove all
# objects from workspace
rm(list = ls(all = TRUE))

# (2) changes the working directory to point to the
# project data directory
setwd("C:\\Project\\wvs")

# (3) load RData file
load("WV6_Data_R_v_2016_01_01.RData")
```

Do Men and Women Differ in Self-Reported Happiness?

The first question we will address using the WVS data is whether there is a gender difference in self-reported happiness. Conceptually, if there is a gender difference, then gender and self-reported happiness must be statistically correlated. If they are uncorrelated, then there is no gender difference.

The logic of statistical inference is to use the sample data in the WVS to draw conclusions about the relationship between the two variables in the population. We will test the following hypothesis.

Null Hypothesis: Gender and happiness are statistically independent of each other.

Alternative Hypothesis: Gender and happiness are not statistically independent of each other.

Before we test the hypothesis, we must first prepare data for the two variables and describe their individual and joint distributions.

Create and Describe Discrete Variables

Create and Describe Dichotomous Happiness Variable

We will begin by tabulating the self-reported happiness variable V10, and then create a dummy variable based on V10. The table() function tabulates the number of observations under each value of the variable V10. As shown, the variable contains values listed in the codebook in Figure 8.1 , such as 1 for Very happy, 2 for Rather happy, 3 for Not very happy, and 4 for Not at all happy.

```
# tabulate self-reported happiness variable
table(WV6_Data_R$V10)

  -5    -2    -1     1     2     3     4
   4   237   505 29430 46092 11482  2600
```

The output also shows values such as −5, −2, and −1, which are missing value codes according to the codebook (note that −5 is not shown in the codebook and it is likely −3 being miscoded). These negative values are missing values, but they cannot be recognized by R as missing values and so need to be recoded as *NA*, as follows:

```
# recode missing values
WV6_Data_R$V10[WV6_Data_R$V10 == -5 | WV6_Data_R$V10 == -2 |
    WV6_Data_R$V10 == -1] <- NA

# tabulate again to confirm coding
table(WV6_Data_R$V10)

    1     2     3     4
29430 46092 11482  2600
```

As shown, the negative values are successfully recoded as missing values *NA*. The frequency count shows that most people in the survey report being very happy (1) or rather happy (2), but many others report being not very happy (3) and not at all happy (4).

It is not easy, however, to see the distribution of the variable based on frequency count. Thus, we also report the proportions of different values. We use the prop.table() function to compute the proportions, with the output of the table() function as its argument. Since we are interested in percentages, we multiply the output of the prop.table() function by 100.

```
# tabulate self-reported happiness variable
100 * (prop.table(table(WV6_Data_R$V10)))
```

```
     1          2         3         4
32.844516 51.439668 12.814160  2.901656
```

As shown, about 84% of the respondents report being very happy or rather happy, 12.8% report being not very happy, and only 2.9% report being not happy at all. The proportions present a clearer distribution of the variable than the frequency counts.

To answer our question on gender difference over reported happiness, we will create a dichotomous variable happy, coded one if V10 is smaller than or equal to 2, and zero otherwise. In Chapter 2, we focused on using the indexing method to create new dummy variables. Since we have become more familiar with R, we will introduce another commonly used function: ifelse(). The ifelse() function has three arguments. It first tests the logical condition specified in the first argument. If the condition is TRUE, then the function returns the second argument; if the condition is FALSE, then the function returns the third argument.

Take the R code below for example. If the first argument WV6_Data_R$V10<=2 is TRUE, then the function returns a value 1; or else, it returns a value 0. The output is assigned to a new variable happy. We then use the table() function to confirm that the dummy variable is created correctly.

```
# create a dummy variable happy
WV6_Data_R$happy <- ifelse(WV6_Data_R$V10 <= 2, 1, 0)

# check variable coding
table(WV6_Data_R$happy, WV6_Data_R$V10)

        1      2      3      4
  0     0      0  11482   2600
  1 29430  46092      0      0
```

Create and Describe Dichotomous Gender Variable

To answer our question, the next step is to create a gender variable. The codebook shows that the variable is V240.

```
V240. (Code respondent's sex by observation):
1 Male
2 Female
```

The frequency count tabulation below shows that the variable also needs cleaning, with its negative values to be recoded as missing. Also according to the codebook, for V240, the value 1 represents male, and 2 female.

```
# tabulate frequency count
table(WV6_Data_R$V240)
```

```
  -5    -2     1     2
  40    51 43391 46868
```

As shown, 43,391 respondents are male, 46,868 female, and some 92 respondents have missing values in V240.

Based on V240, we will create a new gender variable. We first create a new variable, male, as a copy of V240, then recode its negative values as missing, and next recode its value 2 (for women) as zero. Thus, the variable male is coded 1 for men and 0 for women. The output below confirms the creation of the dichotomous variable male.

```
# create a copy of V240
WV6_Data_R$male <- WV6_Data_R$V240
```

```
# recode missing values
WV6_Data_R$male[WV6_Data_R$male == -2 | WV6_Data_R$male ==
    -5] <- NA
```

```
# recode value for women
WV6_Data_R$male[WV6_Data_R$male == 2] <- 0
```

```
# double check frequency count
table(WV6_Data_R$male)
```

```
    0     1
46868 43391
```

Cross-Tabulate Two Discrete Variables: Two-Way Contingency Table

To describe the relationship between two discrete variables, we always cross-tabulate them, generating a two-way contingency table and showing their marginal and joint distributions. This resembles the scatter plot and correlation coefficient between two continuous variables in Chapter 4. A 2x2 contingency table of two dichotomous variables is a cross-tabulation of two discrete variables, each with two levels, and a total of 4 cells of frequency counts.

The R code and output below shows a 2x2 contingency table, with male being the row variable and happy being the column variable. As shown, 7,369 respondents are women who self-report being unhappy, 6,708 respondents are men who self-report being unhappy, 39,148 are women who self-report being happy, and 36,291 are men who self-report being happy.

```
# cross tabulate frequency count
table(WV6_Data_R$male, WV6_Data_R$happy)


      0     1
  0  7369 39148
  1  6708 36291
```

We may report the sample proportions instead of frequency counts in the 2x2 table, using the prop.table() function. Each cell contains a cell proportion, which is the cell frequency count divided by the total sample size. About 43.7% women report being happy whereas 40.5% men report the same. In contrast, about 8.2% women report being unhappy whereas 7.5% men report the same.

```
# cross tabulate sample proportions
prop.table(table(WV6_Data_R$male, WV6_Data_R$happy))

           0          1
  0 0.08232048 0.43732964
  1 0.07493632 0.40541356
```

Note that both the table() and prop.table() functions are crude. To obtain more information, we can use the CrossTable() function from the gmodels package. Of course, we need to install and load the package first. Note that the spelling of the function is case sensitive.

```
# cross tabulation install.packages(gmodels)
library(gmodels)
CrossTable(WV6_Data_R$male, WV6_Data_R$happy)


   Cell Contents
|-------------------------|
|                     N |
| Chi-square contribution |
|           N / Row Total |
|           N / Col Total |
|         N / Table Total |
|-------------------------|

Total Observations in Table:  89516
```

```
                    | WV6_Data_R$happy
WV6_Data_R$male |         0 |           1 | Row Total |
----------------|-----------|-----------|-----------|
            0 |      7369 |     39148 |     46517 |
              |     0.397 |     0.074 |           |
              |     0.158 |     0.842 |     0.520 |
              |     0.523 |     0.519 |           |
              |     0.082 |     0.437 |           |
----------------|-----------|-----------|-----------|
            1 |      6708 |     36291 |     42999 |
              |     0.429 |     0.080 |           |
              |     0.156 |     0.844 |     0.480 |
              |     0.477 |     0.481 |           |
              |     0.075 |     0.405 |           |
----------------|-----------|-----------|-----------|
   Column Total |     14077 |     75439 |     89516 |
              |     0.157 |     0.843 |           |
----------------|-----------|-----------|-----------|
```

The R output includes a lot of information worth clarification. As noted, each cell contains five numbers: the frequency count for a combination of the row and column variables (N), the so-called Chi-square contribution, the conditional proportion given the row value (N/Row Total), the conditional proportion given the column value (N/Col Total), and the cell proportion (N/Table Total).

Take the first cell (male=0, happy=0) as an example. It indicates the combination of unhappy women. Among the total 89,516 observations in the sample, 7369 of them are women who self-report being unhappy. Among all women (row total: 46517), the proportion of women being unhappy is 0.158 or 15.8%. Among all unhappy respondents (column total: 14077), the proportion of women is 0.523 or 52.3%. Among the entire sample (table total: 89516), the proportion of unhappy women is 0.082 or 8.2%.

We often think of the cell proportion as a joint probability of a combination of events. For example, the probability of a woman being unhappy is 0.082. Also, we think of the row or column proportion in a cell as a conditional probability. For example, given that a respondent is a woman, the probability of being unhappy is 0.158.

The values of the marginal (row or column) totals are also worth noting. In the sample, 52% of the respondents are female and 48% are male; 15.7% report being unhappy and 84.3% report being happy.

Statistical Inference

The key to the substantive question asked earlier is whether the two variables male and happy are statistically independent of each other in the population.

If they are independent of each other, then there is no gender difference in self-reported happiness; if they are not independent of each other, then there is a gender difference in self-reported happiness. *For a two-way contingency table of two discrete variables, statistical independence means that the joint probabilities are equal to the product of the marginal probabilities.* In light of this information, the null and alternative hypotheses can be rephrased as follows:

Null Hypothesis: male and happy are statistically independent of each other. (Technically, the joint probability for each cell is equal to the product of the corresponding marginal probabilities, which holds for all four cells.)

Alternative Hypothesis: male and happy are not statistically independent of each other. (Technically, the joint probability for at least one cell does not is equal to the product of the corresponding marginal probabilities.)

A commonly used test is the Chi-squared test of independence, the details of which will be skipped here for the sake of space. Following the procedures of statistical inference in previous chapters, we compare the p value of the test statistic with the acceptable Type I error rate, α, and draw our conclusion.

The R code and output are as follows:

```
# cross tabulate frequency count
freq.output2 <- table(WV6_Data_R$male, WV6_Data_R$happy)

chisq.test(freq.output2)

Pearson's Chi-squared test with Yates' continuity
correction

data:  freq.output2
X-squared = 0.96243, df = 1, p-value = 0.3266
```

The p value is 0.33, far larger than the typical $\alpha = 0.5$ threshold. Hence, the null hypothesis fails to be rejected. The substantive conclusion is that there is no gender difference in self-reported happiness between men and women.

Do Believers in God and Non-Believers Differ in Self-Reported Happiness?

For another example, we can test the hypothesis of whether believers in God and non-believers differ in their self-reported happiness. The variable V148 is a dummy variable on whether a respondent believes in God or not.

V148. Do you believe in God?

1 Yes

2 No

Below are the R code and output for data preparation and cross-tabulation between religious belief and self-reported happiness.

```
# tabulate belief in God V148
table(WV6_Data_R$V148)

  -5    -4    -2    -1     1     2
  36  8291   483  2061 67846 11633

# create a belief variable
WV6_Data_R$belief <- WV6_Data_R$V148

# recode missing values
WV6_Data_R$belief[WV6_Data_R$belief %in% c(-5, -4, -2, -1)] <- NA

# recode non-believers as equal zero
WV6_Data_R$belief[WV6_Data_R$belief == 2] <- 0

# double check frequency count
table(WV6_Data_R$belief)

    0     1
11633 67846

# simple cross tabulation
table(WV6_Data_R$belief, WV6_Data_R$happy)

       0     1
  0 1576  9927
  1 9842 57514

prop.table(table(WV6_Data_R$belief, WV6_Data_R$happy))

           0          1
  0 0.01998504 0.12588290
  1 0.12480503 0.72932703

# show cross tabulations of belief and happiness
CrossTable(table(WV6_Data_R$belief, WV6_Data_R$happy))


   Cell Contents
```

```
|-------------------------|
|                      N  |
| Chi-square contribution |
|          N / Row Total  |
|          N / Col Total  |
|        N / Table Total  |
|-------------------------|
```

Total Observations in Table: 78859

```
             |
             |       0  |         1 | Row Total .|
-------------|----------|-----------|------------|
          0  |    1576  |    9927   |   11503    |
             |   4.812  |   0.815   |            |
             |   0.137  |   0.863   |    0.146   |
             |   0.138  |   0.147   |            |
             |   0.020  |   0.126   |            |
-------------|----------|-----------|------------|
          1  |    9842  |   57514   |   67356    |
             |   0.822  |   0.139   |            |
             |   0.146  |   0.854   |    0.854   |
             |   0.862  |   0.853   |            |
             |   0.125  |   0.729   |            |
-------------|----------|-----------|------------|
Column Total |   11418  |   67441   |   78859    |
             |   0.145  |   0.855   |            |
-------------|----------|-----------|------------|
```

As shown, 2% of all the respondents are unhappy non-believers, 12.6% happy non-believers, 12.5% unhappy believers, and 72.9% happy believers. Interestingly, among non-believers only (first row), 13.7% report being unhappy, and 86.3% being happy; yet among believers only (second row), 14.6% report being unhappy, and 85.4% report being happy.

The question is whether these differences are due to random noise and sampling error, or result from a meaningful relationship between belief and self-reported happiness in the population. The R code and output for the test are as follows:

```
# test statistical independence
freq.output2 <- table(WV6_Data_R$belief, WV6_Data_R$happy)
```

```
chisq.test(freq.output2)

Pearson's Chi-squared test with Yates' continuity
correction

data:   freq.output2
X-squared = 6.5137, df = 1, p-value = 0.0107
```

The p value from the Chi-square test is 0.0107, smaller than the conventional threshold 0.05. Hence, the null hypothesis that religious belief and self-reported happiness are statistically independent is rejected. The substantive conclusion is that self-reported happiness and religious belief are not independent of each other. The statistical test, however, cannot tell us whether it is because religious belief makes people more or less happy or because unhappy people are more or less likely to become religious. It is hard to establish causality using this type of observational data, an important caveat worth keeping in mind.

Sources of Self-Reported Happiness: Logistic Regression
Conceptual Background

We are interested in finding out whether gender, religious belief, and income influence self-reported happiness or not. The dependent variable happy is dichotomous, with one being happy and zero being unhappy. We are interested in estimating the effects of gender, belief in God, and income on the probability of a respondent reporting being happy. In this type of problem, OLS is not appropriate as it can generate predicted probabilities larger than one and smaller than zero. A widely used statistical technique is the logistic regression.

Conceptually, the probability of a respondent being happy or not can be expressed as being a function of gender, religious belief, and income.

$$\pi_i = p(happy_i = 1) = probability \quad respondent_i \quad being \quad happy$$
$$= \beta_0 + \beta_1 male + \beta_2 belief + \beta_3 income$$

To keep the predicted probability bounded between zero and one, the logistic regression fits an S-shaped relationship between happy and other covariates with the following model:

$$ln(\frac{\pi_i}{1 - \pi_i}) = \beta_0 + \beta_1 male + \beta_2 belief + \beta_3 income$$

where $\frac{\pi_i}{1-\pi_i}$ is the odds of a respondent being happy, which is the probability of being happy (π_i) divided by the probability of being unhappy ($1 - \pi_i$), and $ln(\frac{\pi_i}{1-\pi_i})$ is the log-odds or logistic transformation of odds.

Two issues are worth clarification. First, the βs are regression parameters. Following previous chapters, we will carry out hypothesis testing with respect to the null hypothesis on each β being zero, indicating that a variable has no statistical effect on the dependent variable in the population.

Second, what is substantively most interesting is the value of π_i, the probability of a respondent being happy, under different values of the independent variables. To obtain that value, we can apply the following formula:

$$\pi_i = \frac{e^{\beta_0 + \beta_1 male + \beta_2 belief + \beta_3 income}}{1 + e^{\beta_0 + \beta_1 male + \beta_2 belief + \beta_3 income}}$$

Data Preparation

We already have all four variables in the above model prepared except for income. Hence, we will now get the income variable ready for analysis. The codebook definition for the income variable is as follows:

V239. On this card is an income scale on which 1 indicates the lowest income group and 10 the highest income group in your country. We would like to know in what group your household is. Please,specify the appropriate number, counting all wages, salaries, pensions and other incomes that come in. (Code one number):

Lowest group   Highest group
1   2   3   4   5   6   7   8   9   10

The tabulation shows that the variable has several negative values indicating missing values. They will be recoded as NA.

```
# tabulate variable
table(WV6_Data_R$V239)

  -5    -2    -1     1     2     3     4     5     6     7
  17  1736  1371  6758  6280 10030 12076 18665 13536 10650
   8     9    10
6123  1778  1330

# create an income variable
WV6_Data_R$income <- WV6_Data_R$V239

# recode missing values
WV6_Data_R$income[WV6_Data_R$income %in% c(-5, -2, -1)] <- NA
```

```
# confirm recoding
table(WV6_Data_R$income)
```

```
     1      2      3      4      5      6      7      8      9     10
  6758   6280  10030  12076  18665  13536  10650   6123   1778   1330
```

One more caveat is that our data come from cross-national surveys in heterogeneous countries. Hence, it is important that we correct the sample based on national distributions of key variables. This is like in the Bénabou et al. paper in Chapter 7. The weight variable in WVS is V258, defined as follows:

```
V258. Weight variable (Provide a 4-digit weight variable
to correct your sample to reflect national distributions
of key variables. If no weighting is necessary, simply
code each case as "1." It is especially important to
correct for education. For example, if your sample
contains 10 percent more university-educated respondents
as there are in the adult population, members of this group
should be down weighted by 10 percent, giving them
a weight of .90).
```

The inclusion of the weight variable sometimes makes a difference to the results; other times, it does not. If the goal is to make inferences about the population, it is preferable to apply the weight variable in survey regression models.

Another source of heterogeneity is from the cross-national nature of surveys. This may be explicitly modeled in regression, an issue we will discuss further below.

Estimation and Hypothesis Testing

We will first estimate one model specification. In the R code below, the glm() function performs logistic regression analysis, and it operates like the lm() function for the linear regression model. The glm() function implies generalized linear model. It contains four main arguments: the formula y ~ x specifying the dependent and independent variables for the model; family=binomial indicating a binomial distribution is assumed and thus, requesting logistic regression; data=filename for the dataset used; and weights= specifying the survey weight variable.

```
# estimate model and assign output to a data object
model1.logit <- glm(happy ~ male + belief + income, weights = V258,
    family = binomial("logit"), data = WV6_Data_R)
```

```
# display model output
summary(model1.logit)

Call:
glm(formula = happy ~ male + belief + income, family =
    binomial("logit"),
    data = WV6_Data_R, weights = V258)

Deviance Residuals:
   Min       1Q    Median       3Q      Max
-7.2209   0.3464   0.4745   0.6003   3.5918

Coefficients:
            Estimate Std. Error z value Pr(>|z|)
(Intercept)  0.743994   0.036816  20.208  < 2e-16 ***
male        -0.019371   0.020861  -0.929  0.35312
belief      -0.112190   0.030635  -3.662  0.00025 ***
income       0.252452   0.005195  48.597  < 2e-16 ***
---
Signif. codes:
0 '***' 0.001 '**' 0.01 '*' 0.05 '.' 0.1 ' ' 1

(Dispersion parameter for binomial family taken to be 1)

    Null deviance: 63818  on 76613  degrees of freedom
Residual deviance: 61311  on 76610  degrees of freedom
  (13736 observations deleted due to missingness)
AIC: 61941

Number of Fisher Scoring iterations: 5
```

The results show several interesting findings. First, there is no gender difference in self-reported happiness between men and women. On average, a man is equally likely to report being happy as a woman. Second, the coefficient of belief is negative and statistically significant. On average, believers are less likely to self-report being happy than non-believers. Third, the coefficient of income is positive and statistically significant. On average, a respondent in a higher income group is more likely to report being happy than one in a lower income group.

One issue with the model above is that it has not taken into consideration the fact that respondents from over 50 countries are included in the sample. There are many differences between countries that could have influenced the effects of the covariates. As shown in the Bénabou et al. paper, one common way to address this issue is to control for the so-called country fixed effects by including country-specific dummy variables. As shown in Chapter 7, it is easy to implement in R. The country code variable is V2, and we can simply include factor(V2) in the model to control for between-country differences.

The R code and output for the second model specification are as follows:

```
# estimate model and assign output to a data object
model2.logit <- glm(happy ~ male + belief + income + factor(V2),
    weights = V258, family = binomial("logit"), data = WV6_Data_R)

# display model output
summary(model2.logit)

Call:
glm(formula = happy ~ male + belief + income + factor(V2),
    family = binomial("logit"),
    data = WV6_Data_R, weights = V258)

Deviance Residuals:
    Min       1Q    Median       3Q       Max
 -6.9135   0.2660   0.4137   0.5945   3.4507

Coefficients:
                 Estimate Std. Error z value Pr(>|z|)
(Intercept)     -0.057132   0.089043  -0.642 0.521124
male            -0.014423   0.021497  -0.671 0.502256
belief           0.228422   0.038312   5.962 2.49e-09 ***
income           0.275343   0.005674  48.528  < 2e-16 ***
factor(V2)31    -0.104519   0.110739  -0.944 0.345255
factor(V2)32     0.361841   0.123614   2.927 0.003420 **
factor(V2)36     1.311205   0.132002   9.933  < 2e-16 ***
factor(V2)51     0.372078   0.111800   3.328 0.000874 ***
factor(V2)76     1.219641   0.124467   9.799  < 2e-16 ***
factor(V2)112   -0.676415   0.095659  -7.071 1.54e-12 ***
factor(V2)152    0.300268   0.120422   2.493 0.012650 *
factor(V2)156    0.714094   0.107033   6.672 2.53e-11 ***
factor(V2)158    0.979152   0.129629   7.554 4.24e-14 ***
factor(V2)170    0.959120   0.120723   7.945 1.95e-15 ***
factor(V2)196    0.013178   0.114059   0.116 0.908021
factor(V2)218    1.178045   0.137496   8.568  < 2e-16 ***
```

```
factor(V2)233   0.096109    0.104215    0.922 0.356414
factor(V2)268  -0.307751    0.099505   -3.093 0.001983 **
factor(V2)276   0.440598    0.102354    4.305 1.67e-05 ***
factor(V2)288   0.133932    0.100386    1.334 0.182149
factor(V2)344   0.855843    0.130173    6.575 4.88e-11 ***
factor(V2)356   0.567661    0.085560    6.635 3.25e-11 ***
factor(V2)368  -0.805280    0.099600   -8.085 6.21e-16 ***
factor(V2)392   1.125060    0.119031    9.452  < 2e-16 ***
factor(V2)398   0.548679    0.111889    4.904 9.40e-07 ***
factor(V2)400   0.365182    0.113355    3.222 0.001275 **
factor(V2)410   0.977902    0.125893    7.768 7.99e-15 ***
factor(V2)417   1.635809    0.153731   10.641  < 2e-16 ***
factor(V2)422  -0.376743    0.105305   -3.578 0.000347 ***
factor(V2)434   0.501311    0.103275    4.854 1.21e-06 ***
factor(V2)458   1.514907    0.162582    9.318  < 2e-16 ***
factor(V2)484   1.895852    0.124679   15.206  < 2e-16 ***
factor(V2)504   0.030994    0.106180    0.292 0.770363
factor(V2)528   1.480927    0.128094   11.561  < 2e-16 ***
factor(V2)554   1.529226    0.204527    7.477 7.61e-14 ***
factor(V2)566   0.272201    0.101523    2.681 0.007337 **
factor(V2)586   0.160440    0.111983    1.433 0.151940
factor(V2)604  -0.201879    0.103441   -1.952 0.050982 .
factor(V2)608   0.980598    0.121829    8.049 8.35e-16 ***
factor(V2)616   1.471782    0.158966    9.258  < 2e-16 ***
factor(V2)642  -0.592488    0.096459   -6.142 8.13e-10 ***
factor(V2)643  -0.073535    0.092598   -0.794 0.427117
factor(V2)646   0.717313    0.116207    6.173 6.71e-10 ***
factor(V2)702   1.004679    0.117501    8.550  < 2e-16 ***
factor(V2)705   0.287875    0.119068    2.418 0.015617 *
factor(V2)710  -0.289337    0.086781   -3.334 0.000856 ***
factor(V2)716   0.005633    0.099580    0.057 0.954887
factor(V2)724   0.645725    0.122560    5.269 1.37e-07 ***
factor(V2)752   1.470060    0.156306    9.405  < 2e-16 ***
factor(V2)764   1.508651    0.143401   10.521  < 2e-16 ***
factor(V2)780   0.579790    0.126263    4.592 4.39e-06 ***
factor(V2)792   0.075972    0.104163    0.729 0.465782
factor(V2)804  -0.341644    0.096998   -3.522 0.000428 ***
factor(V2)840   0.805515    0.105347    7.646 2.07e-14 ***
factor(V2)858   0.568272    0.123446    4.603 4.16e-06 ***
factor(V2)860   1.644162    0.160830   10.223  < 2e-16 ***
---
```

```
Signif. codes:
0 '***' 0.001 '**' 0.01 '*' 0.05 '.' 0.1 ' ' 1

(Dispersion parameter for binomial family taken to be 1)

    Null deviance: 63818  on 76613  degrees of freedom
Residual deviance: 57881  on 76558  degrees of freedom
  (13736 observations deleted due to missingness)
AIC: 58557

Number of Fisher Scoring iterations: 5
```

Interestingly, after controlling for between-country differences, the effects of male and income remain as before, but the effect of belief has become positive and statistically significant. Once controlling for between-country differences, believers are more likely to report being happy than non-believers.

As before, below we report the model results in a formatted table using the stargazer() function. We have made two modifications in the R code below. First, we use the omit= option to specify that the country-fixed-effects dummy variables are omitted from the table for the sake of space. Second, we use the ci= option to request confidence intervals to be reported instead of standard errors.

```
# report regression results
library(stargazer)
stargazer(model1.logit, model2.logit, type = "text", no.space = TRUE,
    omit = "factor", ci = TRUE)
```

```
============================================================
                            Dependent variable:
                      --------------------------------------
                                    happy
                            (1)              (2)
------------------------------------------------------------
male                       -0.019           -0.014
                      (-0.060, 0.022)  (-0.057, 0.028)
belief                    -0.112***         0.228***
                      (-0.172, -0.052) (0.153, 0.304)
income                     0.252***         0.275***
                      (0.242, 0.263)   (0.264, 0.286)
Constant                   0.744***        -0.057
                      (0.672, 0.816)   (-0.232, 0.117)
```

```
------------------------------------------------------
Observations           76,614            76,614
Log Likelihood       -30,966.460       -29,222.430
Akaike Inf. Crit.     61,940.920        58,556.870
======================================================
Note:                        *p<0.1; **p<0.05; ***p<0.01
```

Interpret Size of Effect

We can use null hypothesis testing and confidence interval construction to interpret the output of the logistic regression model. One important caveat is that a coefficient estimate in the logistic regression represents the marginal effect of an independent variable on the log odds of the dependent variable. It is hard to understand what log odds mean substantively.

There are two ways to interpret the estimated coefficients in a substantively more meaningful way. The first method is to exponentiate a coefficient estimate. This allows us to interpret the new quantity as the marginal effect of x on the odds ratio of the dependent variable.

Take model2.logit as an example. We can exponentiate its coefficient estimates as follows:

```
# odds ratio
exp(coef(model2.logit))

   (Intercept)             male           belief            income
     0.9444699        0.9856804        1.2566151         1.3169824
 factor(V2)31     factor(V2)32     factor(V2)36      factor(V2)51
     0.9007574        1.4359713        3.7106421         1.4507466
 factor(V2)76    factor(V2)112    factor(V2)152     factor(V2)156
     3.3859721        0.5084365        1.3502210         2.0423357
factor(V2)158    factor(V2)170    factor(V2)196     factor(V2)218
     2.6621971        2.6093993        1.0132650         3.2480196
factor(V2)233    factor(V2)268    factor(V2)276     factor(V2)288
     1.1008791        0.7350980        1.5536355         1.1433149
factor(V2)344    factor(V2)356    factor(V2)368     factor(V2)392
     2.3533568        1.7641355        0.4469628         3.0804031
factor(V2)398    factor(V2)400    factor(V2)410     factor(V2)417
     1.7309647        1.4407757        2.6588725         5.1336119
factor(V2)422    factor(V2)434    factor(V2)458     factor(V2)484
     0.6860925        1.6508844        4.5489975         6.6582211
factor(V2)504    factor(V2)528    factor(V2)554     factor(V2)566
```

```
      1.0314794       4.3970215       4.6146022       1.3128508
factor(V2)586 factor(V2)604 factor(V2)608 factor(V2)616
      1.1740271       0.8171935       2.6660488       4.3569903
factor(V2)642 factor(V2)643 factor(V2)646 factor(V2)702
      0.5529501       0.9291037       2.0489203       2.7310307
factor(V2)705 factor(V2)710 factor(V2)716 factor(V2)724
      1.3335899       0.7487595       1.0056492       1.9073692
factor(V2)752 factor(V2)764 factor(V2)780 factor(V2)792
      4.3494958       4.5206278       1.7856638       1.0789325
factor(V2)804 factor(V2)840 factor(V2)858 factor(V2)860
      0.7106009       2.2378484       1.7652143       5.1766686
```

The coefficient of `belief` 0.228 turns into 1.2566 after being exponentiated. This means that as `belief` increases by one point, i.e., from a non-believer to a believer, the odds of being happy increase by $(1.2566 - 1) * 100$ percent, i.e., 25.66%.

We can apply the following R code to compute the new quantity for each variable as follows:

```
# odds ratio
(exp(coef(model2.logit)) - 1) * 100

   (Intercept)           male          belief          income
    -5.5530137     -1.4319585      25.6615140      31.6982430
 factor(V2)31   factor(V2)32   factor(V2)36   factor(V2)51
    -9.9242650     43.5971309     271.0642109      45.0746568
 factor(V2)76  factor(V2)112  factor(V2)152  factor(V2)156
   238.5972134    -49.1563485      35.0221011     104.2335740
factor(V2)158 factor(V2)170 factor(V2)196 factor(V2)218
   166.2197120    160.9399309       1.3265014     224.8019620
factor(V2)233 factor(V2)268 factor(V2)276 factor(V2)288
    10.0879108    -26.4901960      55.3635536      14.3314938
factor(V2)344 factor(V2)356 factor(V2)368 factor(V2)392
   135.3356813     76.4135454     -55.3037152     208.0403145
factor(V2)398 factor(V2)400 factor(V2)410 factor(V2)417
    73.0964656     44.0775746     165.8872465     413.3611854
factor(V2)422 factor(V2)434 factor(V2)458 factor(V2)484
   -31.3907493     65.0884398     354.8997467     565.8221110
factor(V2)504 factor(V2)528 factor(V2)554 factor(V2)566
     3.1479358    339.7021458     361.4602188      31.2850785
factor(V2)586 factor(V2)604 factor(V2)608 factor(V2)616
    17.4027086    -18.2806526     166.6048771     335.6990284
```

```
factor(V2)642 factor(V2)643 factor(V2)646 factor(V2)702
 -44.7049907    -7.0896329   104.8920329   173.1030748
factor(V2)705 factor(V2)710 factor(V2)716 factor(V2)724
  33.3589933   -25.1240457     0.5649219    90.7369218
factor(V2)752 factor(V2)764 factor(V2)780 factor(V2)792
 334.9495839   352.0627766    78.5663846     7.8932547
factor(V2)804 factor(V2)840 factor(V2)858 factor(V2)860
 -28.9399146   123.7848404    76.5214346   417.6668608
```

As income increases by one unit, the odds of being happy increase by 31.7%. The value for each factor variable refers to the change in the odds of being happy between the country and the reference country for the model.

A second method for interpreting logistic regression coefficient estimates is to find the effect of a variable on the probability of the dependent variable taking on a particular value. For example, the probability of being happy for a male non-believer in the income group of 5 in the baseline country is:

$$\pi_i = \frac{e^{-0.057-0.014male+0.228belief+0.275income+0}}{1+e^{-0.057-0.014male+0.228belief+0.275income+0}}$$

$$= \frac{e^{-0.057-0.014*1+0.228*0+0.275*5}}{1+e^{-0.057-0.014*1+0.228*0+0.275*5}}$$

$$= 0.79$$

In contrast, the probability for a male believer in the same income group in the baseline country is:

$$\pi_i = \frac{e^{-0.057-0.014male+0.228belief+0.275income+0}}{1+e^{-0.057-0.014male+0.228belief+0.275income+0}}$$

$$= \frac{e^{-0.057-0.014*1+0.228*1+0.275*5}}{1+e^{-0.057-0.014*1+0.228*1+0.275*5}}$$

$$= 0.82$$

Hence, the difference in the probability of being happy between a male believer and a male non-believer in income group 5 is 0.036. Religious belief is associated with a very small increase in the probability of being happy. It is important to note that since this is a non-linear model, the substantive effect of one variable often depends on what values other variables take. Therefore, instead of focusing on the odd ratios, it is preferable that we compute the substantive effects for all the scenarios of interest.

Where to Find More Data

Data for replication and original research have become widely available in the last decade. The phenomenon has been driven by both the movement toward more transparent and reproducible research, and the fast development of technology and big data. An exhaustive discussion of available data is impossible since a wide variety and almost infinite quantity of data are available online these days. Here we provide a discussion of only a small number of exemplary data sources as a way of introducing students to the abundant data sources out there.

Replication Data Sources

Many journals now start to make replication data and program files available to researchers. One good example is the *Journal of Peace Research*, which has made available the datasets for published articles since 1998. Readers may find those at https://www.prio.org/JPR/Datasets/. Another good example is the *American Economic Review*, which has made available the datasets for recently published articles as well. Readers may find those at https://www.aeaweb.org/journals/aer/issues.

Many individual scholars make the datasets for their published articles available at the Harvard dataverse project, located at https://dataverse.harvard.edu/. Currently, there are over 65,000 datasets available, covering a wide range of disciplines. From the Harvard dataverse site, one may also find links to various other dataverses, such as World Agroforestry Centre, Population Services International (PSI), International Food Policy Research Institute (IFPRI), Murray Research Archive, CfA Dataverse, *American Journal of Political Science* (AJPS), Brain Genomics Superstruct Project (GSP), and Bill and Melinda Gates Foundation.

Original Data Sources

Many large data projects supported by national governments and international organizations have also made their data available. Here is an illustrative list.

- World Value Surveys, located at http://www.worldvaluessurvey.org, provide data from nationally representative surveys in almost 100 countries with respect to individual beliefs, values, and motivations on issues such as development, religion, democratization, gender equality, social capital, and subjective well-being.
- International Social Survey Programme, located at http://www.issp.org/, provides data from surveys in some 53 countries regarding a wide range of

topics, such as the role of government, social networks, social inequality, religion, environment, changing family and changing gender roles, and national identity.

- U.S. government's open data, located at https://www.data.gov/, provides access to some 185,397 datasets in agriculture, business, climate, consumer, ecosystems, education, energy, finance, health, local government, manufacturing, ocean, public safety, science&research. For example, datasets include consumer complaints, demographic statistics, weather, international trade in goods and services, college scorecard, and so on.

- UNCTAD, located at http://unctadstat.unctad.org/EN/, provides a wide range of data from national and international data sources. Its data center covers 150 time-series on a wide range of topics, including trade, investment, commodities, population, external resources, information economy, creative economy, iron and ore, and maritime transport.

- World Bank, located at http://data.worldbank.org/, provides free and open access to global development data, including many datasets such as worldwide governance indicators, poverty and equity database, world development indicators, education statistics, gender statistics, and health nutrition and population statistics.

- Miscellaneous datasets curated by various analysts. For example, Kaggle, located at https://www.kaggle.com/datasets, provides access to over 100 datasets, including tweets targeting ISIS, airplane crashes throughout the world since 1908, Zika virus epidemic, 2016 US Presidential debates, and more.

For another example, Awesome Public Datasets, located at https://github.com/caesar0301/awesome-public-datasets#education, provides data collected and tidied from blogs, answers, and user responses, covering topics in agriculture, biology, climate/weather, complex networks, computer networks, contextual data, data challenges, economics, education, energy, finance, geology, GIS/environment, government, healthcare, image processing, machine learning, museums, natural language, physics, psychology/cognition, public domains, search engines, social networks, social sciences, software, sports, time series, transportation, complementary collections.

Data Packages Available in R

A large quantity of data has now become available through R packages. For example, we have used two packages on economic data in this textbook: pwt and wbstats.

Another great data source, Quandl, located at https://www.quandl.com/, provides financial and economic data from hundreds of sources via API or directly through R and other softwares. Data covers stocks, futures, commodity, currency, interest rate, potion, asset management, industry, and economy. All databases and datasets on Quandl are available from within R, using the Quandl R package.

The following site, https://ropensci.org/related/, presents a growing list of R data packages covering a wide variety of disciplines and topics, such as ecology, Genes, earth science, economics, finance, chemistry, agriculture, literature, marketing, web analytics, news, media, sports, maps, social media, government, data depots, Google web services, Amazon web services, and so forth.

REFERENCES AND READINGS

Analyzed Readings

(1) Anscombe, F. J. 1973. "Graphs in Statistical Analysis." *American Statistician* 27 (1): 17–21.

(2) Bénabou, Roland, Davide Ticchi, and Andrea Vindigni. 2015. "Religion and Innovation." *American Economic Review* 105(5): 346–51.

(3) Braithwaite, Alex. 2006. "The Geographic Spread of Militarized Disputes." *Journal of Peace Research* 43(5): 507–22.

(4) Frankel, Jeffrey A., and David Romer. 1999. "Does Trade Cause Growth?" *American Economic Review* 89, 379–99.

(5) Iversen, Torben, and David Soskice. 2006. "Electoral Institutions and the Politics of Coalitions: Why Some Democracies Redistribute More Than Others." *American Political Science Review* 100(2): 165–81.

Data Sources

(1) Heston, Alan, Robert Summers, and Bettina Aten. Penn World Table, Version Mark 5.6 and Version 7.0. Center for International Comparisons of Production, Income and Prices at the University of Pennsylvania.

(2) Piburn, Jesse. 2016. wbstats: Programmatic Access to the World Bank API. Oak Ridge National Laboratory, Oak Ridge, TN. http://web.ornl.gov/sci/gist/.

(3) World Values Survey Wave 6 2010–2014 Official aggregate v.2015 0418. World Values Survey Association. www.worldvaluessurvey.org. Aggregate File Producer: Asep/JDS, Madrid, Spain.

(4) Zeileis, Achim, and Guan Yang. 2013. pwt: Penn World Table. R package version 7.1-1. http://CRAN.R-project.org/package=pwt.

R Packages

(1) Auguie, Baptiste. 2016. gridExtra: Miscellaneous Functions for "Grid" Graphics. R package version 2.2.1. https://CRAN.R-project.org/package=gridExtra

(2) Dowle et al. with contributions from R. Saporta and E. Antonyan. 2015. data.table: Extension of Data.frame. R package version 1.9.6. https://CRAN.R-project.org/package=data.table

(3) Gandrud, Christopher. 2016. DataCombine: Tools for Easily Combining and Cleaning Data Sets. R package version 0.2.21. https://CRAN.R-project.org/package=DataCombine

(4) Harrell, Frank E., Jr. with contributions from Charles Dupont and many others. 2016. Hmisc: Harrell Miscellaneous. R package version 4.0-0. https://CRAN.R-project.org/package=Hmisc

(5) Hope, Ryan M. 2013. Rmisc: Rmisc: Ryan Miscellaneous. R package version 1.5. https://CRAN.R-project.org/package=Rmisc

(6) Højsgaard, Søren, and Ulrich Halekoh. 2016. doBy: Groupwise Statistics, LSmeans, Linear Contrasts, Utilities. R package version 4.5-15. https://CRAN.R-project.org/package=doBy

(7) Paradis, E., J. Claude, and Strimmer, K. 2004. "APE: Analyses of Phylogenetics and Evolution in R Language." *Bioinformatics* 20: 289–90.

(8) R Core Team. 2016. foreign: Read Data Stored by Minitab, S, SAS, SPSS, Stata, Systat, Weka, dBase .... R package version 0.8-67. https://CRAN.R-project.org/package=foreign

(9) R. Core Team. 2016. R: A Language and Environment for Statistical Computing. R Foundation for Statistical Computing, Vienna, Austria. https://www.R-project.org/.

(10) Robinson, David. 2016. broom: Convert Statistical Analysis Objects into Tidy Data Frames. R package version 0.4.1. https://CRAN.R-project.org/package=broom

(11) Solt, Frederick, and Yue Hu. 2015. interplot: Plot the Effects of Variables in Interaction Terms. Available at The Comprehensive R Archive Network (CRAN). https://CRAN.R-project.org/package=interplot.

(12) Venables, W. N., and B. D. Ripley. 2002. *Modern Applied Statistics with S* (4th ed.). New York: Springer.

(13) Warnes, Gregory R., et al. 2015. gdata: Various R Programming Tools for Data Manipulation. R package version 2.17.0. https://CRAN.R-project.org/package=gdata

(14) Warnes, Gregory R., Ben Bolker, Thomas Lumley, and Randall C. Johnson. 2015. gmodels: Various R Programming Tools for Model Fitting. R package version 2.16.2. https://CRAN.R-project.org/package=gmodels

(15) Wickham, Hadley. 2007. "Reshaping Data with the Reshape Package." *Journal of Statistical Software* 21(12): 1–20. http://www.jstatsoft.org/v21/i12/.

(16) Wickham, Hadley. 2009. *ggplot2: Elegant Graphics for Data Analysis*. New York: Springer-Verlag.

(17) Wickham, Hadley, and Romain Francois. 2016. dplyr: A Grammar of Data Manipulation. R package version 0.5.0. https://CRAN.R-project.org/package=dplyr

(18) Wickham and Chang before Wickham and Francois. 2016. devtools: Tools to Make Developing R Packages Easier. R package version 1.12.0. https://CRAN.R-project.org/package=devtool

(19) Xie, Yihui. 2014. "knitr: A Comprehensive Tool for Reproducible Research in R." In Victoria Stodden, Friedrich Leisch, and Roger D. Peng, editors, *Implementing Reproducible Computational Research*. Boca Raton, FL: Chapman and Hall/CRC.

(20) Xie, Yihui. 2015. *Dynamic Documents with R and knitr*. (2nd edition). Boca Raton, FL: Chapman and Hall/CRC.

(21) Xie, Yihui. 2016. "knitr: A General-Purpose Package for Dynamic Report Generation in R." R package version 1.15.

(22) Zeileis, Achim. 2004. Econometric computing with HC and HAC covariance matrix estimators. *Journal of Statistical Software* 11(10): 1–17. http://www.jstatsoft.org/v11/i10/.

R References

(1) Hogan, Thomas P. 2010. *Bare-Bones R: A Brief Introductory Guide*. Thousand Oaks, CA: Sage Publications.

(2) Muenchen, Robert A., and Joseph M. Hilbe. 2010. *R for Stata Users*. New York: Springer.

(3) Spector, Phil. 2008. *Data Manipulation with R*. New York: Springer.

(4) Teetor, Paul. 2011. *R cookbook*. Sebastopol, CA: O'Reilly Media, Inc.

(5) Wickham, Hadley. 2009. *ggplot2: Elegant Graphics for Data Analysis*. New York: Springer.

(6) Zuur, Alain, Elena N. Ieno, and Erik Meesters. 2009. *A Beginner's Guide to R*. New York: Springer.

Statistics

(1) Agresti, Alan, and Christine Franklin. 2009. *Statistics: The Art and Science of Learning from Data*. Upper Saddle River, NJ: Prentice Hall.

(2) Dougherty, Christopher. 2016. *Introduction to Econometrics*. Oxford: Oxford University Press.

(3) Kutner, Michael H., Christopher J. Nachtsheim, and John Neter. 2003. *Applied Linear Regression Models*. New York: McGraw-Hill.

(4) Wooldridge, Jeffrey, M. 2009. *Introductory Econometrics: A Modern Approach*. Mason, OH, USA: South-Western Cengage Learning.

Statistics Using R

(1) Crawley, Michael J. 2007. *The R book*. Hoboken, NJ: Wiley

(2) Dalgaard, Peter. 2008. *Introductory Statistics with R*. New York: Springer

(3) Hothorn, Torsten, and Brian S. Everitt. 2014. *A Handbook of Statistical Analyses Using R*. Boca Raton, FL: CRC Press.

(4) Kabacoff, Robert. 2015. *R in Action: Data Analysis and Graphics with R*. Shelter Island, NY: Manning Publications Co.

(5) Maindonald, John, and John Braun. 2006. *Data Analysis and Graphics using R: An Example-based Approach*. Cambridge: Cambridge University Press.

(6) Monogan, James E., III. 2015. *Political Analysis Using R*. New York: Springer.

(7) Verzani, John. 2014. *Using R for Introductory Statistics*. Boca Raton, FL: CRC Press.

INDEX

Note: Figures and tables are indicated by italic "f" and "t" following page numbers.